DRIP

YARNS

A season with Lewes FC

OWNER
2011 2012
LEWES
FC

STUART FULLER

Blackline|Press

First published in 2011 by Blackline Press

ISBN 978-0-9563238-7-3

www.blacklinepress.com
Blackline Press 15 Lister Road IPSWICH IP1 5EQ
info@blacklinepress.com

Blackline|Press

DRIPPING YARNS

A season with Lewes FC

STUART FULLER

ALSO BY STUART FULLER

Passport To Football
A Fan's Guide: European Football Grounds
Fuller's Fans Guide to German Stadiums 2005/06
Fuller's Mini Guide to Germany 2006
The Budget Airlines Guide to European Football

FOREWORD
By Paul Hayward

"With the mutation of the Premier League into 20 entertainment corporations, people across England have been reporting strange sensations. Hauling themselves away from HD screens or expensive seats in luxury arenas, they have gathered at non-league football grounds to stand behind goalposts and watch the game they played as children. This is a game that can be heard, smelt, felt and almost touched. It engenders a sense of belonging, of recognition. It's not an act of worship or tribalism or consumerism. There is no swarm of intermediaries between you and the players, you and the game. The smallness of the stadium adds to the intensity of the spectacle.

This calming sense is hard for people to articulate. And in no way should it preclude raucous support for the team.

At Lewes FC, home of the Rooks, and now community-owned, Stuart Fuller saw something of the essence of his love of football, and began recording his impressions for this book.

It doesn't present Lewes as some fortress of virtue, but instead shows what a joy the game can be when it belongs to people who care about it, and know its simple pleasures.

It will always be there, so long as we are, too."

PAUL HAYWARD

Introduction

Until late October 2008 I had never heard of the East Sussex town of Lewes, let alone the fact that they had a football team which were playing at the time in the Blue Square Conference, the highest level of Non League football, the highest level the club had ever appeared at.

A chance email conversation with converted non League fan Danny Last from the website European Football Weekends set the wheels in motion with an invite to visit his team down on the south coast, a start of a journey that like finding a new love saw me turn my back on family tradition. After just one visit to the Dripping Pan, the home of Lewes FC I was hooked.

Just over a year later I had committed to tearing up my West Ham United season ticket and adopting Lewes as my team. Now any man will tell you that switching football teams simply does not happen but thanks to my growing disillusionment with the game I was going to do just that. I thought that there was a compelling reason for me to make the switch.

I needed to find my mojo for football again. I had become a disenfranchised fan of the sanitised Premier League. I followed other fans like sheep into the so called "cathedrals of football", buying my £5 burger and my £3.50 programme which contained more spin than a political party manifesto. I wanted to be part of my club, able to give more than just £60 for a bit of plastic to put my bum on, and be thanked for my contribution.

As luck would have it a revolution was taking place back down in Lewes. After the traumatic events of the previous season when the club had firstly came close to ceasing to exist completely due to a winding up order from the Inland Revenue and then saved themselves from relegation on the last day of the season a group of local businessmen who were supporters of the club had got together and negotiated a deal to buy the club, warts and all.

The group, known as the Rooks 125, in acknowledgement to the fact that Lewes had been formed 125 years ago in the Royal Oak pub in the town centre, had one common interest. An interest to build something special, dare I say unique in terms of a football club. Realism at this level of the game is essential. Many a club has fallen foul of ideas above their station with all the right intentions. The six new owners set about a plan that would steady the club, re-engage with the fans and the local community which would ultimately see some success on the pitch.

This is the story of that first season. With a club at this level it is not hard to get close to the fans, the players, the manager(s) and ultimately the owners of the club and this is my account of what transpired in that first year of the rebirth of the Rooks.

The drinking man's football club

On the 8 July 2010 the deal was done. All of the paperwork had been prepared, the T's crossed, the I's dotted and the six new owners of the club sat back in the Royal Oak wondering if this is how the original owners of the club had felt some 125 years previously. The whole idea of taking over the club had come out of the blue a few months before. All six were local to Lewes, a couple known as DFL's which was what the residents of Lewes called people who were "Down from London" and all had something to bring to the table. A money man who understood exactly what the term "contingent liability" meant. A couple of marketing men, plugged in to the local community as well as ties back into London. A man on the inside, someone who knew a bit about the club and what it was capable of, and someone who had no visible value add apart from boundless enthusiasm, a Can Do attitude and an Oscar nomination. The six became known as the Rooks125 in honour of the forthcoming anniversary for the club.

This was no ordinary take over though. The Rooks125 group spent many hours talking to the likes of AFC Wimbledon, FC United of Manchester as well as Supporters Direct to see if a Community-based model could work for Lewes. The more they looked, the more they saw this was the solution they wanted for the best interests of everyone in and around Lewes FC. The word "Community" kept coming up. The ground, the Dripping Pan should be a hub for the local community. The team should be working with schools in the local community and the club should forge closer links with local businesses in the community. This was not rocket science but in a world of private ownership of football clubs the huge financial rewards prevented most clubs ever considering this route of a symbiotic relationship.

The six set out a manifesto of their own. They wanted to rid the club of its hand to mouth existence, avoiding any repeats of last minute fingernail biting as the fate of the club was decided in a closed court room. So in order to move the whole project forward the club needed finance. They reached out to the local community and asked for "Pioneers" as they put it, that would be willing to financially back the club. They were not asking for "investors" they wanted something different as they outlined in their manifesto:-

"To be clear this is not an investment and there is no return on the money you put in other than the knowledge that by helping us now you'll be one of the fathers (or mothers) of the revolution. People will speak of your name in reverent tones for centuries to come. And even if they don't, you'll still know that you were there at the start, not just of an exciting local venture but of something that might just change football ownership for good."

So why did they get involved in the first place. Patrick Marber, an Oscar nominated screenwriter, and hardly your typical Non League club owner put his reasons in an award winning style:-

"I'm a new supporter. I started coming to the Dripping Pan with my 8 year old son at the beginning of last season. We loved it. I soon found out that the club was in peril. I wanted to carry on supporting the club. I met with Ibbo and we talked. I found him inspirational and I wanted to help him and the club, so I made a donation to them. I was introduced to Charlie (Dobres) through a mutual friend and we talked about the vision of a not-for-profit, supporter-owned community club. We met Eddie (Ramsden) and Ben (Ward) and talked some more. The name Rooks125 came from the forthcoming anniversary of the club and the fact we wanted to be seen as a working group and not just a pipedream. We then met Alex (Leith) and Nick (Williams) from the magazine VivaLewes and asked them to join us. The next few months were spent in meetings, talking about what we could do.

Sometimes there are things you just have to do. This was one of them. I can't explain it. I don't fully understand it. It just had to be done."

The other members seemed to echo these sentiments.

"I wanted to help. I feel very patriotic about Lewes and want to see its institutions survive for the next generation. Some guy called Patrick called me and said we need to do something to safe a great club in a great town. Last season the club was in serious danger of folding altogether which would have been a huge loss to the town. Rooks125 seemed like an opportunity to preserve the club at the same time as creating something distinctive and new in how it's run.

I was approached at the end of last season and knew that the club would go under if nothing was done. I realised the diverse skill sets and dynamism of the over members and that we would have a fighting chance of launching a new, healthy era for Lewes FC."

With the ownership of the club now finalised matters turned to the team. Nobody wanted a repeat of the end of season drama from just a few months previous, none more so than manager Steve Ibbitson, a man who had almost single handily carried the club both on and off the pitch last season. There were occasions, when times were especially dark that we expected the long since retired Ibbo and his assistant Jason Hopkinson would strip off their tracksuit tops and bring themselves on as substitutes.

Both Ibbo and Jason had overseen a complete overhaul of the youth team set up at Lewes in the previous few seasons and now the club were benefiting from seeing some of their "investments" being given a chance to play for the first team. But as Alan Hansen famously once said "You will win nothing with kids" and so they needed to blend the team with some experience. The only problem here is that experience, even at this level, costs money, and money is what the club didn't have. Almost every week went by with another loan player drafted in, almost living hand to mouth.

With events becoming settled off the pitch Ibbo could concentrate on building a team that could compete at the Blue Square Bet South level. On the eve of the new season Ibbo told the fans that "when all the new signings were fully fit they would strengthen the young squad significantly".

The sense of community was clear to see. But could they put the plans into practice? Only the next nine months would tell. Shall we begin?

Saturday 17th July 2010
A new beginning

This was no "Glazer Out" take over, nor did the Lewes fans turn up at the ground in strange coloured scarves wanting their heritage back. As with most things relating to Lewes Football Club it was done in a dignified manner, with scaremongering kept to a minimum. Nor will the vast majority of the fans be saying good riddance to the old directors. On the contrary they were responsible for the club's rise up the non-leagues in the past few years. They invested their own money in the club to help get Lewes on the map, and to a large extend achieved this very means. Ten years ago when Martin Elliott and Kevin Powell stepped in, the club were in the old Isthmian Division Three with basic facilities in the ground. Today the ground, in my opinion, is one of the nicest to watch a non-league game at and has real character, mixed with some half decent facilities, and of course has witnessed non-league football at the highest level. With events off the pitch shaping up nicely it was time to concentrate on what was going to happen on the pitch.

The new squad met in early July for the start of pre-season. There were three notable absentees from the team that finished the previous season in such excellent form. Rikki Banks, outstanding for most of the season in goal had moved on down the road to Eastbourne Borough, hoping for a quieter life (By mid November, Eastbourne had conceded 38 in 19 games - hardly the quiet life he would have expected). Top scorer, and vastly under rated midfielder Joe Keehan had also headed upwards into the Conference to try his luck with Rushden & Diamonds. He was the Frank Lampard of the team, timing his runs into the box to take advantage of those mistimed clearances. The third absentee was not a permanent departure. David Wheeler, England under17 international and the fans player of the season last time out was in Ghana. Footballers are often knocked for their selfish attitude, and in some cases it is fully deserved. But Wheeler could never be put into that bracket. He was to miss pre-season and some of the first games of the season as he was helping building a school in Ghana as part of his studies.

Two weeks of hard work followed as the coaching team worked on areas of weakness from the previous campaign. Ibbo publically stated that he wanted a tough pre-season schedule, and their first test came down the

A27 at Ryman League South side Worthing - a spicy local derby if you could have such a thing in these parts on a hot Saturday afternoon in July. Worthing, or the "Rebels" to give them their favoured moniker, had a good season last time out. Finishing in the playoffs of Ryman League One South they lost in extra time to Godalming Town in the play offs, and thus were having to endure another season at this level - that is if the Isthmian league ever got round to publishing fixtures. Danny Last takes up the story from Worthing.

Worthing 0 Lewes 0 - Woodside Road aka The A2B Stadium

West Sussex met East Sussex and the fans came out in force. It is rare that pre-season games attendances top average league ones but there was a good few hundred in the ground for the first meeting of the teams in quite a few years. Woodside Road seemed as good a place as any to see in the new season. The Rebels have a great fan base themselves. They've also had the mandatory financial issues. Towards the end of last season their players were issued with an ultimatum: accept 30 quid a week or off you go. To their credit they stayed. Fast forward to 2010/11 though and they had a new manager and one or two (OK eleven) players who've joined from Horsham YMCA.

If you think I'm going to tell you that I once played at Woodside Road you've got another thing coming. The last thing I want to do is sit here and tell you how I once scored a 22 yard screamer into the roof of the net at this very stadium. It has changed a bit since then that day I am not going to mention. They've added a few new stands, things are in colour and it's no longer called Woodside Road - it's the A2B stadium or something similar.

As well as Stuart and myself, the game also saw the long awaited reunion of the Lewes Lunatic Fringe after their summer break. West Ham United had their ICF, Portsmouth the 657 Crew, Millwall the Bushwhackers and Lewes has the LLF. Well, sort of. Firstly, the LLF are a group of peaceful fans who support the Rooks through thick and thin. Some away games it is literally only the LLF and a couple of others there. You will get to meet them throughout the season but for this game the stalwarts included Big Deaksy and Cynical Dave, a wild Scotsman who has a passionate dislike of the Premier League and most referees. This favourite chant is "cheat, cheat, cheat" (repeat to fade, arrest or a punch from the official in question). But he knows his football. So much so that his 23 team European accumulator is the stuff of legends and often leads to strange requests for updates from Union Berlin versus Augsburg, Kalmar versus Halmstad or Plzen's vital away game at Hradec Kralove.

Sensible pricing for this game saw a bumper home crowd. You cannot go wrong for £5 admission and we were soon talking tactics with two of the new owners, Alex Leith and Patrick Marber. The sun was out; the grass was green so the only thing missing was a beer. As you will see as the season progresses Non League Football and beer go hand in hand. So we headed into the bar, purchased our ales and went to return to pitch side. "Sorry mate, no beer to be taken outside" said the steward on the door. Obvious question - why? Apparently this game had been deemed a "Category A high profile game" due to the proximity of the two clubs and there could be a danger that the fans may start throwing glasses at each other. Let's just rewind for a minute. We are at the A2B Stadium in Worthing. Worthing not Leeds United or Stoke City. The last time there was any public order offences in Worthing was when Russ Abbot tickets went on sale at the Pavilion Theatre.

One familiar face in the crowd was Ryan Storrie, ex-tricky left winger at Lewes who was sponsored by The Ball is Round last season. Unfortunately he quit the club in the New Year to gain a regular place at Eastbourne Town. Did he give us a refund on our money? Did he ever, but he is a top lad and as usual had his legion of followers all around him. Some of them were also ex-Lewes players and they took up a spot next to the dugout along with a few of the other old Lewes players trying to persuade Ibbo to give them a game in the style of Yosser Hughes "Gissa game, go on mate".

And so onto the actual game. In all honesty I cannot remember a lot about it. Catching up on the news of the club, the take over and further plans for the Rook Inn redevelopment that Danny and I had undertaken during the summer took up most of the time in the first half. Worthing came closest to scoring, hitting the bar in the opening minutes of the game.

After a brief interlude in the bar, we emerged for the second half. Or so we thought. The Worthing team had been replaced in its entirety not just in terms of the players, but also their kit. Gone was the all red strip and replaced with an all blue one. This would be a despicable marketing ploy if it happened in the Premier League but here it was simply that everyone was a bit sweaty after the first half and nobody wanted to swap kit.

The kit change didn't really do any good. This was a first work out for both teams although Lewes did show some nice "plinky-plonky" football at times as if it was like watching Spain which was ironic as most players had probably just returned from a couple of weeks in Magaluf. It wasn't a classic and it was never going to be. It was hotter than Greece for a start and many players hardly knew each other's names let alone their style of play. The highlight of the match occurred when the ball bounced into the electricity substation underneath one of the floodlights. Thoughts turned to those 70s public information films and, indeed, Charlie says. Charlie says don't talk to strangers and don't expect too much entertainment in a pre-season friendly. To add even more confusion to the events the red ball made an appearance. This was supposed to be a "limited" edition version of the Ryman ball just brought out for Red Nose Day last season. Based on the way these leagues are run, expect a fine for a breach of some sub-rule or regulation somewhere Worthing FC.

How many grounds have you been to where a local pole dancing club advertise pitch side? Well beggars can't be choosers in the non leagues and they will take any advertising they can get. Highly amusing moments occurred whilst the LLF wandered around the pitch behind the advert board for Le Chic, raising their arms in celebration for the point earnt not knowing the amusing advert they were creating for the rest of the crowd.

We decided to head away from the ground for our post match tipple. We love to invest in non league clubs but the bar had a bit of an Eau to sweaty socks so we found ourselves in the Cricketers. A pub with live music and a beer festival was always going to catch our attention. Pints of Burpy Bottom and Wobbly Tummy went down ten treats.

There weren't too many alternatives in the vicinity of Woodside Road. Sadly, the Clifton has now closed its doors; we hadn't been in Chapmans for fifteen years and didn't intend to change that. Then there is the Jolly Brewers and the Richard Cobden. It was either of those or do as the locals do and sit on the kerb with a can of cider. Not my words those before you write in, those of Larry from Lancing. Of course Larry from Lancing.

So what will the next nine months bring? Last minute winners, over priced cheeseburgers, quality clubhouses, banter, changing ends at half time, Harvey's and something else positive that I can't quite put my finger on now but I will do in the course of time.

Next up was supposed to be Crawley Town in the first game at the Dripping Pan. A relatively local derby against a team who had spent heavily in the summer would have drawn a big crowd. But then less than a week before the game, Crawley pulled out. They did offer to send their under18's team which would have been a farcical. Their reason? They had arranged a training camp, to "bed" in their new players such as £70,000 signing Matt Tubbs, £100,000 Sergio Torres and £200,000 Richard Brodie. Let me just re-affirm that this was a non league club spending this money. Madness, sheer madness.

Tuesday 27th July 2010
Horshing around

So after the disappointment of the Crawley game Ibbo did what he does best. He picked up the phone and made some calls to see who he could bring to the Pan. Rumours spread that Queens Park Rangers could be the visitors, whilst others who claim to have overheard a conversation in the Rook Inn were convinced it was Horsens, the Danish Superliga team (OK I admit this one was from me). It was neither, but Horsham (Horsens, Horsham - you can see where my story got lost in translation) of the Ryman Premier League stepped into the void left by money bags Crawley Town and send down their first team.

Midweek games cause a problem for Danny and myself due to our various work commitments and locations, so we sent Big Deaksy down to report on this one. The good news is that their report was concise. The bad news was that it was Blackberry instant messenger concise. Ginger Jones having a blinder; Wormie doing the business and Gradders wrist fallen off were three examples of their unique reporting. So please excuse the brief match summary below but this is pieced together from the messages and the help of my 10 year old daughter who has a degree in SMS translation.

Lewes 3 Horsham 0 - The Dripping Pan

The good news was that this was a pre-season friendly and not a league game. It could have been the latter if results hadn't improved at the end of the season. The better news was that pre-season training seemed to be going well. Three well taken goals for the Rooks were enough to see Lewes home and extend their clean sheets to a second successive game. Who needs Rikki Banks eh!

The Rooks went ahead in the first half when youngster George Jones ran with the ball from inside his own, evading four challenges on the way before slotting the ball home in a goal that had the home fans whispering the G word...Not Gazza, Giggsy or Georgie Best but Ginger. With a bright mop of orange hair and a name like George the poor lad will forever be known as Ginger George. One became two before half time after Simon Wormull played in Rob Gradwell and he produced a neat finish to give the Rooks a two goal half-time lead. The last time Lewes had been two nil up had been over six months ago against Weston-Super-Mare. An omen of good things to come? We will see - after all this is Lewes and you need to suspend all normal belief when talking about the future on the pitch.

The second half saw a number of changes on both teams but the Rooks continued to impress. It takes some guts to wear flashy coloured boots at this level but young Tom Murphy could pull it off. The lad is confident beyond his young years and despite being released in the close season by Gillingham and potentially any thoughts of making it in the Football League he had dusted himself down and put in a fantastic performance on the wing, capping his game with a clever goal from a very tight angle. What could be better for the team? Well what about some action for new keeper Chris "Winnie" Winterton? Signed after the departure of Banksie, Winterton had been more recently playing in Finland before being snapped up by Ibbo in the summer and he made his mark in his game by saving a penalty as time ticked down.

At least I think this is what happened, but how can be sure based on the live updates we had from the LLF.

Saturday 31st July 2010
Hayes & Wedding

The purpose of pre-season friendlies is to test your s... pre-season preparations. It is not about the result. Well, ... are always told anyway, especially after your team has been s... ...d at home by a virtually unknown Greek second division team. Lewes's first real test of the season was against Blue Square Bet Premier outfit Hayes & Yeading, who had surprised everyone by holding their own in their first season in the top level of non league football, passing Lewes on the way down at the end of the 2008/09 season.

Unfortunately I was indisposed. Well, actually I was on holiday in Wales meaning that for the second successive game I had to rely on the text updates from Big Deaksy, who wasn't actually in the best of places after a rather heavy work leaving do the previous evening. So whilst the LLF were enjoying some fine Harveys beer in the Rooks Inn I was watching Neath FC conceding 5 late goals to Hereford United in their pre-season cup final. The Brains beer was going down nicely but it would be even better if Lewes could extend their unbeaten streak to a third game.

Lewes 1 Hayes & Yeading 2 - The Dripping Pan

Unfortunately it was not to be. Lewes lost their unbeaten pre-season record although they did not go down without a fight. The Rooks were worthy opponents throughout much of the first half and took the lead midway through to the delight of the home fans as ex Hayes & Yeading striker Rob Gradwell pounced on a loose ball after a tackle on keeper Lee Harrison before slotting into an empty net. Now this was good news for one of us. Danny. Following on from our sponsor a player competition last season, we agreed to do it again this year. My choice, David Wheeler was still doing good things in Africa, but Danny had picked Mr Gradwell and he was on white hot form. Last year the story was similar with Danny's choice Sam Crabb putting in an impressive pre-season before jumping ships to Whitehawk.

With two weeks to go before the start of the season Ibbitson made a couple of changes to the team at half time but it was the visitors who turned things around in the second half. Just six minutes after the break Elliott Buchanan, ng to be yards offside, turned the ball past Winterton for the first he had conceded in nearly 250 minutes. Cynical launched into his encouragement for the "Assistant Referee", causing him to move a few yards onto the pitch, looking over his shoulder at Dave's pint of Harveys in his hand and wondering whether he may get an early shower.

Lewes put pressure on the visitors goal and but for a great save from Harrison from Jordan Laing's header it would have been the Rooks who took the lead. Instead it was the visitors who made it two one when Buchanan scored his second goal with a strong cross shot after Lewes had failed to clear the ball when the opportunity arose. Winterton had no chance with this one but when called into action he did not disappoint. His saves late on from Holmes and Buchanan again were enough for Ibbitson to know he had found his number one for the start of the season. Right up until the final whistle the result could have gone either way. Substitute Tim Rivers should have done better with a late header and Murphy could have taken a shot instead of trying to beat his man again. Ifs, buts, coulds, shoulds. That is what pre-season football is all about.

Wednesday 4th August 2010
Prior history

Some rivalries are based on geography, some are based on history and some are based on factors such as religion or even class. And some rivalries aren't really rivalries at all. Take Lewes and Eastbourne Borough for instance. Eastbourne is actually a town of three football clubs with a "Town" a "United" and "Borough", but the latter who currently play at the highest level were only formed in 1964. Due to their progress through the leagues there wasn't much interaction with the other sides in the town meaning they had to look elsewhere for their rivalries. And where better than down the A27 at Lewes.

In 2008/9 season when Lewes were in the Conference for their one and only season the teams met twice over the Christmas period and over 2,400 squeezed into both games. Both teams had been promoted the previous season and there had been an element of jealousy from Eastbourne as Steve King's Lewes team romped to the league. However, when things started to go wrong on and off the pitch for the Rooks, there was a general sense of amusement from Eastbourne which irked the Lewes fans.

The clubs themselves, like in so many instances, actually have a good relationship, and a number of players have moved between the clubs, underlined this season by the swap of goalkeepers that saw Rikki Banks go to Borough and Chris Winterton go the opposite away. This cordiality was underlined by Lewes agreeing to play in a testimonial for Ray Tuppen and Dean Lightwood. Both of these backroom boys had been at Eastbourne for 11 years and had been unsung heroes in Eastbourne's rise up from county football to the level they are at today.

Friendlies are one thing but testimonials are a whole different bag of chips. They are normally played at a snail's pace, and the people whose testimonial it is will invariably end up scoring from a soft penalty. Unless they feature a foreign team whereby it is necessary normally for players to be forcibly substituted to avoid all out war. One of the last testimonial games I saw was for Julian Dicks some ten years ago. The visitors were Athletic Bilbao, and Dicks with his knackered knees came on as a sub for about ten minutes, kicked a few players, nearly started a fight with Paolo Di Canio and then departed in a sulk straight down the tunnel. Which type of game would this be? Do you really need to ask?

Eastbourne Borough 3 Lewes 1 - Priory Lane

Lewes's preparations for the game had been spoilt by injuries to key players. There was still no David Wheeler, Anthony Barness and Lewis Hamilton were injured at the back and a number of other players weren't fit.

Unfortunately the losing continued from the weekend as Lewes were second best for most of the game, although Ibbo had put faith in some of the promising youngsters in a side that probably only featured 4 of the first choice starting XI (Winterton, Sutton, Wormull & Gradwell).

Eastbourne took a deserved lead in the 25th minute when Winterton flapped at a cross and Ollie Rowe scored from close range. One became two on the hour mark before Lewes had had a chance to really create a chance of their own. Lewes defender Andy Pearson failed to pass back hard enough to Winterton under pressure leaving Jamie Taylor free to score into an empty net as Winterton was out of position.

The goal signalled a move by Eastbourne to make some mass changes, and they brought on 8 players in the space of a few minutes. The substitutions broke the rhythm of the home side and Lewes sensed a chance to get back into the game. In the 67th minute Wormull sent over a decent free kick and Scott Manning headed in unmarked to make the score 2-1. Despite a few more chances, Eastbourne came back into the game and with time running out Pearson completed a miserable evening by scuffing a clearance in the box straight to Eastbourne's new striker Richard Pacquett and he made no mistake. Still there was always Friday night's game with Eastbourne Town and a chance of revenge...sort of.

Friday 6th August 2010
Some unfinished business...

One year ago to the day Danny rang me up. "Stu" he said "I've got a plan. Let's sponsor a couple of players, make it into a competition and have some fun." Never one to turn down a challenge nor missing an opportunity to put something back into the grass roots of the game, we came up with the EuropeanFootballWeekends/TheBallIsRound Challenge and picked two players at Lewes who we would both sponsor, and like a real life fantasy football, would award them points for their contributions. Centre forward Sam Crabb was Danny/EFW's choice whilst mine as we already know was tricky left sided player Ryan Storrie. We announced the competition with a great fanfare and soon details found their way onto Facebook where both players ribbed each other on their performances and points total.

As we know the season was a tough one for Lewes and both Sam Crabb and Ryan Storrie found themselves squeezed out of the first team and both deciding to seek their chances elsewhere - Crabb down the A27 with Whitehawk and Storrie with Eastbourne Town. So we put the cup back in the trophy cabinet, and the champagne on ice, trying to work out a way to award it to the winner, failing and instead quaffing the whole lot a few weeks later.

One year on and Lewes were completing their pre-season fixtures with a game down the road at Eastbourne for the second time in three days. Eastbourne Town had come mighty close to losing their place in the Ryman League South at the end of last season. They had in fact finished bottom of the league but retained their position after the demotion for non footballing reasons of Ashford Town (the Middlesex flavoured one). And would you believe it, lining up for Town would be Ryan Storrie and Sam Crabb - a perfect opportunity to complete some unfinished business.

Eastbourne actually has a third team too, with Eastbourne United (once coached by the legendary Ron Greenwood) playing in the Sussex League giving the town a strangely three way rivalry. However, Eastbourne is known as "Gods Waiting Room" for a reason and so passions do not really run high when the football season starts. Town are actually the oldest of the three teams, but had only played at the county level for more than seventy years before they finally made the Isthmian league in 2007.

So back to the whole EFW/TBIR Cup competition. My daughter Lolly was keen to see Ryan again. After we did the sponsorship deal for him last season she went back to school and told her classmates that "Daddy bought a footballer during the summer" and genuinely bigged him up. He in turn gave her his shirt from the previous season that fitted her like a glove. Lolly is 10, so you may get the impression that Ryan isn't that tall. But he does pack a punch down the wing and so we expected him to rise to the challenge of playing against his old club. With Danny at work interviewing Oliver Kay from the Times, and Big Deaks tempted by another leaving do it was up to Cynical Dave, Terry Boyle, fresh from his jaunt up to Scotland and myself to provide the lunatic fringe element for the team. Lunatic in the sense that everyone else bar us three had better things to do on a Friday night

Eastbourne Town 1 Lewes 0 - The Saffrons

A week after watching a game in a constant drizzle in Llanelli whilst on our holiday and thinking "this is summer", we arrived in Eastbourne just as a similar constant drizzle descended on the town. The Saffrons is certainly a lovely venue for football. A park-like setting sandwiched between a cricket ground and a bowls green a stone's throw away from the town centre. The main stand is unusually behind the goal, and it has one of the most unique food bars in the game which is basically a converted conservatory complete with comfy chairs to wait for your order. The crowd was no more than a hundred or so and most took refuge in the main stand to watch Eastbourne tear into a Lewes team containing some experienced players.

Storrie and Crabb played well in the first half, combining to create a couple of chances. Having joked with Ryan Storrie in the days leading up to the game that I had never seen him score he told me to put a bet on him to get the first goal here, and he certainly looked up for it. Lewes on the other hand seemed comfortable in midfield, although there was an over tendency to keep playing the ball along the back four which served little purpose. Half time was a welcome relief from the weather as well as the less than inspiring football, and a trip next door to the cricket bar was needed, although with darts, pool and Norwich City v Watford on the TV made it very tempting to stay in the warm and dry.

But I am now a loyal Lewes fan so I have to take the rough with the smooth and the frequent rain with the sunshine so we went back outside. The good news was that Eastbourne had taken off Storrie, who did seem to be a thorn in veteran Anthony Barness's side. However, the home team continued to try and beat the Lewes offside trap and it was inevitable that if there was to be a goal it would be through a marginal offside decision and that is exactly what happened. A simple ball through the middle should have been flagged and the Eastbourne forward just beat keeper Winterton to the ball to push it into the net. Dave wasn't impressed and launched in to "Cheat, Cheat, Cheat", positioning himself behind the dugouts much to the annoyance of the Eastbourne manager.

Lewes's best chance came with five minutes left when they were awarded a penalty. Sure it was a foul on the Lewes player but from our position it appeared outside the box. Referee looked at linesman, linesman looked at referee, sort of shrugged his shoulders and put his flag across his chest unconvincingly, wary of Cynical's position behind him no doubt. Rob Gradwell stepped up but saw his penalty tipped onto the post by the Eastbourne keeper, which I think from memory was the only shot on goal they had had all night. Not a good night for Gradwell as he had started from the bench after turning up to the game late.

Farnborough and ex-Lewes manager Steve King was in the crowd. Hard to see what would have worried him about Lewes's play, although perhaps he was looking at the likes of Storrie and Crabb who could both still do a job in the Blue Square Bet South. But at the end of the day only a fool takes bragging rights from a friendly, says he wearing the latest Gold and Sullivan West Ham merchandise - the 5 out of 5 T-shirt celebrating our pre-season wins versus Peterborough, Milton Keynes Dons, Borussia Monchengladbach, Ipswich and err someone I cannot remember. The real test starts in 7 days with Staines away. Come on you Rooks!

Interview with the World Toad in the Hole Champion

By his own admission, Ben Ward is the third best known writer on the board of Lewes FC. Bearing in mind there are only 6 members in total that is some going. And we are not talking about just a run of the mill local newspaper journalist here (not that there is anything wrong with such a noble tradition). Ben is an award winning writer, nominated on numerous occasions for his writing and winning a number of BAFTA's on such Childrens TV programmes as Tracey Beaker and Horrible Histories. There can be few higher accolades from his peers than this.

Being Lewes resident almost his whole life it isn't really a surprise that Ben is today involved in the football club. He still rates the fact he "owns a football club" as something more to be proud of than his BAFTA awards and nomination. Living almost 250 miles from the city, and owning a subscription to Sky Sports makes Ben an obvious Manchester United fan, so what does he really know about football? Well, quite a bit actually.

His passions in life are his membership of one of the famous Lewes Bonfire Societies, football, and Toad in the Hole. The last one of those may seem strange, but we are talking about the game rather than the English contribution to world cuisine here. For those of you who (like me) have no idea what the game involves, let me enlighten you:-

"Toad in the hole is a pub game, involving throwing brass coins at a lead topped table with a hole in the middle. Toad in the hole is a more refined version of the coin-throwing game Pitch penny.

The only known league in the country is based in East Sussex, and has three divisions, involving roughly 21 teams based in pubs around the county. There is also a major "International Competition", run by Lewes Lions Club and held in Lewes every year."

Ben is a member of the Laughing Fish, who are the current World Champions, similar in a way to whoever wins the Major League Baseball World Series each year earns the right to be crowned world champions despite only American and a couple token Canadian teams being able to take part.
Part of the reason why Lewes FC is trying to change the face of how football

clubs are run at this level is the energy of people like Ben. Lewes FC are lucky in the fact that out of the six directors, five have flexible working arrangements. Ben's writing schedule means he is able to devote his time and creativity to the club when he is not working on a project. He has always been someone to push his deadline to the limit (and over it on such occasions).

The story of his involvement in the club is part evolution, part community spirited. He lives on the High Street with a view out of one window of the comings and goings of the lives of the townsfolk whilst from his back window he has a view, through the buildings down the hill of the main stand at The Dripping Pan. His front door displays his current passion - every single Lewes FC match poster so far this season. Nobody could ever accuse Ben of not believing in the dream of Lewes FC as the centre of the community.

He went to the same school as Eddie Ramsden, the financial expert from the board of directors, although he is a year or so older. He had spoken to Eddie for quite awhile about getting involved in a community-based project. They had looked at owning a pub for instance but nothing really stuck out with the "wow" factor. That is until one day he got a call from Eddie about the potential of getting involved in the football club. He had been an infrequent visitor to The Dripping Pan through the years and knew little about their plight last season. He went along to a meeting at the Kings Head one evening after a game and met Patrick Marber and Charlie Dobres for the first time.

Over the next few weeks a plan started to form. The club was in a desperate state and was unlikely to make it to the start of the following season. There was a danger that their approach of looking at the situation as fans would simply prolong the dire situation. In hindsight it seemed that the one moment of success in recent years that the club had, in winning the Conference South in April 2008 was actually the downward tipping point for the club.

The plan was devised and began to be executed during the summer. The dream was always to put the club at the heart of the community as well as putting the community at the heart of the club, a saying I would hear considerably more of this season. The sole objective for the short term was, and still is, to save the club and make it self-sustaining. Past that it is about developing the community benefit for everyone in Lewes. Changes off the field would eventually translate to on the field success but it was clear from day one the financial security of the club was priority number one.

Ben is under no illusion that this is not a short term flight of fancy. He understands football, he now needs to understand the mentality of your average football fan and translate that into an evolutionary approach to Lewes FC. Themed events such as the Bonfire society drummers, the delayed Christmas match in February or the "Beat my Mother" Mothers Day event are certainly unique. He became a Manchester United fan because of peer pressure from his brothers, having first been a Manchester City fan, so he knows full well how peer pressure can be used to influence your choice of team.

One final question for him got him thinking. FA Cup third round draw. Lewes are pulled out of the hat first. They have 63 other sides to wish for. So who would he want to be pulled out next? No question - Manchester United. But he would be willing to take the game to Old Trafford. And which red scarf would he wear on that day? The red and black of Lewes of course.

Saturday 14th August 2010
A Massive game

At a time in football where profit seems to be everything, Lewes FC went into the new season as a community-owned club "putting its money where its mouth was" by donating their shirt sponsorship to charity. And not just a half hearted gesture either as they decided to donate their "prime inventory" as commercial managers would call the shirt fronts to two different charities.

The Home shirt would feature the name of the much-loved Lewes Victoria Hospital, which was currently celebrating its 100th year in the midst of looming cutbacks. David Jones, the Manager at the Hospital commented *"We are already incredibly fortunate to have a very active League of Friends who support us, but the offer of so many local people seeing the hospital's name on the club's shirts and in our centenary year was one we were very surprised at, but delighted to accept."*

The Away shirt was being donated to the NSPCC. Founded in 1884, its vision is to end cruelty to children in the UK, something that all the staff at the football club felt very strongly they wanted to support. Russell Squire, NSPCC community fundraising manager for Sussex commented "*We are always looking for new ways to get our message in front of people. Lewes FC have shown that they put young people before profit and I'm impressed to see are also putting their hands in their own pockets to start the fundraising. Come on The Rooks!*"

And to emphasize their support for the idea, all the players signed up to a Donate As You Earn scheme that would see a percentage of their salaries go to the charities. Can you imagine the difference this scheme would make to some charities if all footballers in this country adopted such a scheme? Steve Ibbitson, Lewes FC Manager added: "*I'm proud of the Club for doing this and setting out its principles, especially when things are still tough for us. I hope the fans and local business community will support us in this very special initiative.*"

The opening day of the football season, coming at the end of a scorching hot week in the South East of England can only mean one thing. Rain. And plenty of it down on the banks of the Thames in Ali G country. As would become a common theme for me over the course of the season the journey to Staines was hampered by the world's biggest car park, the M25. So much for buying a decent Sat Nav with live traffic updates. Approximately ten minutes after I hit the mother of all traffic jams it kindly told me to avoid the next 10 miles of tarmac as it was "experiencing difficulties". Not sure if it meant the road or the SatNav but sitting watching a lorry driver pick his nose for 10 minutes was not my idea of fun.

The hour delay did not dampen my appetite for the new season and when I entered into the smart bar at the top of Staines Town's main stand to see the familiar faces of the loyal Lewes away following I knew I was back at the heart of the football I was beginning to love. Staines Town can be mightily proud of their ground which was funded by a progressive local council. The £6.5m main stand that also houses a fitness club and community facilities is well used seven days a week, especially the bar facilities that has its walls adorned with signed shirts, including one from local "boy made good" Darren Rose, one of the world's best golfers. On the big screen the Spurs v Manchester City game was winding down whilst the fans from both teams mingled, hoping that this season would be "the one" for their side. Last season Staines had played in the Blue Square South for the first time and for a period in the spring actually looked like they may be challenging for a playoff spot before finishing in a very credible 8th.

So day one, minute one and Lewes were joint top of the league. Could we end the season here and take a share of the spoils? Of course not. Ninety minutes would give us an idea as to how the off the field events had influenced the team. And what did the Rooks125 predict for this season?

Nick Williams - Play Off contenders
Ben Ward - I really don't know. Most of the excitement seems to have been off the pitch in recent years
Charlie Dobres - Really well, a great mix of youth and experience AND the ball will stay on the ground
Patrick Marber - Formidable
Eddie Ramsden - Midtable based on our playing budget
Alex Ward - Injuries permitting, top half of the table

We shall see shall we.

Staines Town 1 Lewes 0 – Wheatsheaf Park

Ninety minutes later and the Lewes fans had that familiar sinking feeling in their stomach as they had lost another away game by a single goal. In what has been a common theme in the past twelve months, and what would become a familiar story in the next 12, Lewes went down to one nil to Staines Town. It was a weakened Lewes side that kicked off the season and Staines made their inexperience pay in the opening exchanges.

Tom Murphy had the first chance of the game when he hit his shot wide of the upright after Gradwell alongside him had created an opening. Lewes keeper Winterton, making his debut at this level was the busier of the two keepers although some of the Staines finishing left a lot to be desired for a team that were one of the playoff favourites. Michael Kamara followed the finishing quality of his namesakes Titi and Henri by blazing over the bar for the home side when it was easier to score. But it was Staines who took their chance eventually in the 39th minute when former Lewes striker Griffiths fired home from 20 yards after Scott Manning failed to cut out a cross from Rene Steer. Lewes almost got back into the game immediately but the one player you probably do not want in a goal scoring position is captain Anthony Barness who is yet to score for the Rooks in over 100 games.

After a disappointing opening half, Ibbitson had to try and rally the team into life and whilst Lewes played a lot better in the second half they rarely threatened to grab an equaliser. The Lewes travelling support launched into a long version of "Oh when the Rooks" but it had no effect. Big Deaks started muttering about latest scores from the Bundesliga which is a sure sign that he was bored. We had already lined up a post match venue for some darts, which was becoming more and more appealing as the game wore on and we realised that the game would obviously end 1-0. But we do not leave games before the end - any right-minded football fan should never leave early. Would you walk out of a film before the end "to avoid the traffic?" No of course not so why do people do it at a football match. However, as soon as that whistle was blown we were out of there and straight into the Beehive for a few legs of the Netherlands second biggest sport.

Staines manager Steve Cordery summed up the game at full time quite well:

"With all due respect to them, they didn't really cause us any major problems, but we didn't really do enough going forward, and didn't do enough with the ball when we had it"

Lewes boss Steve Ibbotson essentially echoed this view *"We were struggling to cope with their full backs coming from deep and making late runs. We changed our formation around a bit in the second half. We went 4-3-3 and that nullified them but to a degree it nullified us as well. We had more of the play than in the first half but we didn't create any chances."*

Whilst the result was disappointing Lewes fans should remember that just seven months previously when this game was last played many thought it would be Lewes FC's last game with a huge tax bill and a winding up order from HMRC just days away. Football is a funny game and things can change in the blink of an eye. With forty one games still to go we can still win the league, can't we?

Wednesday 18th August 2010
Pan o ramic

After the disappointment at Staines, the question that most fans were asking was whether the buzz around the club in the summer would translate to people coming through the gate. The club had sensibly decided to keep the same pricing structure from the tail end of the previous season which saw yours truly step through the turnstile with Lolly for just £10. The Lewes fans knew that the transition from strugglers at the end of last season to a team that could hold its own would take a few months, especially as the teams coming into the division in the form of Farnborough and Dartford were both well fancied, and above all appeared (as much as it can in the non leagues anyway) to be financially sound. The key to any success this season had to be some decent home form. Last season the club had won only 6 games at home and this eventually was the main reason why they found themselves in the bottom three for most of the campaign. Manager Steve Ibbitson had targeted this as a "must do better" and the foundation to this he believed was the support the team got.

And as a measure as to how far the club had taken things off the pitch the crowd of 601 was better than all bar two of the crowds in the previous campaign but more importantly almost 250 people up on the same fixture, ironically played on the same day as the previous year. That game had been a disappointing draw, although the three sendings off did liven things up slightly in the second half. But it was three points The Rooks needed after Saturday's defeat and that was the only thing Ibbo would accept.

Lewes 2 Thurrock 1 - The Dripping Pan

Steve Ibbitson made two changes from the side which had lost 1-0 at Staines Town on the opening day of the season, with Sonny Cobbs and George Jones replacing Lewis Hamilton and Tom Murphy in the starting line-up. In a fairly tentative start by both sides, the ball spent much of the first 15 minutes or so in the midfield, with each team finding it difficult to put the opposition under any sustained pressure. It was Thurrock who had the first real openings, though, with Joe Collins cutting inside from the left wing and dragging his shot just wide of Chris Winterton's near post, before Cliff Akurang sent a powerful shot from just outside the penalty area straight at the keeper. The Lewes fans, standing on the Jungle, the open terrace behind the east end of the ground, so called because, erm, we couldn't think of anything better to call it, simultaneously exhaled. Things were not looking rosy.

However, the Rooks soon found their feet, with midfield lynch-pin Simon Wormull the architect of a superb move involving George Jones, which saw Ross Sutton scuff his shot wide of the target. If you haven't ever seem Wormull play then close your eyes and imagine a cross between a sober Paul Gascoigne, a better timer of the tackle than Paul Scholes, but with a bad back. He can put the ball on a six pence from forty yards, although afterwards he has to have a "little sit down".

After 25 minutes, Lewes took the lead and with it opened their account for the season. The goal came courtesy of Lewis Ide, who met Jones' cross with a superb diving header from just inside the penalty area, giving Andre Charles-Foster in the Thurrock goal no chance. Diving headers these days are becoming as rare as seeing a genuine young English player make it through the ranks at Chelsea, and one from such distance not only took the Thurrock keeper by surprise but also the whole crowd.

This goal gave the Rooks momentum, allowing Wormull to take control of the game, after his little sit down and be involved in every Lewes attack, with his range of passing and quick thinking posing the visitors a number of problems. Just minutes later, Ide nearly scored a spectacular second goal. The impressive midfielder showed great awareness to lift the ball over a Thurrock defender before trying his luck in chipping the keeper, only to see his chip go just over the bar.

The one thing that Lewes has always lacked is that self belief. Holding the lead were not something the team had been used to so it became worrying that they let Thurrock back into the game as the half wore on. They nearly got their equaliser through a bizarre incident that saw Thurrock keeper Charles-Foster send a long free-kick forward from midway inside his own half which evaded everyone apart from Winterton who had to back pedal quickly to touch the ball over the bar as the bounce caught him off guard.

Thurrock started the second half as they had finished the first, with Lee Flynn seeing his powerful volley from the edge of the area go just wide. Minutes later, Lewes nearly spectacularly doubled their lead with Wormull, in almost Beckham territory now, spotting Charles-Foster off his line and sending his half-volley on the turn from 40 yards out just wide of the post. This was a mere warm up for the midfield maestro who had the crowd convinced we had a new international star in our side as in the 63rd minute he had a second chance at a spectacular goal from distance and this time he made no mistake from around 45 yards, flighting the ball over Charles-Foster, turning to give him a wink before celebrating as if to say "told you I could do it".

Funnily enough Lewes had held 2-0 leads twice towards the end of last season, away to Worcester City and Hampton & Richmond, only to give a goal away and frantically hang on for a win, so it was no surprise to see Thurrock back in the game within two minutes as Akurang latched onto a through-ball after a slip by Andy Pearson, held off two further Lewes defenders and fired home via the near post.

Despite Thurrock enjoying more possession, Lewes had a chance to make the game safe as it entered the final 15 minutes, with Rob Gradwell firing a shot right across the face of goal after being set up by a killer ball from substitute Jordan Lang. A goal at this stage would have killed any hope of a comeback, but instead Thurrock pushed more men up front and in the final few minutes saw Kenny Clark's header come back off the post.

Despite this pressure, Lewes held on to record their first win of the season. So played two, won one. Expectations for the season are modest to say the least but for the fans who have endured two very difficult seasons it is all about seeing the team trying to compete. After the game, Ibbo was as upbeat as a dour northerner could be.

"Yes, I am pleased with the win - the result was great but I wasn't so pleased with the performance. At two-nil up we should have killed the game off but instead we concede a silly goal and we are left to hang on. Both our centre backs could of and should have cleared that ball when it was pinging around the area. We have to learn to kill teams off. However, we are having to play some of the youngsters due to injury and they are bound to make some mistakes - that is all part of their apprenticeship. I am very proud of what we have developed here as a club"

One final notable figure was the crowd. The takeover had put the buzz back into the town, and for the first time in years the club had reached out and promoted itself into the community in the lead up to the game and the result was a crowd of 601.

"We want to be a big part of the community. We want the town to come down and enjoy the football with us" was Ibbo's final quote on the game. Here here.

Saturday 21st August 2010
Open for Business

Our appeal first went out in late June. "Wanted. Scarves, pennants, badges, shirts. Anything accepted, nothing refused. Help us turn the Rook Inn into a proper European Fans Bar. Danny and I love nothing better than heading off on a jet plane to the four corners of Europe and sharing a beer, some tales of bravadery, some banter and an exchange of mementos, consequently building up such a collection that in 2006 I opened the first ever Football Memorabilia, Tack and Press Pass museum in South East London in my garden. Even today visitors head for TBIR towers wanting a glimpse at the Hertha Berlin egg cup that shouts "Tor!" when you crack the egg, or the unique South Korean World Cup stadia jigsaw puzzle postcards that you were supposed to make then post to your friends, although just picking them up caused them to crumble to 32 pieces. So we decided to find a more permanent home for our collections, and what better place than the Rook Inn.

The bar at the Dripping Pan had seen better days and wasn't exactly welcoming. There is very little we can do to improve the size of the bar, or removing the pillars that support the club offices above, but we could adorn the walls with a bit of colour, sparkle and mystery. And that is exactly what we did. Over the summer the walls were painted white, like a fresh canvas awaiting an old masters brush. And along we came with literally a hundred scarves, from clubs like Forest Green Rovers, 1860 Munich, Atalanta and err Tottenham Hotspur. We chose the best and started adding them to the walls, forming a colourful backdrop for the number events that the bar hosted, and featuring in the Times no less when our new owners were profiled and snapped a few days after our work was done.

We arrived early on a glorious August to put the finishing touches to the latest arrivals including a 70's style pennant from Leeds United. Now what would look good on that would be a signature from a Leeds legend of the era perhaps? Hang on. Isn't that Frankie Gray just walking through the door? Of course, we had forgotten that Lewes's opponents for their second home game of the season Basingstoke Town were managed by former Leeds United man Frankie Gray. Frankie was just a bit too young to feature in Brian Clough's 44 days in charge at Leeds United that had just been immortalised by the film Damned United. In fact in the film he was the only real player of that Leeds squad who wasn't featured. Clough obviously liked what he saw as along with John McGovern and Archie Gemmill he soon had him in his squad at Nottingham Forest, winning almost every cup going including the European Cup in consecutive years, a feat that no other English team has ever matched. I could imagine Cloughie liking Lewes. I could see him waltz into the car park, flicking a couple of quid at a kid to buy a ticket from the machine. Wandering in through the gate, stopping to have a chat with Edna about her corns before wandering into the Rook Inn and "taking a quick medicinal" for the circulation. Walking along the touchline from where the players enter the pitch he would stop, ruffle some young chaps hair before giving a thumbs up to the Jungle....If Carlsberg did dreams about non league football eh!

Lewes 0 Basingstoke Town 0 - The Dripping Pan

Home form would be the make or break for Lewes and so after the win against Thurrock and another crowd of over 500 expectations were high. Unfortunately it wasn't to be. Despite starting well with Wormull and Gradwell going close in the early exchanges the visitors created their own opportunities to win it as well, so a draw was a fair result.

The lively Basingstoke forward Nathan Smart had the best chance of the first half in the 31st minute when he skipped past Scott Manning and Sonny Cobbs, but saw his 20 yard shot tipped around the post by Winterton at full stretch. Nerves started to spread across the Jungle and even the appearance of Cynical Dave's emergency pint, only pulled out in extreme cases of tension could not settle the nerves. Despite this only being the third game of the season, six points from three games would be a start beyond expectations. Half time was a reflecting walk back into The Rook Inn, a furtive nod at Patrick Marber biting his fingernails, whilst simultaneously smoking two cigarettes said it all.

The visitors opened the second half with Greg Draper's shot across the face of the goal causing a collective gasp from the terrace but neither side was able to take a controlling interest in proceedings for much of the second period. Basingstoke centre back Ross Adams had two great chances within a minute with a volley from a free kick and a header from a corner, whilst substitute Jason Downes was denied by the legs of Winterton. Squeaky bum time.

Frankie Gray was on his feet, fingernails in his mouth knowing that his Basingstoke team should have been in the lead. But football is a fickle master and it was Lewes who ended the stronger with Chris Breach's header finding its way fortunately into the arms of Tardif in the away goal. Big Deaksy let out a sigh, Dave a long drag on his roll up, Danny stopped Tweeting and I scratched my head - I am sure I had brought at least one daughter to this game, but in the tension I hadn't seen her for the whole second half. Good old Lolly. Seeing the tension on our faces she had gone off to buy (out of her own money I should add) bacon rolls all round. I swear if the law allowed she would have been at that bar carrying pints of Harveys backwards and forwards all afternoon.

Deadlock it was then. A fair reflection on the whole and Lewes manager Steve Ibbitson reluctantly agreed with after the game:-

"Two home games gone and we had targeted six points but we cannot complain in the end. We still have players out and haven't played very well in any of the three games. Today we couldn't get the shape right and they could have been 2 or 3 up early on. Injuries mean we have the wrong players in the wrong positions, although the team needs to listen to what we say before the game and play in the positions we ask!

We seem to be taking two steps forward and three back in terms of injuries at the moment. Sonny Cobb's groin is a bit tight (snigger from interviewer Patrick Marber at this point). *The good news is that David Wheeler is back, although he is still not fit. He has a parasite in his system that he needs to pass. Granted he is a lovely passer of the ball but I do not want to be sitting next to him on the bench until that thing is out of his system!"*

Three wins, four points and all seemed to be progressing....or was it?

Mint - An interview with Dave Lamb

Dave Lamb is fantastic yet few people know the name, or even the face. But the voice? Well that is up there with Patrick Allen, Marcus Bentley and Alan Dedicoat (the voices of Black Adder, Big Brother and The National Lottery respectively) as the most recognisable on Television. He is the voice of Come Dine With Me, the Channel 4 reality cooking show that pits four or five contestants cooking and hosting skills in the ultimate game of one upmanship. I used to roll my eyes and lower my bottom lip when my wife would flick over to Channel 4 after the football on a Sunday. And then I actually watched it and had to stop myself from giggling at the verbal soundtrack delivered expertly by Dave Lamb. And that is why he is fantastic.

Lamb has more strings to his bow than just Come Dine With Me. He's appeared on a plethora of television and radio programmes and is, as you might expect, a comedy genius. But to us his most impressive trait is his taste in football, a fan of Lewes FC. We caught up with him standing in his favourite spot just by the flagpole on the Mountfield Road bank early in the season.

How come you've ended up supporting The Mighty Rooks?
As a life-long Manchester United fan born and raised in the south east of England, I've taken a fair amount of stick over the years. It's got to me if I'm honest. I now agree completely that it's vital to support your local team. So whilst I won't be giving up United - you can't just give up your allegiance even if you suspect it may be wrong on many levels, I made a decision in good faith as a six year old and I'll stand by that - my passion has been localised. When I had this revelation I was living in Dorset so became a Weymouth season ticket holder for two years. As a Weymouth fan I developed a taste for relegation battles, financial difficulties and defeat. So when I moved to Brighton just over two years ago The Rooks and I were clearly going to be a perfect match. Also my good friend and ex-writing partner Ben Ward is one of the directors and he made me come at first until I was bitten by the Rooks bug.

The Dripping Pan is a majestic place to spend an afternoon watching football no?
The Dripping Pan is simply the finest place I've ever watched football. I am an absolute bugger for a pint of Harveys, and to be able to sup a pint whilst

breathing in the air and taking in the South Downs is spectacular. Sometimes I get so caught up in the experience that I forget there's a game on - but not for long.

Are you fully supportive of the new board of directors and its 'Community Club' ethics?
Very much so. I think what they are doing is beyond reproach. Their determination to ensure that the club survives first and foremost and then finds a natural level for itself is admirable and wonderful. Theirs is not an ego thing, it's a love thing.

You've been sprinkling Come Dine With Me with your magic for the thick end of a decade now. Is that something you still love doing? *It's all right.*

Do you ever commentate on the Lewes games in your head in the same bitingly sarcastic manner as on Come Dine With Me?
No. Because Lewes are brilliant, unlike most of the people on Come Dine With Me.

Right, be prepared to roll your eyes at the final question: who would be your dream four guests at a Come Dine With Me dinner party?
Henry the Eighth, Gillian Mackeith, Wayne Rooney and Susan Boyle. I can't see Rooney's agent agreeing to it though.

Tuesday 24th August 2010
Written in the Cards

Work dictates that neither Danny nor I cannot get out much during the week. I have to endure overpriced beer, tall beautiful blondes and the least corrupt country on earth as I scratch out a living in Denmark. Danny is still training to be a vampire so he has to be selective about his games. In fact it has to be a very special occasion, like for instance, the Finnish branch of the Lewes Supporters Club travelling from Helsinki to Woking on a Tuesday night just to see The Mighty Rooks. That is a special occasion no?

The Lewes Lunatic Fringe of course need no introduction. Stalwarts Cynical Dave and Big Deaks were keen as the proverbial mustard as well for this game and why wouldn't they be? This was going to be the best day of our lives - again as we told our respective partners.

Trying to find a pub that won't drain the life and soul out of you between Woking Station and the Kingfield Stadium isn't as easy as one might think. A simple search using the word "Woking" on the website Beer in the evening results in a belly laugh as good as that bloke who always dresses in red, works one day a year and lives up north. So we decided to go all militant for this seasons visit to Woking. The Woking Railway Athletic Club looked to have some characters in there, but, not being life members of the Railway, we were refused entry. In hindsight, we should have taken a punt and said that Paddy, Mick, Scouse or Jock would sign us in. Comrades indeed!

What would Woking's favourite son Paul Weller do in this situation? Write 'Town Called Malice', and then head to the Snooker Club probably. So that's what we did, after we'd walked through the infamous park near to the ground. Infamous in that even the Woking FC website recommends that, for personal safety reasons, women and young children do not walk unaccompanied. It was actually rather pleasant and, as luck would have it in bloom. An idyllic setting for joy riding I am sure.

Snooker clubs all conform to stereotypes from the 1980's in my book. Well, yes they are full of snooker tables of course, but it is the hushed atmosphere, the dim lighting and the lack of anyone who looks healthy. You can only look at fat blokes playing snooker surrounded by mandatory cartoon etchings of Tony Meo and Jimmy White for so long can't you before you crave some culture. So, being short of that we headed off to the ground.

Kingfield, home of Woking FC. I did ask around as to why it was called this. Nobody seemed to know. I am sure that at some point in history a King has parked his horse in the field here (perhaps he too was trying to get into the Railway Athletic Club) and someone thought long and hard, trying all combinations of name such as Regal Fallow, Royal Meadow and the like before coming up with the current name. But we had no time for such philosophy. We were here to extend the geographical boundaries of the Lewes fan network and meet the biggest (and probably only) Finnish member of the Lewes Supporters Club, Helsinki Branch. Our man in the land of mobile phones, lakes and er Mixo Patalaenan is called Ville Miettinen. Ville is a freelance football journalist, and pleasingly, a very nice chap. He even presented us with Finnish scarves for the Rook Inn. We like Ville and quickly ratified the existence of the FLSC (Finnish Lewes Supporters Club) over a round of the nearest beer we could find to being Finnish, Carlsberg.

Days before the game Woking had announced it had a small issue. Nothing to worry about at the back chaps, just a little cashflow problem. When clubs talk in such words as "cash flow", "working capital" and "we haven't got any money" alarm bells should ring. In Woking's case it seemed to be a tad more serious. They were on the well worn path to administration, as most non league clubs are I should add until somewhat reluctantly, former Chairman Chris Ingram dug deep to find £200,000 to plug a huge funding gap. Ouch. Realistically will Chris ever see that money again? Probably not. But football is reliant on men like Chris and never should we forget it.

Beers drunk, Finnish words for "Oh when the Rooks go swooping in" learnt and stomachs fed, we headed onto the terraces to welcome the Lewes machine onto the pitch. Stand anywhere in the Kingfield Stadium itself and I challenge you not to say "This is a right old mixed bag of goodies". Two marvellous old stands that, if you squint your eyes and use your imagination, could pass for the pavilion at the Sydney Cricket Ground. They're dwarfed though by an enormous new stand behind one goal. It is the size of a bus. In fact it's the size of about two hundred buses. And it's shiny. The stadium is also in the Guinness Book of Records, or it should be, for having a record amount of signs declaring 'No standing in this area please'. I counted 416. Good omens one and all predicted Danny.

Woking 2 Lewes 0 – Kingfield Stadium

So to the match. Beforehand, Danny had told anyone who'd listen that we should fear Cards striker Dave Gilroy. He is the scourge of Lewes Football Club. He looks at the fixture list to see who we're playing, signs for them, scores against us, and then moves on. Until he signs for Lewes, which must be imminent, we hate him. Last season he popped up at Newport County and Weston-Super-Mare, helping himself to a match ball along the way.

Naturally Gilroy scored twice early on as the Cards threatened to run riot. As we looked around the terrace for something to humour us we noticed a couple of familiar faces. The takeover of the club had injected some celebrityness (my new word so hands off) with Oscar nominated scriptwriter, playwright and Alan Partridge's mucker Patrick Marber taking an active part as one of the Rooks125 group. Not content with a place in the directors box he stood firmly on the terrace with the away fans. And tonight he had with him Drop the Dead Donkey's Neil Pearson. Patrick is, as one might expect, extremely good company. The sort of company you need when you're two-bloody-nil down to Woking on a Tuesday night.

The second half was a different story. Lewes came out like caged tigers in a Siegfried and Roy Las Vegas show and took the game to their hosts. Lewis Ide (you will note that Lewes like to play players with the christen name Lewis) began to pull a few midfield strings, substitutes Aaron Hopkinson and Tom Murphy added pace, guile, Coca-Cola Silver badge skills and verve to the attack and youth team prodigy deservedly Jordan Lang pulled a goal back with a cushioned (cushioned!) shot with the inside of his boot to make the last part of the game interesting to say the least. However, in the end the sweaty palms of the home support dried out and Woking clung on for their second win in four days.

Whilst we tucked into a few more beers in the clubhouse, playing a round of Finnish Catchphrase, Lewes manager gave his thoughts on the game.

"Sometimes you can sense a problem in the warm up and tonight both Jason (Hopkinson - assistant manager) and I thought the team didn't look up for it before the game, and we have to hold our hands up for not addressing that. As we saw, ten minutes into the game and we were one down, but it could have more. But after that man Gilroy had scored the opener we

realised we could play and we created a few chances. The second was a real kick in the knackers but when we got the players in at half time we changed it around a bit. We needed to do something - we struggled against their front players and that bloke Gilroy seems to score every time we see him."

"George Jones came on and he played really well. You forget sometimes that players like him are so young - he is only 17. We finished that game with 10 players under 24 which again shows the potential we have at the club. We had 3 or 4 good opportunities after we had scored to draw level. We realised that putting balls into the box would create problems. It is difficult to say we deserved a draw based on the whole 90 minutes but we certainly did base on our second half performance."

No panic then Mr. Manwarring. Not just yet anyway. Next up "crisis" club Dover Athletic. If only we had half of their problems!

Saturday 28th August 2010
Remember Boxing Day?

Romantic breaks away when you have kids are few and far between. With one it is just about possible, but when you have two then people seem reluctant to take them as a package. We are lucky that CMF's parents will have them at the drop of a hat. That is the good news. The bad news is that they life 150 miles away, and due to a number of phobias about the evils of the M25 and crossing "the river" mean that a 600 mile, 11 hour round trip (150 there and back twice) means it isn't always practical. But when an interesting looking envelope fell on our doormat back in April the opportunity of such a break was simply too good to miss.

My good chum Luge lives in New York. He is as Cockney as jellied eels, pie and mash and the O2 Arena and as a true Londoner supports Manchester United. Amazingly, despite spending most of his spare time in Nevada Smith's watching beam backs from the Premier League in good old blighty he had not only managed to find a beautiful American girl, but also managed someone to convince Katie to marry him. The wedding day? Saturday 28th August 2010. And we had been invited. Frantic arrangements made, childcare sorted for the children and we were on that British Airways flight across the Atlantic. Not only would we be missing Manchester United versus West Ham, which was obviously a shoe-in for a home win, but we would also be missing the visit of Dover Athletic to The Pan.

Last season Lewes rarely moved out of the bottom three whilst Dover challenged all season for promotion, missing out in the end in the play offs to Woking in what was a relative shock. When the teams met on Boxing Day last season it seemed to be a foregone conclusion. And just thirteen minutes into the game Dover were two goals to the good.

And then something happened. Something that for those few hundred who were there will one day say to their Grandchildren "I was there at the Pan on Boxing Day 2009". If this game was at Upton Park, The Emirates or most of the plastic Premier League grounds the home fans would have been making their way to the exits with just a sixth of the game gone, preferring the pub to the pain on the pitch. But for some reason the crowd sensed something was about to change.

Five minutes later and the arrears were reduced by Joe Keehan's volley. Then it was all square when Brinkhurst smashed it in from distance. Could it get any better? Well what about a Dover own goal to take the Rooks in ahead at half time. Scoring three at home in the league for the first time in what seemed like years was enough to send the fans for the bar, fearing a Dover onslaught in the second half. But two more from Keehan and a late effort from David Wheeler made the score Lewes 6 Dover 2. Probably the most surprising result of the season.

So could they do it again? Could they make my afternoon some 3,000 miles away? Hmmm..

Lewes 0 Dover Athletic 3 – The Dripping Pan

There was no six appeal this time around as a disappointing performance from Lewes saw the visitors comfortably claim the points. An own-goal from Anthony Barness and strikes from Elliot Charles and Harrison Crawford did the damage both in East Sussex and in downtown Manhattan as the score filtered through.

Lewes manager Steve Ibbitson made three changes to the side which had lost 2-1 at Woking in the previous game, with Chris Breach, Marc Pullan and Ross Sutton being replaced in the starting line-up by Anthony Barness, Arron Hopkinson and Lee Carey making his debut. Following on from an impressive second-half performance at Woking on Tuesday night, Lewes started brightly, with the Rooks enjoying the majority of the possession in the opening exchanges and created the first goal scoring opportunity, with Rob Gradwell just being beaten to a superb through-ball from Lee Carey by Ross Flitney in the Dover goal.

The Rooks continued to have a lot of possession in midfield, though, and after some excellent play in midfield from Simon Wormull, were unlucky to see Gradwell's powerful shot from a tight angle inside the penalty area deflected just wide. However, it was Dover who took the lead after 17 minutes. The goal was scored by Lewes captain Anthony Barness, who met the impressive Harry Baker's cross with a header which caught Winterton off his line and ended up looping over the unfortunate goalkeeper and into the back of the net.

Half time couldn't come soon enough for manager Ibbitson so that he could try and sort out the dysfunctional team. However, it was Dover who started the second half as they had finished the first, with Jon Wallis capitalising on a slip in the Lewes defence, only to see his pull-back scrambled clear by Winterton at his near post. It was only a matter of time though that a second would come and on the hour mark it was Elliot Charles who slid in to meet a pinpoint a Baker cross to score.

Perhaps remembering their two-nil lead from last season Dover went for the kill, punishing Lewes for not making the most of the openings they had created and they added a third goal after 69 minutes. The goal came courtesy of substitute Harrison Crawford, who had only been on the pitch for two minutes, after the striker fired a low shot from a tight angle across Winterton and into the far corner.
Despite the points now being wrapped up for Dover, the Rooks continued to work hard in midfield and were unlucky not to pull a goal back just minutes later when Hopkinson saw his shot from inside the penalty area parried wide by Flitney after a perfectly-weighted through-ball from Carey. From the resulting corner, the impressive Scott Manning, sent a powerful header just wide.

Tom Murphy then saw his shot which seemed destined for the top corner saved by Flitney after the substitute had done well to get past Olly Schulz in the build-up.

Three nil was perhaps a bit harsh on The Rooks but that is football. A downbeat Ibbo faced up to the grilling from Patrick Marber after the game as he explained what went wrong.

"*I feel annoyed because it wasn't a 3-0 game, We asked the players not to start as we did against Woking where we lost the game before we had started playing and it worked. We were brighter at the start of the game but then conceded that own goal. Barney (*Anthony Barness) *has never scored a goal in a Lewes shirt but we didn't want his first one to be an own goal. He has probably never scored one like that before and I doubt he will score one like it again!*"

"*On reflection we need to say we gave them all three goals. They deserved to win the game as they were stronger than us especially up front. We are still struggling with injuries and had three players fail fitness tests pre-match. However the positive was that we saw David Wheeler on the pitch for the first time this season. It is frustrating every week to have 4 or 5 players out injured who would be in the match day squad. But we cannot complain too much as we are giving some very talented youngsters a chance to get some first team football."*

Only one win from three successive home games was not the return that Lewes wanted. Still there was always Welling away to look forward to.

Monday 30th August 2010
A local club for local people

Some years ago when I first flirted with divorcing West Ham I looked around at where I could spend my Saturday afternoons. Welling United's Park View Road ground is approximately 3.5 miles from my house. I could cycle there. Actually, based on the fact that I have completed three (three!) 5km runs in the past year I could run there, and it would only take me about an hour. So I gave it a try. I got to know a few people at the club, even helped out with the odd match report but the more I learnt about the club, the more I felt there was a dark centre in the club so I decided to renew my vowels at Upton Park.

I had been back a few times, standing on the Park Terrace watching the buses drive past. Last season a pre-season friendly against Gillingham was enough for me. I simply couldn't enjoy the afternoon. I couldn't put my finger on it. Nobody seemed particular happy to welcome me, as a "neutral" fan there. Now I am not every expecting a red carpet, but as part of my pre-match research I always drop the club a note, looking for someone to touch base with. I tried numerous times to get someone from the club interested in this free publicity, as well as at their official supporters club. Not a dicky bird.

Despite being the closest team to The Ball is Round Towers circumstances have dictated that for the past two seasons neither Danny nor I have attended the home game against Lewes. Last season the game co-incided with our annual European Ocktoberfest - a meeting of nearly 40 football fans from around Europe for a weekend of football, beer and er...beer and football. This year I was on the other side of the pond sans children still enjoying the Luge Pravda festivities. Annoyingly with virtually every game in Europe being shown on TV somewhere, the haunt of the Expats in the Big Apple, Nevada Smiths were not showing this game so I had to rely on updates via Twitter from Big Deaks.

Welling United 2 Lewes 1 – Park View Road

After three games Lewes had four points and sat healthily in mid-table. Six games on they still had those same four points and had dropped into the bottom quarter of the Blue Square Bet South after a third successive defeat.

Despite a Simon Wormull penalty in injury time it only proved to be a consolation at Park View Road. Despite major concerns off the pitch for the future of Welling United, on the pitch the tales of woe don't seem to have got through as the team continued to hold a top five spot.

Lewes manager Steve Ibbitson made three changes to the side which had lost 3-0 at home to Dover Athletic just two days previously, with Marc Pullan, Sonny Cobbs and George Jones effectively replacing Scott Manning, Lewis Ide and Arron Hopkinson in the starting line-up. Although Lewes had a lot of possession in the opening exchanges, the Rooks fell behind after only five minutes when Welling centre-back Graeme Andrews flicked home an in-swinging Jack Obersteller free-kick from the right-hand side. Another game, another early goal conceded.

However, the Rooks continued to play with confidence and saw Tom Murphy force Welling's Charlie Mitten into a relatively comfortable stop with a half-volley from the edge of the penalty area after latching onto a Rob Gradwell knock-down. Just minutes later, Lewes went close again, as George Jones sent his far-post header from an Andy Pearson cross just over the bar.

Not long before half-time, the hosts believed they should have been awarded a penalty when, following some intricate passing in midfield, Welling's Tom Whitnell was brought down in the penalty area. However, referee Nigel Lugg waved away the vocal protests of the Welling players. Now whether Lugg knew he had got this wrong, or he was simply a rubbish referee we will never know but he levelled up the unjust penalty decisions. Lewes's Tom Murphy did well to capitalise on a defensive mix-up to round Mitten and send an effort goal-wards. The ball was diverted onto the crossbar by the outstretched Obersteller on the goaline, but Andy Sambrook headed the ball back towards the goal, where there were suspicions of the ball crossing the line and of handball. The long walk back to the tunnel at half time saw Mr Lugg's opinions in great demand but of course referees are accountable to no-one and he kept his reasons for giving neither decision to himself.

The Rooks started the second half brightly, with young winger Jordan Lang going on a run and sending his low shot straight at Mitten.

This lively start to the second half gave Lewes confidence as they enjoyed lots possession in the opening ten minutes of the half although, as with the first half, they were unable to turn this possession into any clear-cut chances. With this being the case, Welling always posed a threat and were unlucky not to double their lead when Jack Parkinson saw his powerful shot from a tight angle acrobatically saved by the impressive Winterton.

Just when it seemed as though Lewes were beginning to put Welling under an increased spell of pressure, the hosts scored a second after 69 minutes to give themselves some breathing space. The goal was scored by Pugh, who received a pass from substitute Joe Healy and unleashed a wonderful curling shot from the edge of the area into the top corner.

To their credit, the young Lewes side did not give and continued to create one or two chances. Substitute Tim Rivers had the most notable chance, as he connected superbly with a Lee Carey corner at the back post on the volley, only to see his effort drop just wide.

However, Welling also continued to create chances as the game entered the final ten minutes. The best of these saw Luis Cumbers drag a left-foot shot from the edge of the area just wide after an excellent run.

With four minutes indicated as the time to be added on, Lewes finally got some reward. Tom Murphy was again at the heart of the action as he burst into the penalty area before being brought down by a combination of Welling's substitute Femi Omegbehin and Sambrook. Up stepped Simon Wormull and it was two-one. But it was too little too late despite another chance falling to Murphy in the final seconds.

After the game Ibbo was furious. *"To concede a goal like that after a couple of minutes was a nightmare, especially after the games in the past few weeks. We have specifically worked on defensive free kicks but went to sleep, simple as that, and they scored. Rob (Gradwell) held his hands up at half time and said he let the player go which led to the goal but it is really annoying to have conceded the goal."*

Things had to change soon for the team. But what would those changes be?

Saturday 4th September 2010
National Non League Day

"Fewer attended matches last season than at any other point in this club's history. Hardly anyone offers to volunteer for match day duties; almost no-one attended the Quiz night nor the Race Night previously arranged for fans. Hardly anyone gets their friends to join our lottery scheme; fewer people have renewed their supporters trust subscription. And so on. And so on.

We can all remember when the previous chairman told us year in year out that the club needed to be self-financing to continue to operate in the future. Most of us ignored it and he, along with the other committed directors continued to finance the club out of their own pockets. Then one day they stopped putting the cash in and the Trust had to step in to ensure the survival of the club.

I am today telling you again, as the Trust's Chairman that this club needs to be self-financing and soon. Our cash reserves are declining rapidly and will be completely depleted soon. You can ignore me if you want but if you do, you might want to start thinking about how you are going to spend you Saturday afternoons and Tuesday evenings in future.

We have enough money for this season, and probably for the next, but if we are not able to improve our financial position and get a few more volunteers on board then we will be out of business in two or three years.

It is as simple as that.

I am doing as much as I can to keep the club alive. So are the other members of the Trust board. Are you? We cannot do anything more that we are already doing based on the resources we have to work with. Can you? Please do not wait until it is too late.

Your club needs you NOW!"

This intro could apply to 90% of most non league teams up and down the country. It was written by a Chairman of a Supporters Trust of a team in the third level of the non-league pyramid - a level that has already seen a number of clubs simply give up since the end of last season, unable to find a way to carry on in the current climate where costs are increasing and revenues are falling.

The simple fact of the matter that the majority of football going fans drive past non league grounds week in week out to head off to the cathedrals of Old Trafford, The Emirates and the B2Net Stadium. With England's first qualifier for the 2012 European Championships moved to a Friday night and with no games in the Premier League and the nPower Championship, Saturday 4th September was built up as National Non League Day. A day when fans of the bigger clubs were urged to attend a game at the grass roots level. Brainchild of James Doe, a Harrow Borough (and QPR) fan, he managed to mobilise the media to getting behind the initiative. It was music to my ears. Someone else coming out and saying it's not all about the Premier League. This weekend was all about trying to encourage those fans to experience something new. The first designated Non League Day was not meant as a charitable act - in fact many non league clubs slashed their prices to encourage more people to attend a local game. If 10% of the fans who go to watch the Premier League every week paid just £10 to watch a non league team then there would be £350,000 more going into the pockets of clubs who desperately need it. And if a fraction of those came back to watch a game then the state of football at the lower levels would see a small improvements.

Four months ago when the 2009/10 Premier League season came to a close, and West Ham United hung onto their place on the gravy train for another season I made a monumental decision. I was going to turn my back on the Hammers and follow Lewes FC instead. In the past few seasons I had been all over the country watching the game in all levels of the non leagues and had simply "seen the light". And looking back now I saw a number of reasons why I kept coming back, pointing my car down the M23 and along the A27 instead of through the Blackwall Tunnel. Here are just a few.

Because you never know who you will bump into

Want to meet a West Ham legend? Head into the bar of the Beveree at Hampton & Richmond, or The Waterside at Walton Casuals and you can chat to Alan Devonshire and Tony Gale. What about one of England's finest wicketkeepers? Well that will be Jack Russell sitting in the stand at Forest Green Rovers. A European Cup double winner? What about Basingstoke's manager Frankie Gray. It's the way I tell them? Well certainly at Chasetown where a regular visitor is Frank Carson. Lewes has a Whose line is it anyway dream team of celebrities with Patrick Marber, Mark Williams, Neil Pearson and Come Dine With Me's Dave Lamb all regulars through the gates at the Pan.

Because the players are playing for the love of the game

Few non league clubs are full time, and so players are expected to feed themselves outside of the game. This means that they are human, understanding the pains that fans feel themselves. It also means that sometimes they have to miss a game to work (one non league coach regularly misses midweek games as he can earn more money as a taxi driver doing airport runs) or to study for exams. Want to say well done to a player on a great performance? Buy him a bee, but just the one as the manager is watching (unless you buy him one too).

Because the fans are realists

Sure, every club has a website forum, and debate can rage about any issue. But it is never malicious or vicious. You will rarely meet a non league fan who thinks his team have a god given right to be top or constantly challenging for promotion nor one who is spoiling for an argument. That is unless they suddenly "inherit" a lot of money and start spending it like they are the Manchester City of the south.

Because at the start of every season every team has some hope

It is very unusual for any fans to get above their station at the start of the season. With some very very rare exceptions the season kicks off with a relatively level playing field. Even last season when Newport County ran away with the Blue Square South title they were not even in the bookies top 3 bets prior to the start of the campaign.

Because it is great value for money

In the Blue Square South Bet this season the most you will pay to get into a game is £12, the least £9. Most clubs charge £10. And the kids? Well Lewes and Farnborough Town don't charge a penny for under 16's and most clubs only charge a couple of pound. Or of course you could buy a programme and a burger at The Emirates for the same price...that is after you have paid your £50 to get in. Anyone who has been to a game at Upton Park in the last few seasons will notice no difference in the atmosphere between the 250 at Thurrock or the 30,000 against Wigan Athletic.

Because you are still allowed to have a beer

I am not going into the rights and wrongs of the Taylor Report but I fail to see how being allowed to have a nice pint of Harveys on the terrace at The Dripping Pan this season is allowed, yet if they are promoted to the Blue Square Premier or it is an FA Trophy game it is illegal and I could be arrested. Beer and football have always gone together and at this level to many clubs bar sales are vital income streams. After all it's not like you cannot spend four hours in a pub (or seven if it happens to be a Weatherspoons on a Saturday) sinking as many pints as you want before you head into the ground.

Because the hospitality is heartfelt

The people who work behind the scenes at the non league level often do so for nothing more than the pleasure in seeing people smile. They go out of their way to try and provide a warm welcome, a nice environment and a cheery goodbye. Few are paid yet every week rain or shine they are there with a smile for you selling you raffle tickets, Golden Goals or providing cups of tea to the visiting officials.

Because the clubs are pioneers

Last season Mansfield Town came up with the idea to "pay what you want" for their game against Gateshead - the result a sell out 7,000+ crowd. Myfootballclub's takeover of Ebbsfleet United anyone? Some may say it failed to deliver what it was supposed to but is it any co-incidence that during that first season Ebbsfleet United reached, and won, the FA Trophy Final at Wembley Stadium. Free entry for under 16's? Lewes, Farnborough Town and others have given this one a go. Half price admission for season ticket holders at Premier and Football League sides has been in place at clubs like Thurrock and Basingstoke Town for some years with success at getting "floating fans". And then there are the grounds...A twelve foot wooden man holding up a roof with grass on it? Dartford said sure why not. None of your identikit stadiums here.

Because you can make a difference

Contact a Premier/Football League club and ask if you can help out in any way and they will either point you in the direction of their commercial webpage or to the company that provides the stewards. Do the same at a non league club and you may end up serving behind a bar, painting the changing rooms, giving our leaflets in the town centre about the game or contributing to the match programme. And afterwards they say "thank you".

Because there is always the chance that this year will be THE Cup run
Blyth Spartans reached the fifth round of the FA Cup in 1977/78, Harlow got to the fourth round in 1979/80 and in January 2008 who can forget Havant and Waterlooville taking the lead in the FA Cup third round against Liverpool at Anfield. Every year a couple of teams from the non leagues make it through to the third round and will financially secure them for years to come. Every year the chairman of all non league clubs pray this year it will be them.

I could go on. I feel more at home now standing on the terrace at a non league ground (or even a simple grass bank) than I ever was at Upton Park in my plastic seat. I feel I have more in common with the people around me rather than the Premier League branded blinkered fans I used to share my Saturday afternoon with. And finally, I feel I belong to something more than a faceless brand - I feel like I belong to something worthwhile. Viva Non League Football. Viva Non League Day!

Lewes 1 Hampton & Richmond Borough 2 - The Dripping Pan

For such a day of friendship amongst the Non Leagues it was apt that the visitors to the pan were Hampton & Richmond Borough; a club where enjoying the day rather than the result is the main priority. And it is a good job that the result wasn't the most important thing today as Lewes lost by the odd goal in three for the second game in a row.

This was a special day so the Fuller Family was out in force. The Current Mrs Fuller loves a bit of football, but youngest Fuller isn't that keen so she normally has to take her shopping to amuse her whilst Lolly and I watch a game. So this was special as it was to be their first ever visit to the Dripping Pan. I didn't want to spoil the surprise of mine and Danny's hard work too early in the day so I dispatched them with Patrick into town to do some leafleting of the Lewes Saturday afternoon whilst I headed into the Rook Inn to collect the latest parcels of fan joy from around Europe. A fine collection this week from Norway, Germany and our first effort from Poland. Fans started arriving "early doors", obviously with the news of our fine supporters club bar reaching far and wide.

Hampton & Richmond Borough's genial manager, ex-West Ham legend Alan Devonshire wandered in and had a quick drink with us as we discussed the general state of affairs at Upton Park. It must be hard for ex-professionals like Devonshire. He came from an era where there simply wasn't the opportunities to progress in clubs. The off the field staff in the 1980's consisted of a manager, an assistant if the team were flush and the kitman/physio whose only qualification was normally the ability to dip the "magic sponge" in freezing water. Coaching qualifications were hardly rigorous although they meant nothing to clubs. So like other ex-players from that era, such as Basingstoke's Frankie Gray Devonshire started at the bottom of the managerial ladder with the likes of Maidenhead United, working his way up. However, the world started to change and the next era of pros such as Iain Dowie, Chris Coleman and Steve Bruce found more opportunities in the professional game to start. But is he bitter? Not at all - I get the feeling that he loves the game at this level just as much as we do.

So Lewes kicked off on the first ever National Non-League Day in the midst of a huge first team injury crisis. Six regular starters were forced to sit this one out, with a couple of loanees drafted in to the side to try and ease the problem. However, it was the visitors who started the better, forcing Winterton into action early on.

The high point of the half was a fine spot by James Boyes on the touchline of Jonathan Pearce in the crowd. With no Premier League games he had decided to give his dulcet tones a rest for the day, or so he thought. It would have been rude not to ask on such a special day whether he would mind reading out the half time scores, which being the professional and gentleman he is, he duly obliged. Not that Jonathan was the only celebrity visiting the Pan on the day. Mark Williams, formerly famous as one of the two main characters in The Fast Show and now better known by the younger generation as "Arthur Weasley" from the Harry Potter films was also enjoying a pint or three in the sunshine on the terrace.

It would be nice if I could report that Lewes had turned a corner, and the three successive defeats were laid to rest. But I can't.

The visitors went ahead in the 33rd minute when Scott Manning was the last person to touch Barrie Matthews' corner, scoring the second Lewes own goal in consecutive home games. Queue the Lewes team standing around looking at disbelief at each other as if they had forgotten the words of the play. Half time came and went, with the bar of the Rook Inn almost at breaking point but non league fans being hardy souls, they waited patiently for their pint of Harveys.

Weeks of frustration and woe was washed away in the 55th minute when Simon Wormull's perfect free kick levelled the scores. We have said in previous weeks about his deadball abilities and he showed his skill with this effort, bent around the edge of the wall and into the top corner. Cue some high fives between Deaksy and Dave on the terrace and general back slaps all around. But the fun never lasts and with ten minutes left on the clock some lax defending from a Hampton free kick led to the ball falling to man of the match Charlie Moone and his strike sent the fifty or so Hampton fans home around the M25 happy.

In some ways football had been the winner. With crowds already up by more than 46% from the corresponding period last season, the attendance at the Pan for this game was a best of the season 694. But manager Steve Ibbitson wasn't in any kind of mood to celebrate after the game when Patrick Marber caught up with him.

"It was a winnable game as they were not the best side we will see down here this season. But again we are conceding silly goals. The first was another own goal and the second was simply poor defending. We had two or three chances to clear the ball but we didn't. It is not the time to be playing football when the ball is pinging around your six yard box. The one positive was that we did start playing some nice football in between the two goals. We have brought in a couple of new loan signings for today and we need to work on integrating them into our system. But overall I am pissed off. We have lost another game that we will come to regret later in the season."

Saturday 11th September 2010
Spitfired

One of the most frustrating elements of watching Non League football is the lack of information about games being on when the weather is poor. No clubs at this level have the luxury of a spare blanket to put across the pitch, let along undersoil heating. So when the weather turns nasty it can often lead to games being called off quickly. A few clubs have adopted Twitter as their method of communicating with their fans but even so there are occasions when you simply have to take a chance and head off to a game. One such occasion was last November when torrential rain had put most games in doubt. With Lewes away at Eastleigh we set off for the 95 mile trip down the M3 to Southampton Airport, where round the corner is the Silverlake Stadium.

When we arrived the game was 95% off. The club needed volunteers to help fork the pitch. We chose to help by pumping vital funds across the bar, safe in the knowledge that our afternoon would see us not move an inch, watching Jeff Stelling on TV instead. But amazingly their hard work paid dividends; the referee turned up and said "Let's play". Oh how we all laughed when Lewes scored an opening minute own goal to gift Eastleigh a win.

Ninth months later and it was time for revenge surely? The weather was certainly better when the Lewes Lunatic Fringe pulled into the car park sans Mr Last or myself. Danny was sunning himself on the north coast of Spain, or actually trying to eat his way through a ten day fiesta of meat and red wine whilst I was enjoying the delights of the English seaside at Whitstable with the little Fullers. So today's report would be brought to you by Deaksy's one line Twitter updates.

Eastleigh 2 Lewes 1 - The Silverlake Stadium

Despite the recent run of poor form which had seen one point gained from a possible fifteen, and an injury list that would shame most Premier League treatment rooms, Lewes took on Eastleigh from the first whistle creating some early chances when Wormull and Wheeler, back in the side at last after his little visitor in his stomach had departed, went close. But the same problem that had dogged the team all season paid a visit in the eleventh minute when a lack of concentration at the back led to a cross coming into the Lewes box that was turned in by Jamie Slabber.

Now here is an interesting thing. I feel as if I have known Jamie for years. He is one of those players that if you buy in Championship Manager for your Non-League team he will score you a bucket of goals. I first bought him in my initial spell at Grays Athletic, before taking him to Oxford United and then into the Championship with Leeds United. I'd love to be a professional footballer so that I could buy myself in games like Championship Manager. I know from talking to professionals that they also buy themselves when they play these games, refusing to ever sell themselves even when their form went downhill.

Anyway I digress. Lewes had conceded first for the sixth time in seven Blue Square Bet South games. Ibbo and Jason Hopkinson slumped back into the dugout, utterly confused as to what to do next. Well, as if by magic the team picked themselves up. A quick break from the kick off saw Simon Wormull advance up the right wing to plant a cross on David Wheeler's head, as the midfielder snuck in between two giant defenders to equalise. Lewes took confidence from their equaliser and began to boss proceedings. The pace of the midfield saw them a little more mobile in comparison to the Eastleigh defence, and Wormull was running the show from midfield with his passing and vision.

A lively counter-attack almost saw Wheeler score his second but his shot was too high having been played in by Kane Wills.

Rob Gradwell's advancing run saw Eastleigh keeper Gareth Barfoot come out of his area to clear the danger and he was forced into action again when a superb header from Lewis Ide from fully 25 yards had to be tipped over the bar. For the first time this season Lewes could say with authority that they had bossed a half of football.

In a complete reversal of fortune, Lewes came out after the break devoid of ideas and attacking intentions. Slabber and Tom Jordan had early opportunities as Eastleigh sought the lead. Jamie Brown was moved into the Spitfires' attack and his movement caused problems for the Lewes defence who had their hands full. Richard Graham and Brown both combined for chances and with Lewes struggling to produce anything of danger at the other end, the smoothness of the first half at times gave way to some more desperate defending. Chris Winterton made a fine save to tip Danny Smith's 83rd minute shot around the post, but then a minute later, Lewes succumbed to a powerful header from substitute Chris Holland direct from a corner which saw Eastleigh snatch all three points.

It was a disappointing end for an injury-plagued Lewes side that finished on the losing side for the fifth game in a row. In what was becoming a common theme, Ibbitson was again fuming after the match that the Rooks had conceded an early goal.

"I cannot believe I am standing here again complaining that we again gave a poor goal away early on - we should have defended that better. The rest of first half we played well and stood up to their long ball game. If we can get a little bit more up front and a little less predictable we will start to get some goals."

The Second half saw four of our players tiring which is the downside of bringing back the injured players. There were some positives though. David (Wheeler) return was a real boost and I was really pleased with our goal - an exceptional goal. Great build up and Wheeler got in front of their "monsters""

The facts though made grim reading. Played seven, won one, drawn one, and lost seven.

Monday 13th September 2010
Dib Dib Dib

After a weekend of FA Cup 2nd qualifying round excess I returned to the office in London on Monday, looking forward to my next game, the class of the titans in the Swedish Allsvenskan when 1st place Malmo were due to take on 2nd placed Helsingborgs in just 24 hours. The advantage of looking after two offices is that I can attend the occasional match in the Nordics. Whilst I love my non league games, and all of the quirkiness that comes with it I do enjoy returning to a packed stadium full of atmosphere (you can see why I stopped going to West Ham now!). At 11.30am on that Monday morning I had a routine email from Mr Boyes informing me that Lewes had been drawn at home in the FA Cup 2nd Qualifying round to Bethnal Green United or Harlow Town who had drawn 1-1 on Saturday. Ibbo had wanted a home tie against a lower division side so this suited everyone down to the ground.

Now I knew that this was the only replay in London and the South East from the crop of games played on Saturday which was in itself unusual. For a few seconds I contemplated going to the game as it was so close to home but thought a third game in as many days, coupled with my weekly trip to Scandinavia may result in a straight red from CMF and a subsequent ban from the "bottom draw". And of course this particular Monday saw the long long awaited return of the Inbetweeners on E4.

But then my life was momentarily turned upside down. A simple email from Patrick Marber, one of the new owners of Lewes FC arrived on the trusty Blackberry. *"Could I just pop along to the game and take a few notes?"* Of course I could. He said an email would follow from Ibbo with what was required, and he kindly sent a "get out of jail free" email for CMF that read:-

"Dear CMF. It is not your husband's fault that he has to go to football. The Club Board insist that he goes. He has no choice in the matter. He didn't want to go to a football match on such an important night but circumstances commanded it"

She couldn't refuse, and with a promise of some petrol station flowers, my pink note was duly signed. I then got my instructions from Ibbo. So much for "a few notes". He even sent me a template to fill in. Of course not knowing who we could play I would have to complete one for each team until it became obvious who the winner would be. Some of the things he wanted were:-

Formation - 4-4-2, 4-5-1 or 4-3-3
Attacking corners - Danger Men? Anything special they do - e.g. short corners
Attacking free kicks - anyone with a special shot or talent?
Defending corners - Any weaknesses? How do they handle different attacking styles? What does the keeper do?

This was on top of a breakdown of strengths and weaknesses for each player plus a comment on their type of play - direct, physical, counter attacking. And there was me thinking that all of these options in Championship Manager were irrelevant.

So at 7.30pm I walked into the Mile End Stadium, home of Bethnal Green United. I put on my special Lewes hoodie to add some authenticity to the night, as well as carrying my clipboard. Oh how well prepared I was - apart from one item. My glasses. I can see well enough on a bright sunny afternoon with a nice elevation in the stands, and the pitch close to the terraces. But put me at pitch level, at night in an athletics stadium and I struggle a bit. Well, OK not a bit, a lot.

The Mile End stadium is one of the most basic grounds you will see an FA Cup game being played at. Bethnal Green United were playing regional football until a few seasons ago, moving up to the Essex Senior League after only 10 years in their existence. This is essentially level 5 of the non league pyramid. Facilities are in keeping with the status of the club - basic. So it was with some surprise that I entered the ground to find a programme and printed match tickets. I went in search of a team sheet so I could start preparing my reports but was told there wasn't one. Instead a chap from the Essex Senior League wrote the numbers down in my programme - useful if it wasn't for the fact that he listed visitors Harlow Town with two number 9's and a number 31 and had handwriting that would have made a doctors look good.

The original game had been Harlow's for the taking, and it was only a last kick/head of the game that salvaged a draw for Bethnal Green. The Isthmian League North team had obviously been firm favourites for the game and were probably none too happy to have to replay the game.

Bethnal Green United 0 Harlow Town 4 - Mile End Stadium

The game kicked off and I furiously started to take notes on both teams, on formations and who was playing who. With a severely restricted view my eye sight stretched to about half way across the pitch and no more. Fortunately a knight in shining armour arrived, as one of the veterans from my trips watching England abroad Vinny turned up, shortly followed by his wife (what else would you do on a Monday night in London apart from come to an FA Cup 1st Round Qualifying replay eh?) who helped me on the simple things like shirt numbers.

The worst thing that could happen was of course a close game that went to penalties after extra time as I would have to continue to take notes on all 22 players throughout the two hours. Certainly for the first half an hour it seemed like that would be the case as both teams seemed to be happy to sit back and defend. I duly noted the formations and then tried to put shirt numbers against positions, only to realise in Harlow's case that according to my notes they had 10 men. I made extensive notes for the corner formation for Bethnal Green, describing their approach of all standing on the corner of the box and running into as the ball was delivered as a shambolic shotgun tactic, and I described the home team's as fat Peter Cech simply due to his luminous orange kit.

I was under no illusions about the importance of my task with emails flying in from Patrick, James Boyes and even Danny over in Spain, reminding me that the accuracy of my report could be worth £4,500 in prize money in the next round, and to "remember Leiston" from the Eastern Counties League who had beaten Lewes two seasons ago when they were a Blue Square Premier club.

It was certainly an interesting crowd. Nearly 200 people squeezed into the old stand and along the side of the pitch and they were certainly vocal. The unusual but easily recognisable smell of cannabis was also a feature of most of the game, perhaps relaxing me more than normal as I soon got into the rhythm of delivering stinging critics on all of the players. The first goal came just after the half hour mark. A Harlow corner (big men up from back, man to man marking) was met by Jon Stevenson, not with his head as he initially intended, but with his knee - hmm how do I write that one up?

I had imagined half time would be spent with some of the big wigs from other clubs in a room somewhere discussing players and tactics but instead it was spent queuing up to use a vending machine for some cold tea. I have seen on TV countless times Premier League managers at other clubs "having a look at future opponents" but none of them ever seem to be scribbling furious notes; Capello is always at games yet he just goes to look like a miserable Italian. Who takes notes for him?

The second half started, fortunately with no changes on either side and gave me the opportunity to fill in the other half of the pitch on my sheets. Harlow had adopted the traditional 1-11 numbering with the defenders using 2, 3, 4 and 5 but throwing in a spanner with their play maker and central midfielder Danny Cowley wearing number 9. Bethnal Green, well let's just say I used the word "fluid" to mask my deficiencies.

Fortunately my work got a little easier in the 47th minute when Cowley scored a magnificent free kick from 25 yards right into the top corner of the net. A box ticked for me for "men to look out for at free kicks I think". He then added a third ten minutes later, finishing off a nice move that ran from box to box in just 5 passes (Counter attacking style - tick). Vinny's wife Becky provided the commentary as I was hastily scribbling down the defensive formations, trying to find other words for "He hoofs it".

Three nil up and soon playing against ten men, when Bethnal Green's captain Lee Ryan was sent off for dissent meant I could rip up one of the forms and just concentrate on Harlow for the last fifteen minutes, a fact further underlined by a fourth a minute later when Clark Akers slotted home from just inside the penalty area. But what else could I write? The full backs "got up and down the line well", the central midfield "has a good engine on him", and the centre forward Akers "held the ball up well". Let's face it I was out of my depth. There is a website called Zonal Marking. It is one of the finest pieces of work known to man, dissecting every game in terms of positional play. Do you know what I don't understand a word of it. I am not cut out to watch a game in such a theoretical way. To me football games are won on a) luck, b) referees decisions and c) one team being better than the other. I am sure tactics play a massive part - it’s just I cannot get how.

So a successful evening? Well I was home in time for Inbetweeners at 10am but from a scouting point of view? Ask me in two weeks when hopefully Lewes have beaten Harlow Town, are in the draw for the 3rd Qualifying Round and are £4,500 better off. If not then I can see my new career coming to a premature end.

Saturday 18th September 2010
125 Not Out!

On the 18th September 1885, the union of Eastern Rumelia and Bulgaria was announced in Plovdiv to cap an amazing week in history. First we had the ridiculous Arbroath 36 Bon Accord 0 scoreline that would have had James Alexander Gordon repeating that a few times (to this day Bon Accord fans still claim the 7th goal was miles offside) and then we had the news that Jumbo the elephant had been killed in a train crash whilst working for P T Barnum's circus. Sad days indeed. But down in East Sussex a story that got no press whatsoever broke.

A normal night of karaoke at the Royal Oak pub in Lewes turned into something quite special as a group of fine Victorian gentlemen, fed up with the butchering of Wired for Sound (Cliff is that old surely?) decided to form a football club. And so was born Lewes FC. They agreed with the local council that they could play in a boggy area of the town known as the Dripping Pan and have called that place home since - in itself quite an impressive achievement. That group of men who played their first ever match a few weeks later wore green shirts to reflect the picturesque South Downs overlooking the ground.

Fast forward 125 years and the team ran out onto the pitch at the Dripping Pan. Remarkable because less than 6 months ago it seemed that Lewes FC would be no more. We are all familiar with the trials and tribulations of last season but it is fair to say that without the change in ownership in the summer it is doubtful that the club would be gearing up for this momentous occasion.

The week running up to the game had been filled with special events for the club. The team had met up at the ground, posing for photos dressed up as if they were back in 1885. Local brewers Harvey's had been busy putting the final touches to a special Lewes 125 Ale which was launched at the 2nd Annual Beer Festival at the club, and Danny, James and myself had been busily handling message of congratulations for the match programme from clubs such as Manchester United, Arsenal and West Ham United.

Our day had started early. In preparation of the arrival of the Football Focus cameras (yep, we move in exciting times now at Lewes) I had been putting up our latest influx of scarves in the Rook Inn. Welcome to Dagenham & Redbridge, Lincoln Moorlands Railways and Malmo into the hall of fame - you are most welcome, and if anyone wants to see their club colours showcased them please send a scarf c/o The Rook Inn.

Unfortunately, Mr Last was absent without leave in the north of Spain preferring to take in Racing Santander v Real Zaragoza if you please, but you are never on your own at Lewes - in fact Cheers bar stole our motto of "friends you haven't yet met". And with Harvey's brewing a special 125th Anniversary beer for the occasion what could make the day go any better? Well how about a guest announcer, some live music and not forgetting some welcome opponents in the form of Chelmsford City.

The first few games hadn't exactly gone according to plan for Lewes with just four points from their opening eight games. The positives were that attendances were up significantly at the Pan, the negatives, well six defeats is something you can't gloss over. Chelmsford on the other hand had started as everyone expected them to - 100% at home and mixed away. Let's just hope the only thing they would be taking away from the Pan would be one of those very nice anniversary beer glasses.

You couldn't have asked for a better day for a birthday party. The sun was shining when I arrived at the ground and the bar was still filled with barrels of beer from the previous nights Beer Festival and the BBC had arrived with their Football Focus cameras to report on the day. Fans started arriving from 1pm to take advantage of the wide range of ales on offer, although the special Lewes 125 Ale, brewed by those masters Harveys down the road would be held back for half time. Chelmsford's directors arrived and kindly gave the club a special 125 shirt as well as a certificate marking the occasion - a very nice touch indeed.

By 2pm the bar was packed. Six deep would be a fair reflection. The club had eight people working to try and serve as many as possible, and the ales were slowly disappearing. The Football Focus team were interviewing all and sundry, giving some special attention to the work we had carried out in the Rook Inn. The birthday cake arrived soon after, which would be ceremonially cut on the pitch at half time by a group of former players. Just before kickoff I received a message of good luck from our Danish (Ben) and New York (Luge) correspondents, who had found a pub in Copenhagen with

Harveys on draft and were raising a few in Lewes's honour. It was like my wedding day all over again, and as if I was blessed The Current Mrs Fuller was here at my side to wipe a tear of emotion from my eyes when the 125 children, dressed in their Lewes finest formed a guard of honour for the teams, and I don't think I was the only one in the ground to shed a tear.

Lewes 0 Chelmsford City 1 - The Dripping Pan

Everything we could have done to make the day special had been done. It was now up to the team and try as they might they couldn't find that opening to exploit. Chelmsford are a difficult team to break down, and despite some excitement when the back line was breached, James Pullen in the Chelmsford goal wasn't tested in the opening period, whilst at the other end Chris Winterton was showing why he was a worthy replacement to Rikki Banks. Chelmsford almost scored the opening goal after only eight minutes when Sami El-Abd manoeuvred past keeper Chris Winterton at the far post but Anthony Barness was on hand to head off the line.

The best Lewes move came on 27 minutes when Tim Rivers played in Redwood who was able to lose his marker. The on-loan Brighton winger then crossed into the area where Rob Gradwell's header couldn't be reached by a stretching David Wheeler much to the anguish of the Jungle. The game continued to ebb and flow with Chelmsford now coming back into the game .Under pressure from Robert Edmans, Lewes keeper Winterton produced a fantastic save on the half hour, clawing the ball away for a corner which Matthew Lock bounced off the top of the bar direct from the kick. Edmans caused no end of trouble for Lewes with his height and made Winterton stretch to keep out his low shot just before half time.

Half time saw the launch of the 125 Ale and the queues were testament to its popularity. The cake was cut and later divided up so that the two hundred or so kids all got a piece. "Football club giving away free things to kids in the crowd shock "eh! However, the rest of the Lewes fans were going to leave empty handed as just four minutes after the break Chelmsford scored the only goal when Sam Higgins shot from the edge of the box hit the back of the net. After this strike City's goal was rarely in danger as the best Lewes move ended with Leon Redwood blasting a decent chance high into the stand. Kane Wills was forced into another goal line clearance but despite Chelmsford's threat subsiding after Edmans substitution, Lewes didn't get the present they were hoping for on their birthday.

Bugger....Ibbo was furious and explained after the game why

"Their goal was horrendous. When it went in we went bananas. Such a poor goal to give away. I was talking to my tubby friend over there (Jason) about this - You cannot turn your back on the ball and argue with the referee over a decision. Our centre back was away with the fairies, debating what was happening and they scored. I felt we should have got at least a point."

"If we weren't conceding these poor goals we would not be losing games. Six on a row now is a cause for concern. But there is lots of hope and optimism - crowd was amazing and it was a great day. We need to turn it around and look forward to the next 125 years"

So it was another pointless afternoon for the Rooks. The crowd of 1,346 was the biggest at the ground since local rivals Eastbourne Borough visited on Boxing Day 2008. The league was beginning to take a familiar shape with Bromley, Braintree, Dover and Chelmsford in the top five, a similar situation to most of last season, whilst the smaller clubs who were expected to struggle were so.

With Mr Last being away I caught up with another blogging star, Mr Ian King from the excellent Twohundredpercent blog who is becoming a regular visitor at the Pan. The pitch still looked fantastic, the balloons were still up and kids played on the terraces - just like football used to be. The world may have moved on but some things are more important and 125 after they were formed, Lewes Football Club still remember that. There's always the FA Cup next week anyway!

Saturday 25th September 2010
The Magic of the FA Cup

After I had provided Ibbo with a full scouting report on Lewes's first opponents in the FA Cup I faced a bit of a quandry. Of course I wanted to be there to stand up and say "I told them that" when Lewes exploited a hole in the Harlow Town plan, but what if I cocked it right up? What if I had got the tactics all wrong, the players I said were crap were actually quite good, and the one "danger" player I identified turned into a crock of crap? I would be the laughing stock of the club. It wasn't as if it was a secret report either. Everyone in and around the club knew I had written it, and it had even been mentioned in the previous week's post match manager's interview.

I decided not to go. Whilst it seemed to be disloyal, I could not face the people who had put faith in me if it all went wrong. After all Harlow Town were two divisions below Lewes, and whilst the club had painful memories of a defeat to County League side Leison a few seasons ago AND whilst they were on a run of six consecutive defeats they were expected to win.

Instead I was going to spend the day with my wonderful family. My girls. Because that is what is important in life isn't it? Family. Not football. 1pm came and I had done all my chores, been food shopping, cut the grass and generally been "best Dad in the world". But CMF could see a sense of frustration on my face. I was pacing and she could see the pain I was in, so at 1.30pm she brough me a cup of tea and said:-

"Angel. If you want you can go to football."

That was the words I wanted to hear so I burnt my mouth drinking boiling hot tea, not wanting to appear rude, rounded up Lolly and we were away. But of course this is Saturday, and Saturday's mean only one thing. Delays due to a crash at junction 5/6 on the M25. Without fail around about lunchtime on a Saturday this occurs. There are two ways I can get to Lewes - the shorter but much longer in time cross country route, taking in some of Kent and East Sussex's finest countryside and villages, or the longer in distance but shorter in time round via the motorways. Inevitably I chose, or should I say am advised wrong by my SatNav and today was no exception. Rounding the bend after passing junction 5 on the M25 I hit (not literally) a traffic jam. After crawling for the next few miles my ever so accurate and updated SatNav told me there was an accident ahead, and to "avoid". It is prone to these errors once in a while. On the A20 near TBIR Towers if often tries to get us to take a detour home, across the central reservation and three lines of traffic. It once took me down a dead end street in North London and was telling me to cross the railway line on a footbridge.

We sit and brooded for thirty minutes, slowly realising that we would not make kick off. Ten more minutes and the game was now kicking off. Do we turn around if and when we got to junction 6? Well that would depend on the score I thought and when eventually we were through I got a message from CMF that Lewes were one up I could hardly go home could I? Fifteen minutes later as we bombed down the M23 the phone beeped again.

"One nil Dad, Mum says"

Decision made then...onwards and upwards.

Lewes 2 Harlow Town 0 - The FA Cup 2nd Qualifying Round - The Dripping Pan

It did cross my mind that CMF had been winding me up, but despite her often teasing I do not believe she would be that cruel. As we pulled into the car park and found our regular space I could see through the part open gates that the second half had just got underway. Less than a minute later we were on the terrace, standing next to Patrick who replayed the first half action to us, complete with simulations of both goals, both scored from the head of Chris Breach, who had exposed the weakness of Harlow at set pieces in picking up the "big men". I thank you. Move over Mourinho I am officially a tactical genius.

Harlow Town had brought a large and vocal contingent to the Dripping Pan hopeful of a shock result against the Rooks but it was the home side who had controlled much of the game so far. Sonny Cobbs had hit the woodwork early on and then Gradwell had missed the sitter of a rebound, still without a goal all season. The first goal came in the 32nd minute when Wormull's corner was met with force by an almost unmarked Breach. As if to emphasis my scouting prowess, Breach then scored an identical goal just six minutes later.I could retire a happy man, safe in the knowledge that my work had not been in vain.

In the unusual situation of protecting a two goal lead, Lewes offered little in the second half content to spurn the rare opportunities that their opponents worked hard to create. Harlow's Che Stadhart had a chance when he met a long defensive clearance on the half volley, but his effort was easy for Lewes Winterton keeper who had a fairly easy afternoon. Tom Murphy almost capped his best display for Lewes with a great goal from the edge of the area but the Harlow Keeper Madden was alert to tip his 72nd minute shot over the bar. And so it was a final whistle that brought handshakes and backslaps all round, as well as a nice pint of Harveys from manager Ibbo who then gave us his opinion on the game.

"The first half was a great performance. We played some really bright football but then in the second half we looked a bit worried and sat back a bit too much and they came back into the game. We played Tom Murphy up front today in a 4-4-2 instead of the 4-5-1 we had been playing and it seemed to work. The fans on both sides were great today. It is nice to see a club like Harlow bring so many, and make so much noise in getting behind their side."

"At the end of the day we are in the hat for the next round and that is all that matters. A non conference team at home would be ideal"

Saturday 2nd October 2010
The King is dead, long live the King

There is an unwritten law in football that when you play against a former manager you are always going to lose. Last week West Ham finally crushed their voodoo with 'Appy 'Arry at the 8th attempt since he was given the boot back in 2001 in the 1-0 win over Spurs. Last season Chelsea's dreams of a treble were ruined by none other than ex manager "The Special One" then at Inter Milan and who can ever forget the triumphant return to Melchester Rovers by Roy Race when he was at Walford Rovers in 1983.

So when Farnborough Town were promoted from the Zamaretto (Southern) League last season all Lewes fans marked the 2nd October 2010 as a certain away defeat. Steve King, Farnborough manager had legendary status at Lewes after taking them to the Conference South title in 2008. What made this all the more amazing was that on the eve of the final day of the season it was announced King's contract, along with virtually all of the team's contracts would not be renewed. The result? Lewes played their first season at the highest non league level with a novice as a manager, and a squad ill prepared for the likes of Oxford United, York City and Burton Albion. And King? Well him and a fair number of those players from that Lewes Championship winning squad ended up in Farnborough.

It is exciting times at the Rushmoor stadium. Farnborough are climbing the leagues again, and there has been some serious investment in the ground. Just twenty four hours after the Lewes game then club were due to host the Nepalese national team. Why you may ask? Well apparently due to the proximity of the Gurka regiment's home, Farnborough has one of the biggest Nepalese communities in the UK. Unfortunately heavy rain put pay to the unique game.

The original plan was to meet the rest of the Lewes Lunatic Fringe in the Hawley Arms, a pub that has got the lowest rating I have ever seen on the excellent website Beer in the Evening - a massive 1.8 out of 10. However, Danny, Deaks and Dave in the advanced party informed that the pub had shut down and so instead we would have to make do with the Farnborough Dugout bar. A real hardship as it turned out.

The TBIR team had been delayed in leaving the office. Around midnight the night before there was a large bang from under the stairs and all of our electrics went off. I slipped on the old handyman outfit from the "bottom draw" and with a promise of a "good tip" from CMF when I fixed the problem I began to check all the fuses. All were in order, our neighbours had power and there was no logical reason for the lack of juice. Wind forward 12 hours and we were still without electricity, awaiting a professional. Being such a wonderful woman CMF said I could go and she would wait in for the "handy man"...sometimes I question her motives.

An hour later we parked literally outside the front door of the Rushmoor stadium in Farnborough, took advantage of the excellent family ticket (£10 for me, Lolly and Northern Liam), shook hands with our glorious leaders and found ourselves in the very smart Dugout bar in the main stand. Looking around at the plush surroundings you would be hard pressed to think you were in a Conference South ground. So comfortable were the settings that a number of fans simply didn't move when it was time for the action to start, prefering the multiple TV screens and excellent beers.

Lewes's form coming into the game wasn't good. Apart from the 2-0 win in the cup last week, they were on a run of six consecutive defeats. And with our David Wheeler out injured the signs didn't look good, even when Farnborough announced that eBay would be playing for them - hardly fair including one of the world's biggest online companies in your starting line up.

Farnborough FC 1 Lewes 0 - Cherrywood Road

Whilst these are exciting times for Farnborough, I was actually present at the biggest moment in their history. On 4th January 1992 the club travelled to Upton Park to play West Ham "at home" in the FA Cup 3rd Round and came away with a brilliant 1-1 draw. A few days later they returned for the replay, losing 1-0 to a last gasp Trevor Morley goal. Five divisions separated the clubs on that day. Nearly nineteen years later approximately 21,000 less were in the ground for this game but the atmosphere was almost as good as you get at Upton Park these days.

Faced with just one "end", the Lewes fans took up their position behind the goal with the Farnborough "under fives". The banter was loud and amusing most of the times - a mutual love for King, a mutual mocking of the unfinished stand opposite. Lewes fans threw in songs about Aldershot, Farnborough for some reason assumed that all Lewes fans came from Brighton and started down the "your're from Brighton so you must be gay" chanting. One classic comment when one of the yoofs was asked if he drove a pimped up Nova was "no mate, a Corsa". Classic.

You may get the impression that such incidents distracted us from the football - and you would be right. Lewes played Gradwell up front on his own, and with Wormull sitting deep, created very little in a half ruined by a fussy ref who loved to stop play whenever he could. And it was in the result of one of these stoppages that Farnborough took the lead when Ibe (aka eBay) was allowed to turn in the area and poke the ball past the impressive Winterton in the Lewes goal.

There was more of the same in the second half, especially when Gradwell was replaced by Dan Beck and the game petered out as the rain began to fall again. I cannot remember Lewes actually having one single chance on goal. Farnborough hit the post towards the end of the game, but in truth the referee caused them more problems, booking players at will.

It was left to a debate about what you would put in football's Room 101 if you were in charge of the game. Coloured boots would be outlawed - Farnborough had all eleven players at one point sporting "trendy boots", something that would make our friends over at the Fancy Dan Boots website quiver with excitement. Second up would be cycling shorts - pointless modern day cockpieces and finally Stan Collymore - simple as that although Deaksy's submission that linesmen should be made to wear shin pads because men wearing football socks pulled up "is just wrong" gained a snigger from the portly assistant referee.

Full time and a seven consecutive defeat for Lewes was bad, but when the results started to come through Boreham Wood's surprise win over Dartford meant that the Rooks hit rock bottom of the league - ouch. It's going to be a long long season. After the game, Ibbo was philosophical about the result. Talking to Patrick Marber and noting the "plush" surroundings of the Rushmoore stadium.

"Not the best performance we are going to have this season. We changed the formation to 4-5-1. We felt if we could keep it tight for an hour and then

go 4-4-2 in the last half an hour and inject some pace we may have a chance of nicking the win. We conceded in the 47th minute and it was a killer. Their forward looked like a monster from the sidelines, he could hold off the defenders and turn and that was exactly what he did for the goal. We were incensed that the referee only put up one minute for added time, but they scored with nearly two minutes gone.

We cannot compete money-wise with Farnborough. They have a lovely ground here although there are some mutterings around the corriders about some financial problems. We've got Thurrock in the cup up next. Jason and myself will sit down on the coach on the way home and work out if we approached it wrongly. The fans were again fantastic today and we owe them a decent performance next week."

An interview with Nick Williams

Sitting upstairs in the office at Viva Lewes behind his Apple Mac you would fail to recognise Nick from the same man who ten hours later would be running arms outstretched to embrace David Wheeler on scoring the winner for Lewes against Braintree Town. He looks every part your publisher. Scruffy t-shirt, jeans and of course dark shades which in a few hours would be swapped for a smart suit as he stepped into the role of Chief Executive of Lewes FC.

His background is similar to Alex's, learning his trade at EMAP and Future Publishing, producing Chelsea and Manchester United's official magazines as well as launching the Mens Health title. His involvement in Lewes started last season as shirt sponsors. Being a Portsmouth fan from a very young age he had become used to chaos and disappointment, so being asked to get involved in the club did not bring any shocks. Nick understands the unique Lewes community spirit more than most and saw that the new directors had to re-connect with the local people and businesses.

Could there be a better draw in the FA Cup than Portsmouth at home in the 3rd round of the cup? Probably not, although with a small number of non league teams making it through to the 1st round proper, this must be the first objective.

Saturday 9th October 2010
The magic of the FA Cup

Of course I wanted Lewes to go on a decent FA Cup run. Who doesn't want that for their team. But most fans also want a nice away day as well. Somewhere they haven't been before and a chance to experience a few new pubs, a new ground and some new stories ro tell. Drawing Thurrock at home didn't really tick any of those boxes for me so I was reluctant, despite my new found love for Lewes to go to this one. Instead I decided to go to the FA Cup game down the road at Whitehawk as they took on fellow Ryman League side Hendon.

When I told people I was heading down to Whitehawk everyone who knows Brighton looked at me as if I was mad and shook their head. "Lock your car doors", "Make sure you don't wear your watch", "Don't forget your bullet proof vest" were three such comments. But as a veteran of Zagreb, Bratislava and Arbroath it was water off a ducks back to me.

We drove down the Falmer Road, past the impressive new American Express Community Stadium which will be Brighton & Hove Albion's new ground in just a few months time on a beautifully sunny day. The road takes you high above Brighton, with the road falling down towards the sea. A quick right along the top of Brighton racecourse and the a left literally across the track and down the hill. So far all I saw was neat bungalows and smiling children playing in the sunshine. As you get near the bottom of the hill you through a left, drive past the Caravan Club (a code word for a massive orgy according to Jay in the Inbetweeners) and there is the ground, hidden behind the trees. So where exactly was this war zone?

We parked, paid our £8 and walked into one of the most rural grounds in England. From all parts of the ground you simply cannot see anything apart from greenery. The club after nearly 50 years since their formation had at last left the county leagues, having won the Sussex League last season. They were also just one game away from Wembley in the FA Vase last year, losing to Wroxham in the semi-finals. They were also managed recently by ex-West Ham legend George Parris. This game against Isthmian Premier League Hendon marked their joint furthest progress in the competition.

Fanny's was the obvious choice for a quickie prior to the game, and full sated we took our place behind the goal. The pitch must be a nightmare to play on. It seems to slope in all directions, and is bloody wide – a fact that the home team tried to exploit from the first minute with long cross pitch balls. FA regulations meant that no alcohol could be taken out from the bar, but that didn't stop a number of fans who simply brought out the cans from their bags as if it was part of a normal country picnic.

Still Lolly and I aimed to enjoy our afternoon of FA Cup action. The game ebbed and flowed with both teams creating chances before Hendon took the lead. I had ignored the vibrations in my pocket, knowing full well it was messages of hate coming through from the Pan about my mis-information. After forty minutes it vibrated once too often and I pulled it out to find three missed calls from CMF. I rang her sheepishly and got the lecture about "*What is the point of having a mobile if you never answer it"*. She wanted to know if I could bring home a chinese on my way back and almost as an after thought she said "Oh, and you must be pleased. I've just seen on TV that Lewes are 1-0 up". Sorry, rewind that last bit. Lewes were one nil up?

I told Lolly the latest score, and with maturity way past her ten years she calmly said "*Dad. It's not too late. We could still make the second half*". How could I disagree. As soon as the half time whistle blew we were in the car quicker than Batman and Rob could access the Batcave and we were off down the A27.

Lewes 2 Thurrock 1 - The Dripping Pan

So whilst the sun was shining in East Brighton, just across the downs Lewes were kicking off the second half against fellow Blue Square Bet South strugglers Thurrock in cloudy conditions. Apparently this is known as the South Downs effect, a mystery that even Michael Fish cannot explain. The Rooks only league win this season was against "The Fleet" back in August, and they intended to do the same, having started two men up front for the first time in a while.

And the tactical switch had worked early on as Tom Murphy headed home a pinpoint cross from Kane Wills. When we arrived Director Patrick Marber whispered in my ear that Lewes haven't lost after taking a lead for six months and thoughts started turning to the next round, and the dilemma of a winnable tie, or a big team at home such as Luton Town or Cambridge United. The atmosphere had been boosted by the presence of the Cliffe Bonfire Society drummers, who drummed their life out, taking the team into half time with a slim lead. Our sponsored man David Wheeler came on as sub, himself still getting back to full fitness after a stop/start campaign and teed up Tom Murphy perfectly for the second goal with fifteen minutes to go. The Wheeler curse struck again a few minutes later as he was injured in a tackle with the Thurrock left back, and Lewes were down to ten men to hang on.

Every Thurrock attack was greeted with mass nail-biting but Winterton in the Lewes goal seemed to be unbeatable. It would take something special to beat him, and that is exactly what happened in the 87th minute. James Boyes, Lewes's man on the ground summed it up perfectly - "It was a goal fit to grace any level of football, with the winger chesting the ball down in a goal-mouth scramble, before sending an unstoppable overhead kick past Winterton to give the visitors hope of snatching an underserved replay."

Four minutes of added time were announced and we counted down every second. When finally the whistle went, the 850+ crowd raised the noise another notch and the new owners of the club celebrated with the fans, as well as a big group hug. This was progress, and whilst the Que Sera chants of Wembley may be a bit premature it could well be "Whatever will be, will be, we are going to Grimsby Que Sera, Que Sera."

Afterwards we caught up with a smiling Steve Ibbitson.

"*Eight games away from Wembley! I thought we played well and were the better side for 80 minutes, much the same as when they came down here in the league in August. We scored two good goals but they gave themselves hope with a fantastic goal near the end.*

We know we have good enough players to compete in the league, but we haven't got a squad big enough to cope with injuries, as we saw today when we finished with ten men. We need to look at some loan options up front next week. Unfortunately we appear to have also lost David Wheeler with a knee ligament injury which is such a shame.

The atmosphere here today was fantastic. The drums made such a big *difference to the team today and we have a lot to thank the supporters for. We really need to win next week (*against Dorchester*)."*

Saturday 16th October 2010
Co-incidence or what?

It's old hat now talking about the fact I used to be a West Ham season ticket holder, and how I fell out of love with the club due to the change in owners, and the direction they were taking the club. No? Well refresh your mind here. And it is no secret that I have decided to share my overflowing cup of football affection with Lewes FC.no? Well just read back over the past few weeks and you will see why.

But strangely enough both teams seasons have run in almost complete parallel. Lots of player injuries, although David Wheeler's stomach parasite is much more interesting than Carlton Cole's groin I am sure (to most fans anyway), new owners trying to win over fans (again, I prefer the Lewes under 16's go free approach to the West Ham £36 for a kids ticket to watch them lose to Chelsea) and a surprising run in the cup for both. But it is the league position that is the greatest cause for joint concern. Coming into this weekend's games both West Ham and Lewes were rock bottom of their respective leagues. And to add more spice to the next game, both were playing the teams second to bottom. West Ham travelled to Wolverhampton Wanderers whilst Lewes entertained Dorchester Town.

So guess which game I was going to? I still haven't returned to West Ham this season, although I will admit I have already paid my £80 for a ticket for the games versus West Brom and Blackpool in a few weeks time. But for now Lewes needed my support so I was making the 130 mile round trip to pay them my £10 and enjoy football the old fashion way (beer on the terraces, a chat with a Hollywood celebrity or two and having a an audience with the manager after the game in the bar).

This week Charlie Anderson wrote on Twitter that "The sheer amount of media coverage Lewes FC get is illogical"....then followed it up with "But if it is written by The Ball is Round who cares?" Never a truer word spoken I think so instead of having an extra pint of Harveys I picked up my pen and jotted a few observations from "Demotion Destiny Day".

A few days before the game more honours were bestowed on the club as manager Steve Ibbitson picked up the Contribution to Sussex Sport award, sponsored by The Argus at Brighton's Theatre Royal. An honour indeed, but could he translate his passion for the game into the players for the must win game against Dorchester Town.

Lewes 0 Dorchester Town 2- The Dripping Pan

In this fixture last season Lewes desperately needed a win. With just three games to go, and still sitting in the bottom three, The Rooks needed to beat a Dorchester team who were technically safe from the drop. And did they just do that. Their biggest win for over two years saw them rise out of the bottom three....so what chance a repeat performance today?

Err. None actually. The high point of the afternoon was the continued progress in the Rooks Inn where Danny had started on our European wall. On the field it was soon forgotten as Lewes couldn't make the most of their early pressure that saw Tom Murphy hit a post. Halfway through the first half with the news filtering through that West Ham were losing at Wolves, so to even things up Lewes gave away a needless penalty when Scott Manning tripped up Guiseppe Sole, and the Dorchester man picked himself up and dispatched the ball into the corner to send the 8 away fans into ecstatic delirium.

Injuries have been a major issue for Lewes this season, with every major player suffering at some point bar keeper Winterton. For this game the treatment room included TBIR's own David Wheeler, Simon Wormull, Lewis Hamilton and Chris Breach and this bad luck seemed to seep onto the pitch.

The rest of the half passed most fans by, as did most of the passing on the pitch. An invite into the boardroom at half time lifted our spirits but in truth most fans realised based on that half that this was going to be a long season's fight against relegation. With a sausage roll in my pocket I headed back onto the terraces, narrowly avoiding the latest clutch of celebs to visit the Pan (Mark "Arthur Weasley" Williams and Dave "Come Dine with Me" Lamb) just in time to hear that West Ham had equalised at Wolves. So there was hope after all!

Alas it was not to be. Dorchester kept the door shut, despite constant "fattist" abuse being rained down on their slim keeper (thank God I wasn't out there - I would have been an easy target) and created a final chance in the last minute when just announced Man of The Match Pullen allowed Danny Igs to lob the ball over his head and follow up with a neat finish.

The goal was the signal for most of the crowd to filter out. Frustration was the key word here. Progress is evident off the pitch but on it the team need a bit of luck. The attendance was down by a few hundred on last week's cup exploits but still higher than the same stage last season, in most part due to the initiatives undertaken by the club (and of course our European Football inspired Rook Inn). With a very difficult trip to Cambridge United next week in the FA Cup to look forward perhaps a good performance there could lift the players ready for a tough few league games to come where they must takes some points.

But football is a funny game and there is always hope. Last season the club were all but relegated with a month to go before pulling out 3 wins from the final 4 games to avoid the drop and with the likes of Wheeler and Wormull back in the side things will improve.

Thirty minutes after the final whistle and there was still no sign of the home players. Dorchester Town's squad were digging into seconds of their post match meal unaware that their extra portions were actually for the home team, but for once perhaps the victors did deserve all the spoils. In fact so incensed was Ibbo that he couldn't be found after the game for his regular post match chat.

So much for co-incidence then - West Ham's draw hadn't taken them off the bottom of the table but it had put them level on points with that tin pot team Liverpool.

Saturday 23rd October 2010
From Slovakia with Love

Every year Danny arranges an annual trip for some of Europe's most ardent Football fans. A trip into the heart of somewhere in Europe for a weekend of football, beer and er, well that is about it really. This year's trip was planned during the Spring, and once fixtures came out in the Summer we had a perfect long weekend of games in Hungary and Slovakia.

We always knew that the weekend clashed with the FA Cup Final Qualifying round, but based on previous Lewes form, we thought it was a relative safe bet that we would not be missing a game on this weekend. But we didn't figure on the new found cup spirit that the team had - in fact the magic of the FA Cup. Wins against Harlow Town and Thurrock had put Lewes in the draw, and just one game away from the 1st Round proper and a potential money spinning game against a league team. Just think of the possibilities - Brighton & Hove Albion, Charlton Athletic or Southampton were all just 90 minutes away. The club wanted to avoid a Conference team, especially away from home. Next round they would take anyone, anywhere, but for now it wanted another home tie against a lower ranked team.

When the draw was made on the Monday after the Thurrock game the groan at being drawn against Blue Square Bet National Cambridge United away was clear for everyone to hear. Sure they weren't having anywhere near the season they had in the past, sitting in midtable rather than challenging at the top, but the fact of the matter was they were an old Football League club and they had a Football League mentality about the way they approached games. This was going to be a massive game for the Rooks, and secretly the club were hoping that a draw may be the best result in the circumstances.

So whilst Danny and I flew off into the land of Goulash, we sent James and Cynical Dave up the M11 to give us a minute by minute breakdown on the game.

Cambridge United 3 Lewes 0 - The Abbey Stadium

The Abbey Stadium, or to give it is latest name, The R Costings Stadium, is a proper football ground. What I mean by that is that it ticks a large number of aesthetic features. Big towering floodlights - tick, A rickerty old main stand that has seen better days - tick, a decent covered terrace that runs down the side of the pitch - tick, and some decent food options - tick. A few years ago, the bacon rolls sold at The Abb..sorry R Costings Stadium, won the award for the best football grub when the club were in the Football League. An honour that we would rank higher than a Johnstones Paint Trophy win at Wembley Stadium. However, based on the feedback from the Behind the Goal boys it appeared that reheated burgers were the only food choice.

The Lewes contingent were given the whole of the new stand to use. I always think that this is quite bizarre. Why do clubs almost bankrupt themselves to build new stands, only to put the away fans in it? The South Stand was built during their Football League days and is a smart structure, which looks quite out of place when you compare it to the rest of the stands. It was the first step in a plan to redevelop the whole stadium, but a combination of expectations not being met on the field, the collapse of ITV Digital (it still amazes me how many clubs blame this collapse for the sole source of their financial woes) and change in ownership of the club has seen little more chances to the ground.

I think it is safe to say that eight consecutive league defeats, and no wins away from home since April in all competitions is not the kind of form you would want to take into a cup game, especially one against higher league opponents. However, putting all of that to one side and concentrating on this game, Ibbitson presented an attacking formation which squeezed Rob Gradwell, Dan Beck and Tom Murphy into the starting line-up, although Murphy was played on the right wing.

The game started out in bright sunshine but changed to reflect Lewes' chances in the game, with a cold wind eventually giving way to a downpour in the second half which did little to raise spirits. Simon Wormull had an early attempt for Lewes in the twelfth minute but that was all the Rooks could muster before they conceded in the 23rd minute. Josh Coulsdon launched a route one ball out of the Cambridge defence which Andy Pearson and Sonny Cobbs had difficulty in tracking, allowing Wayne Gray the chance to finish neatly across the face of goal.

The one way traffic continued towards Chris Winterton's goal and further chances were spurned by the U's until eight minutes before the break when Robbie Wilmott's cross saw Danny Wright running into the near post to head home from close range. The game was as good as over and this was certainly the case only four minutes into the second half when an inch-perfect effort from the impressive Simon Russell was lofted past Winterton's hopeful dive to give the home side a three goal lead. At this point, with Danny, Deaks and myself, along with a supporting cast of thirty from six different countries filtering into Spartak Trnava's ground in Slovakia we had hoped that there was some lucky co-incidence that the biggest club in Slovakia, Trnava's choice of home kit with its red and black vertical stripes, was a good omen for events some 750 miles away in Cambridge. But alas the half time report wasn't good so we saught refuse in the bar (Little did we know that this point that Lewes were playing in green - and that is why, in our opionion the magic wasn't working).

Lewes continued to battle on with Murphy shooting over although such was the Cambridge players' desperation to score that they seemed to try to do too much individually when a more measured approach may well have found them more goals, which is of course polite speaking for "they all wanted to score so they were trying to walk the ball into the net".

After the dust had settled, Ibbo faced the camera.

"They are a very strong side and they will turn most teams over here. They played more football than I thought they would. Having said that we gave them all three goals, not defending as well as we could. It was disappointing but there was an improvement from last week against Dorchester. We missed our wide players, Sutton and Wheeler and we could have troubled them if they would have been available. Crellin was outstanding today, and will be a good player in years to come."

The soaked bedraggled faces of the players as they walked off the pitch told one story, but another that would rock the club's fans was about to break.

Monday 25th October 2010
It's hard to say goodbye to yesterday

Unbeknown to virtually everyone outside the club, this season was to be Steve Ibbitson's last in charge of the club. During the summer Ibbo had approached the board and told them his wishes, but also made a private pledge to help find his successor. He also suggested that the process of finding his successor shouldn't wait until the next close season, as any incoming manager would want to start early planning for 2011/12. After the season started, a process for selecting a successor was discussed and potential candidates were aired, one of whom was Tim O'Shea, who had recently resigned from Croydon Athletic.

The Board had preliminary conversations with O'Shea in which he expressed great enthusiasm for coming to the Dripping Pan, but before the end of the season. O'Shea was also attracting very strong interest from several other clubs. As the season had progressed the combination of numerous injuries and a run of defeats in the League prompted the Board to stress to Ibbitson that they were ready and willing to release significant new funds to the current management team to strengthen the playing squad. Ibbitson considered this option, but also felt that a second option should be explored for the good of the club, and, with the Board, he met with O'Shea last week.

Following a hugely productive interview session lasting several hours Ibbitson and the Board recognized that O'Shea was a seriously talented young manager and that this was a major opportunity not to be missed. Consequently, O'Shea was made an offer to take over this season rather than risk him being unavailable at the end of it. O'Shea and his assistant Neil Smith readily accepted the position. The Community Board has agreed a fixed contract to run until the end of this season. Simultaneously, the Board was absolutely delighted to announce that Ibbitson had accepted a new role as club Chairman.

Tim represented the Republic of Ireland at the 1985 World Youth Championship. His clubs included Spurs, Leyton Orient and Gillingham, where he made over 100 appearances. In February 2008, Grays Athletic appointed O'Shea as a senior coach to assist Micky Woodward and Gary Phillips with fitness and tactics. In September 2008, he was appointed as manager after chairman Micky Woodward stepped down, until the arrival of Wayne Burnett as manager two weeks later. He moved from Grays to take the position at Croydon Athletic. O'Shea took the Rams from 2nd bottom in the season he arrived to promotion the following season to the Ryman Premier League, the team scoring 92 goals along the way. O'Shea resigned from Croydon on 4 September 2010.

Assistant Neil Smith started his playing career at Tottenham Hotspur as an apprentice. He went on loan to Gillingham and then signed for them permanently in 1991, going on to make over 200 appearances. He moved to Fulham in 1997 for two seasons, making 75 appearances before joining Reading, where he made 65 appearances in a three year spell. He was part of promotion-winning sides at Gillingham, Fulham and Reading. In 2002 Smith moved to Woking where he played a vital part in the escape from relegation that season. He made 180 appearances for the club. Smith was appointed joint caretaker manager of Woking in March 2007 helping the club to stay in the Conference National and was later appointed as the new manager of Welling United. Smith moved to Grays Athletic as part of their coaching staff in 2008. He then joined Tim O'Shea with whom he worked at Grays, at Croydon Athletic as a coach.

Board member Patrick Marber stated: *"The day I met Ibbo, just under a year ago, he told me that he didn't see his future at Lewes FC as the First Team Manager. He's always been very clear about this in private and in public. So while the timing of this announcement might be a shock for some of the supporters it is something that we have always known as inevitable.*

Ibbo and Jason are beloved at this club. Everyone knows what they did last season, everyone respects and admires them deeply. They are a source of inspiration. The current Board would not have worked to make this takeover happen without their support, guidance and enthusiasm.

Understandably, some people might think, 'Ibbo was pushed'. He wasn't. He was very concerned about our current position in the League, as we all are, but Ibbo cares about the Club first and foremost and he believes the choice to hand over to Tim and Neil will get us back on track. This is typical of Ibbo; it's not about him, it's about what he deems right for Lewes FC.

The club needs Steve at its centre which is why I'm so thrilled he's going to be around as much as ever as our Chairman. Typically, he wasn't entirely sure about the role. He finds the formality onerous. Consequently, we have sanctioned him to wear his shorts in the Board room, on match days and at all FA conferences. Ibbo will be involved in the running and future development strategy of Lewes FC – both on and off the pitch. And he will continue to be at the heart of this fantastic football club."

Chief Executive Nick Williams: *"As well as Ibbo's contribution to the club the Board are very aware that Jason Hopkinson, Simon Gough and Dave Winterton have formed an incredible team around him. Jason's energy and passion for the game is inspiring. His exceptional coaching talent allied to his skill in guiding and developing youth players from Under 18's into the First Team is something we are determined to support and continue with. We have stressed to the new management team that this is a club which wants to give opportunities to young, home grown players. We also want to continue working with Goughy and Dave. They are superb football men and we will be discussing future roles with them too."*

Derrick Parris on behalf of the Supporters Club added: *"We thank Steve for the effort and dedication he has given over the past years. Now a new era begins, we welcome the new manager and his assistant to our club and assure him of our support for the future."*

O'Shea commented: *"On behalf of Neil Smith and myself, I just want to say how pleased and excited we are to be joining Lewes Football Club. The club has a great feel to it - the Board has energy and drive, the supporters are friendly and loyal and we are constantly impressed with the unique transparency and professionalism in the way that the club is run. We are very much looking forward to working with Ibbo, who has done a fantastic job both on and off the field during the club's transition. We are looking forward to the challenge and can't wait to get started."*

A new twist in this most remarkable of season's in Lewes Football Club's history. Only time would tell whether this was a turn in the right direction.

Tuesday 26th October 2010
Dignity

Imagine a football manager agreeing to manage a club for free? What about one who willingly puts his hand in his own pocket to pay an overdue bill for the club? And then one who goes to his own board and suggests there could be a better man to take the club forward and is involved in the interview process? Pie in the sky right? Wrong!

Late on Monday night the news was announced that Steve "Ibbo" Ibbitson was stepping down as manager of Lewes FC and would be replaced by ex-Croydon Athletic manager Tim O'Shea. In an interview with Guardian football writer, and long time Lewes fan Paul Hayward, Ibbo explained the reasons behind this and why it was the right time

"Too many people have sweated blood to keep Lewes FC going and surviving at this level for us to surrender our status easily. The Club needs new impetus to give us the best chance of staying in the BSS. In my opinion, this gives us a better chance of achieving that, at a cost which the Club believes it can afford.

My last word as manager has to be to acknowledge the part my coaching team of Jason Hopkinson, Simon Gough and Dave Winterton have played in the survival of Lewes FC. In particular, for the last five years or so, Jason and I have stood shoulder to shoulder, fighting many battles, both on and off the field, on behalf of the club.

Often, that has been with a team full of kids, who we've seen develop from 15-year-old schoolboys into young adult footballers. That brings a special sort of camaraderie and is something you never forget."

Despite the torrid start to the season that has seen the Rooks win just one league game and more often than not more players unavailable through injury than are fit, there was never any doubt that the new board would wield the axe. Ibbo had agreed that this would be his last season in charge and that he wanted to be part of the process to find his replacement. With funds in place to purchase some new players he felt now was the time to hand the reigns over to someone new.

Dignity - no other word for it. Read any of the message boards and you will see the Rooks fans all saying "We believe in Ibbo". He took over a virtually relegated team in March 2009 after a disastrous first every campaign in the Blue Square Premier.

Last season, with significant financial pressure on the club that resulted in two winding up orders being presented he masterminded some end of season loan signings that saw the club win three of its last four games to stay up. Having a beer with him after the last day win at Hampton & Richmond in April he expressed no surprise that the club had manage to stay up, explaining that he had faith in the players and he knew they would not let him down. The people of Lewes responded by making him Lewes's "Man of the year".

This season with a change in ownership Ibbo became much more open, readily agreeing to be interviewed by the directors on video for all to see and hear (the archive can be found here) and including some very funny moments such as describing David Wheeler's parasite and his reluctance to put him on the bench.

We all have a choice on how we react to the circumstances around us. Watch any match from the Premier League/Football League and you will see the same reactions from the manager. "I did not see that incident", "The goal was offside", "It was handball"...managers are always the first to point the blame at someone else but never at themselves. In the past two seasons I have never seen Ibbo blame anyone for the performance of the team. We have seen some shocking referees in that time, some of whom have cost Lewes valuable points but not once has he spoken out. Again, there is dignity in that.

The good news is that "Mr Lewes FC" was staying on. He was becoming Club Chairman, which I am sure will mean he can still wear his long shorts in all weathers around the club.

The King is dead, long live the king as they say. Well, not quite. Ibbo had agreed to stay for one more game - a very convenient for me local match away at Bromley, re-arranged as Lewes had been in the FA Cup at the weekend. So the travelling Rooks fans could give him a send off. It was all set up so nicely for me as well. A bus trip to the ground, a couple of beers and even the appearance of (in)Active Matt. And then the Slovakian sausage struck.

At some point during the weekend's festivities in Hungary and Slovakia as part of Ocktoberfest 2010 I contracted food poisoning. Not just a mild case but a full blown, pack a spare pair of trousers for the flight home case. Forty eight hours later and 8 pounds lighter the contents of my stomach still seemed to be finding a way out. I was officially on probation from CMF - if I wasn't well enough for work, then football was out of the window too. I resorted to taking tablets - something that never happens in my book just to try and get better, or in this case just to try and make the football. A late 6.30pm fitness test, consisting of eating an apple and keeping it down, was passed and so I was off.

Bromley 1 Lewes 1 - Hayes Lane

Ah Hayes Lane, let me count the ways I love you. I recently chose Bromley's ground as one of my 5 best non league grounds and on a chilly Autumnal night my opinion did not waiver. Stand on the open terrace that runs along the side of the pitch and look to your left and you will see a bench lined stand, to your right a terrace with a unique styled roof. Want a beer, head up to the modern bar where you can even watch the game from the windows. If only all grounds were like this..It was a shame not more fans felt the same way. Lewes's travelling contingent of 12 included 3 of the Rooks125 who like real fan/owners stood on the terrace.

We headed up to the bar to receive all the gory details of the weekends cup game. Patrick introduced me to the new manager, and his assistant Neil Smith which yielded the fact we were almost next door neighbours in BR1 - a fact that could be quite handy when either of us has had a few too many Harveys after a game!

Bromley had started off like a proverbial rocket. Seven consecutive league wins saw them top the table into late September before three wins and finally a surprise 4-1 reverse at Basingstoke Town last week had seen them drop a place or two. Last season Lewes had simply not turned up for this game. On a hot August Bank Holiday they had lost 3-0 to the home side in a performance that would have had Ibbo hopping mad.

The teams emerged with Lewes sporting at least two new faces and a formation that was unlike anything we had seen this season - in one word - attacking. Not only did the Rooks start on the front foot but there was also some bite in there. They were 100% committed into every tackle, chasing every loose ball and making sure every Bromley player knew this would not be a walkover they expected. With the new manager in the stands, and a debt to pay to the departing one, I cannot think what their motivation was!

The game had a few interesting incidents which were viewed differently by both sides. The first in the 30th minute resulted in the opening goal for Bromley. No one doubted the mistake by the so impressive Winterton in the Lewes goal that saw Bromley's Tony Finn lobbing the ball into an empty net from nearly 40 yards, but the Lewes protestations were about the initial through ball that saw a Bromley player clearly in an offside position. But all officials really understand active/passive offside right? I rest my case.

A few minutes later a scuffle over a loose ball ten yards into the Bromley half saw all twenty outfield players involved in some girly pushing and shoving, with Ibbo chomping at the bit to jump into the action in his final game. The result yellow cards all round.

Half time over and Lewes introduced some new blood. New striker Paul Olima had the ball in the net half way through the period but was again wrongly judged to be offside. It was a belter of a half - both teams wanting to score and defending became an irrelevance. Ibbo and Jason could simply stand back and almost say "look what we have done - it's all clicked into place".

And then at last some reward. A complete mess in the goalmouth saw the ball apparently cross the line (according to the lino) but from whom it is unclear. The Bromley keeper came out ended up punching the ball against the bar, Rivers headed the ball into the empty goal but a defenders foot seemed to hook it back. Who scored? Who cares - 1-1 and to see one of the owners of the club jumping around screaming at the top of his voice must have been motivating for the players.

Both teams had chances near the end and Rivers was millimetres away from sealing a famous win when he needed a Peter Crouch leg to get on the end of a fantastic Murphy cross. Bromley then had a free kick on the edge of the box in injury time. The Lewes Lunatic Fringe held their breath and the ball flew off a Lewes shoulder over the bar. And with that the whistle blew. Throughout the second half a teenager had been taunting the Lewes fans about our ineptness. He celebrated like mad that "we had only drawn with Bromley" until his mate pointed out that Lewes were from NEAR Brighton and NOT Brighton, and so a home draw against the bottom team who had lost every home game so far was actually nothing to brag about.

So that was the end of the Ibbo era. He wandered back to the dugout to collect the kit bags (just like Wenger and 'Appy 'Arry do every week) and it was touching to see them share a private moment of chat before they headed back to the waiting throng of press. The players went off to meet the new management team, whilst Ibbo was presented with an old chum who used to play with him from his Scunthorpe days. As has become the habit this season Ibbo (and Jason) conducted their post match interview, in what was quite an emotional moment for all involved.

"Absolutely delighted. We went through it with great detail as to how we wanted them to play, and they did exactly what we asked them to. Their goal was a terrible one to give away. He must have been 8-10 yards offside. But second half we came out and played and I thought we would go on to win it. It would have been great to finish off with a win, but I am really chuffed. This guy (Jason Hopkinson) *deserves more credit and it was nice to share that final moment together in the dugout at the end."*

Hopkinson was then given the mic to say a few things.

"We've been trying. We have put our heart and soul into it. Tonight we tried a lad we had in on loan and we tried a different formation and the players worked tirelessly."

Ibbo and Jason we salute you and wish all managers had a shade of the dignity you have shown everyone around you.

Snap happy

Every club has one, yet normally they just blend into the background, not noticed by the fans. They earn their crust through concentration, anticipation and a steady hand. Ladies and Gentlemen - I give you the club photographer.

James Boyes, as well as doubling up as Lewes FC's website and programme editor is also the club's official photographer. Hardly the easiest of jobs to make sure that every corner of the club is covered, and whilst he relies on a team of able helpers to pull everything together, essentially he is the man behind the public face of the club. Over the past few years he has overseen the evolution of firstly the website and now the match day programme to something that is as far away from the copy cat sites you see through out the Football League, and the PR spin magazines that are more like political party manifestos than football programmes.

One of the essential components of a match day when I was growing up was the programme. Before the days of the Internet (Oi! Grandad - shut up!) it was the only way you could get information on what was going on at the club. In the 1970's and 80's the typical programme was text heavy with few adverts, and those it did carry tended to be for local companies. The concept of syndication had not reached football yet and so each club carried its own exclusive content.

Today, on the main part programmes offer little value. Everyone knows everything about the players at the top level and Premier League match day programmes are rarely of interest or even up to date. The content toes the club line, filling its pages with glossy adverts from premium brands, and bland interviews with players all confessing their love for the game. This was one of the reasons why Fanzines grew in popularity during the early to mid noughties. Today the internet, and mobile communication replaces the need for programmes. Unfortunately, printing deadlines still mean match day programmes are often days out of date - a classic example being Blackpool's recent edition for the game versus Liverpool where the visitors were profiled with Roy Hodgson in charge under the caption "You will never walk alone". Hodgson had of course departed the club some four days previously. And this is why Lewes have tried to be different in their approach, shying away from the information that can be found on the website, and delivering a pot puri of football stories from around the globe for instance.

We caught up with James mid-shot to find out what it is like to be sat on the edge of the pitch with your eye on the lens and a pen in your hand writing the match report.

What are the worst conditions you have had to work in?
I think the wet and the cold are the photographer's enemy. I managed reasonably well in my first season as there wasn't too much rain, but the last two seasons I haven't been so lucky. Last season I tried to brave the rainstorm when we ironically played Bath at the Dripping Pan but five minutes into the second half, the game was abandoned. I was in the back of the stand by then but I did manage to get a photo of a wet referee blowing the final whistle. I couldn't do the puddles justice though.

I think the coldest conditions were when Lewes played at the Kassam Stadium against Oxford Utd in February 2009 in a freezing, biting wind. Fortunately I managed to get home just before the snow which chased me around the M25 and caused more than a few problems for everyone the next morning.

You've worked at a few different clubs in the Non Leagues as a travelling photographer. What are the best media facilities you have come across?
To be honest, photographer's rarely get to experience clubs' media facilities, unlike journos with their cups of tea, radiators and wi-fi, and they certainly aren't allowed in the hospitality areas with their dirty boots and bags of equipment. Sometimes it's even a struggle to get hold of a teamsheet. Again, the facilities vary wildly depending on the club and the league but the Kassam Stadium was quite good (and warm). It was nice to go to Wembley when I photographed the play-off final in 2009, but the fancy press box is in a different section to the photographer's area which is a window-less room underneath the stadium.

What picture are you most proud of?
In terms of football, there are two that stick in my mind. One is of Jean-Michel Sigere celebrating his 94th minute goal which secured a Lewes win against Thurrock in 2008 that kept our promotion on track. He ran towards me behind the goal and I just hit the shutter in hope. The other one is of David Wheeler celebrating a goal against Leatherhead in last season's FA Cup replay. It was a dark, foggy night but I managed to capture the joy and relief that comes with a longed-for goal. Great photos need a lot of luck though.

The photo shoot for the 125th anniversary of the squad and Ibbo as 19th Victorian gentlemen was a stroke of genius. Who came up with the idea, and how easy was it to convince Ibbo to go along with it?
Sadly this was an idea dreamt up by Rooks director Alex Leith and the Sussex Express. I wish I could claim it as my own.

Ever dozed off or been distracted so that you have missed a vital moment?
As I mentioned earlier, good photography is a lot about luck, from chosing the right end to anticipating a key incident. With practice you can reduce the luck level a certain extent but an element of it will always remain. Even more so when you have to take notes during the game for a match report as well as taking photos.

Sometimes I don't see the actual "goal" being scored as I'm following the player who is shooting or the keeper who is diving and it's often the crowd reaction that gives you an initial indication as to what has happened. I've not yet nodded off but it's sometimes been a struggle. It wasn't whilst I was photographing but to answer your question, I was watching Brighton v Leeds at Withdean a few seasons ago with my wife and we missed a goal because we were both, independently, watching a passing policeman putting his glove on.

Which one player would you have loved to have photographed in action?
I can't decide between Bryan Robson, Zinezine Zidane or Bobby Charlton. So I'll choose Eric Cantona.

What do you keep in your camera bag? Any secret hipflask to keep you warm?
Nothing out of the ordinary really. A camera, lenses, memory cards, spare battery, stopwatch, pen, notebook, Conference registration number and some headache tablets. If I'm off to an away game on the train then I might try and stuff some sandwiches in there too. Looking at that lot, maybe I need to get a bigger bag!

Is the job the lonliest in football?
Yes it can be at times. It's normally no problem and there's enough going on to occupy you, but it got so bad when Lewes played at Woking earlier in the season that I upped sticks and went to join Director Patrick Marber and the boys from EFW and TBIR on the terrace when the Rooks were trying to

claw back an equaliser in the last 20 minutes. I enjoyed that. I'm quite humbled sometimes that I am able to go pitch side and behind the scenes at some grounds. I felt like that when I went to Wrexham given the history of the Racecourse Ground. Even Sutton United when I thought of their win over Coventry in the FA Cup all those years ago. Wembley was great too but if I ever get to go pitch side at Old Trafford then it's downhill from there.

Would you want to be a photographer full time?
Sounds like a good thing to do, but it's probably not as easy as it would appear. You'd be expected to get the shot every time with no excuses and you probably wouldn't be able to enjoy the match particularly. I spoke to an Observer photographer earlier in the season at the Dripping Pan and he gave me an insight into the long days and high demands of his job, but one good thing is that he got all his equipment supplied by Canon free of charge, lucky chap, which would be wonderful. Can I plug Canon at this point? At least for me there's not all that much pressure and the lights at the Pan are so bad that even the best of the pros would struggle to get a decent shot. I photographed a good friend's wedding as a favour after Christmas, but it was bloody hard work, I was busy all day and I ended up with almost 1,000 shots to download and sort through. Wedding photographers might seem expensive but I now know they earn every penny.

How much time does the Award Winning* Lewes Matchday Programme take to pull together?
This is my third season as editor but I've still not found the magic formula. It depends on various factors really. The external ones, like family and work, are significant ones I need to be aware of, but I do try and make a tentative plan for each programme, especially when there's a few in quick succession. I guess they take a week or so but some elements like the manager's notes have to be submitted almost at deadline to be topical.

The first season I edited the programme was when we were in the Conference Premier and I had 24 pages of editorial to fill each week. I was doing something on the programme more or less every night of the week for about 3-4 hours and filled it with my own articles and photography. I didn't think I was doing too badly until we visited teams like Wrexham and Cambridge United whose programmes were fantastic, but then I looked in the credits and saw they had a programme team so I didn't feel too bad. Since last season, local student Tom Harper has written match reports when he can get to games and I've recently been aided on the photography front by Lewes-based pro Steve George, who has raised the proverbial bar at the same time. I have also been fortunate enought to regularly include written articles from award-winning members of the blogging community (European Football Weekend, Two Hundred Percent and of course ourselves) which has helped me considerably, not to mention the vast efforts of David Sheppard at Proworx who continually makes the whole thing look presentable. With everyone's help contributing to the programme, on some evenings now I even get the chance to speak to the missus.

With the rise of "quality" blogging, social media applications such as Twitter and a general thirst for the "news now", how long will it be before the programme as we know it will die?
It's an interesting question. "The programme as we know it" already differs dramatically depending on the club and the league they are in and so will the response to social media. Clubs might need to examine what the role of the programme is; what supporters expect from it; can it be adapted to fit in with new technology? "Want to read the matchday programme on the train? There's an app for that" as the advert might say. However part-time clubs will probably find it a huge challenge to keep up with all the possible channels that news now travels in and some clubs will cope better than others.

Most people have got the technology to be constantly informed but does the average non-league club have the capacity to pump out daily news on Twitter, on Facebook, in an email, a podcast or via the website?
Changes might be made if new technology provides a cheaper option than a printed programme but I'm sure clubs will continue to provide something for a supporter to read at half time - besides, league regulations demand it. A subscription-based pdf of the programme is one possibility we've looked into at Lewes (click here for an example) but as a companion to the matchday programme, not as a replacement. Besides, is the programme as much a part of the matchday experience as a pie or a pint? Are we in danger of dismissing the "art" or heritage of the programme too easily? Only time will tell I guess.

You've interviewed a few well known people recently for the programme, who is the most famous?
I was really pleased to interview The Observer's Chief Sport's Writer Paul

Hayward for the Boxing Day programme in 2009 and he was very insightful about football and sport in general. He made me realise that Fleet St journos can actually be decent, genuine people. Using my contacts (ahem) I was able to interview Nick Hornby for the Boxing Day programe last year although that game was postponed so it won't be until February that people will get to read that when the game has been re-arranged. He spoke lovingly about Arsenal and how some of the predictions he made when he wrote 'Fever Pitch' about the influence of money and corporate business on football had materialised. Someone who is not famous but nonetheless a very interesting interviewee was Paul Emerson, the sports psychologist at Lewes. I wanted a quick chat with him so I could give an insight into his work in one of my programmes but ended up talking to him for nearly an hour. He was fascinating to listen to and is obviously someone who is highly regarded in his field.

Sum up James Boyes in a 140 character tweet?

Programme editor, website editor, wannabee sports writer and amateur photographer. Enjoying the ride until someone tells me to get off.

Saturday 30th October 2010
Daylight robbery

Lewes and Bonfires go together like Milton Keynes and roundabouts. Bonfire festivities began when the discovery of the Gunpowder Plot was declared a national holiday. Celebrations in Lewes were not planned or carried out annually, but were more random events that were more like riots. They continued until they were banned by Oliver Cromwell during his reign. However, they were reintroduced when King Charles II returned, but still on a random basis when the townsfolk had something to protest about. Interest waned by the end of the 18th century but in the 1820s large groups, known as Bonfire Boys started celebrating the failure of the Gunpowder Plot with fireworks and large bonfires.

This got a bit too much during the 19th century with police from London regularly being drafted in to keep the peace on Bonfire night as the groups tended to be a bit "exuberant". Societies sprang up, each having their constitutions and their own stripy jumper to the extent today that there are seven groups, each of whom plan their Autumnal events months in advance. Over 80,000 people descend on the town each year to join in with the celebrations, making it the bonfire capital of Europe.

With no game at home on weekend of the 5th November, the match versus Dartford was deemed "Bonfire Special", with an offer of half price admission to anyone coming in smugglers gear, the traditional dress for the Bonfire elite. Add to this that it was the first chance for the Lewes crowd to see and meet the new Tim O'Shea/Neil Smith management duo as well as saying goodbye to Ibbo and the crowd was going to be a bumper one. Dartford are no shrinking violets themselves away from home, taking hundreds wherever they go. The smart money was on a four figure crowd.

O'Shea and Smith had been busy themselves this week, bring in no less than five new players in the past few days through their network of contacts in the non-leagues. Exciting times indeed, and it wasn't just things happening on the pitch that was getting the town talking. In the run up to the match, and in preparation for the firework celebrations, the town launched its own radio station - RocketFM. During the week each of the Lewes owners took it in turns to host a show. Come Thursday and it was the turn of Ben Ward and Patrick Marber to host two hours of mayhem. It was like a party in your living room with special guests all chipping in to add to the chaos. I was invited live on air to try and find ten clubs around the world who played in red and black who we could try and "twin" with.

Dartford holds some fond memories for me, growing up literally down the road from their old Watling Street ground. They had hit rock bottom, dusted themselves down and simply got on with things, climbing slowly but impressively up the leagues, winning honours such as last season's Ryman Premier League along the way. This season, despite the attentions of their old rivals Ebbsfleet United their form has been patchy. Unbeaten at home but without a win away had seen them drop too close to their liking to the bottom three, but the one thing the Darts have is faith in manager Tony Burman who has been in charge for over five years and guided them through thick and thin.

We had another group of special guests. Making their debuts at the Pan were Reading fans Adam and his son Harry. Danny and I had been guests in Adam's five star luxury box at Wembley earlier in the season for the Community Shield so it was only fair we returned the favour here and we gave him his own square on the terrace to stand on. Also making his first visit to the Pan was the founding member of the Finnish branch of the Lewes fan club, Ville Miettensen and his wife. After all who wouldn't want to bring their loved ones halfway across Europe to watch a game at the Pan.

Lewes 1 Dartford 1 - The Dripping Pan

For 92 minutes this was a professional performance, continuing the hard work the team put in on Tuesday night at Bromley. But then a stupid over reaction, a crap refereeing call and then a lapse of concentration saw all that hard work undone and the team and fans trooping off disappointed. How far we have come in just a week that a point earnt is treated in such a way.

Rewind 94 minutes and the teams emerged to a rousing reception from the massed ranks of the various Bonfire Societies, accompanied by drums and bagpipes. Tim O'Shea (officially renamed now as ToSH) had been busy in his three days in charge, bringing four new faces to the starting XI but it was two of the old guard who really shined. When Rikki Banks was lured up the road by Eastbourne Borough in the close season to have a quieter life than he had last year between the sticks for Lewes, no one foresaw that Chris Winterton would be as capable in goal (as well as Banks's Eastbourne conceding 38 goals in 17 games so far), growing in confidence as each game passed, and no one expected to see the kind of Ronaldo style showboating on the wing at the Dripping Pan, but that is exactly what Tom Murphy showed the crowd today.

Both teams got stuck in early, and not for the first time the weak refereeing led to tempers fraying. On the twenty minute mark Andy Pearson was floored by a leading arm from a Dartford player that was unwarranted and would have led to a more competent referee reaching for red instead of the yellow he gave. Lewes gave as good as they got though and it was through this "never say die" attitude that led to the opening goal in the 40th minute. A long ball over the top was chased down by Murphy and he managed to win a corner, which when swung in caused confusion in the box and Paul Olima managed somehow to prod the ball home.

Half time saw the Rook Inn packed as usual, with many admiring a glance up at the new scarves that Danny and Dave had put up pre-match. Young Adam had generously donated a Reading shirt on behalf of the little Berkshire club but even he could not be more impressed by the new names in the wall of fame - FC Siofek, Debrecen and AS Trencin are now immortalised forever (well, until we find some even more obscure ones). One Harveys Blue later and we were back on the terrace, drums beating, bagpipes belching and the crowd urging the team forward, although the addition of the countdown clock in the corner of the ground did give the impression Lewes were hanging on for a win from the 46th minute.

With the atmosphere cranked up to ten, Lewes tried to kill off the game. Tom Murphy literally dazzled the Bankside crowd with some hot shoe shuffles sending the young girls into a Cristiano Ronaldo frenzy. One of the new members of ToSH's management team, a slightly younger looking Ibbo took up a position on the Bank, giving more advice to the linesman than the team.

The new countdown clock kept on ticking. Fifteen minutes to go, Dartford corner, Winterton misses it but there is substitute Hutchinson to hook it clear. Eight minutes to go Barness is out of position, the Dartford full back goes marauding down the line, crosses the ball but there is no one there.

Four minutes to go Crellin loses the ball in midfield and a three versus two attack is averted by some smart thinking from Breach. One minute to go Winterton takes two attempts at gathering the ball. One second to go, Crellin takes the ball into the Dartford half and is literally rugby tackled. As he goes down he flicks his foot out David Beckham style, queue huge "gathering" in the centre circle and once again the referee proves he is not fit to officiate at this standard, by not only sending off Crellin and only booking the Dartford player, but giving the free kick to the away team. Hang on - Crellin was rugby tackled - as far as I am aware this is not the oval ball game. Tackles around the waist are illegal AND reversal of decisions cannot take place.

Less than 45 seconds later and of course the ball is in the back of the Lewes net. Concentration gone, they allow Dartford time in the box and an unchallenged shot from Tom Bonner nestles in the corner. Bollocks. Gutted. Thanks ref.

So, thirty minutes after his Dripping Pan debut, new manager Tim O'Shea faced the video camera of Patrick Marber.

"They had run out of a few ideas at the end. They pumped it long into the box, a deflection and then the ball is in the back of the net. I thought the sending off was harsh. I don't understand why our guy was sent off and not theirs. We had gone 4-5-1 after losing our left back so early on. Tom Murphy and George Porter were both fantastic and once that bit of belief started to grow and we gave as good as we got. It was an encouraging performance. The players cannot go away from today regreting that late goal.

It was an enjoyable day. The crowd were fantastic and the team need to put that effort in as a thank you. Onwards and upwards."

Postscript

Video evidence supplied by Dartford themselves shows that Crellin and the Dartford player both fell to ground wrestling but when Crellin got back up the Dartford number 3 can be clearly seen pulling his hair and it is this incident that caused the issue. Of course the referee did not see this and the Dartford player got away scot free - and of course such evidence counts for nothing in this league.

* The ten clubs we came up who play in red and black stripes were AFC Bournemouth (England), St Mirren away (Scotland), Foggia (Italy), Spartak Trnava (Slovakia), IP Brommapojkarna (Sweden), Eintract Frankfurt (Germany), OGC Nice (France), Flamingo (Brazil), Bohemians (Ireland) and Khimki (Russia)

Saturday 6th November 2010
Weston-travel-nightmare

Anyone who knows Danny and I would think that we spend every waking hour planning trips to football in the most obscure places, and you would not be too far from the truth. About a year ago we were made aware of a crazy, if a slightly bizarre game that takes place twice a year in the village of Spakenburg, around thirty minutes drive south east of Amsterdam. What do you mean you have never heard of it? It is one of the maddest, surreal venues for the craziest game in Europe.

The Spakenburg derby, derby of derbies, where have you been all our lives? You can now lay claim to being the greatest match on earth, and the reason European Football Weekends were invented. Ticketmaster went into meltdown in the Netherlands last week, and not just because Take That were playing at the local EnormoDome. Everybody wanted to lay their mitts on a ticket for the thirty third village derby between the blues of SV Spakenburg, and the reds of IJsselmeervogels.

This was the first time the match had taken place in the newly formed Topklasse Division, the third tier of Dutch football. Previously, these two had been the most successful amateur clubs in the country. IJsselmeervogels Chairman Arian van de Vuurst had been a dissenting voice amongst those who wanted change, "professional football does not fit in with our culture" he harrumphed before the start of the season.

Traditionally, these two clubs have always tried to outdo each other on and off the pitch. When one team builds a new stand, the other will build one slightly bigger. Last season the reds let loose a pig on the pitch as a little dig at their rivals who they consider to be farmers. They themselves are proud to be known as the fishermen of the village. The blues responded by flying a light aircraft over the ground which dispensed inflatable toilet brushes onto the reds terrace. SV Spakenburg also unveiled their new mascot at the derby last year, a giant viking standing over 20 feet tall, brilliant.

So you can see why we had to head off there, knowing that we would be missing another Lewes game. But we had chosen well in some instances. Weston-Super-Mare is a nightmare of a journey to make. Without being disrespectful to WSM I think a number of clubs breathed a sigh of relief when they were relegated last season from the Blue Square South, simply for the fact of the four hour plus journey most teams have to make. However, due to a number of reasons they retained their place in the league and as soon as the fixtures came out it was the one we looked at to give it a wide berth.

Last season we headed off on a five hour train trip to Weston-Super-Mare which provided enough laughter for a whole DVD box set. Not that much of it came on the pitch as Lewes went down to a 3-2 defeat in a game watched by barely 200 fans. But the pre and post match entertainment was first class. This season it would be left to Deaks and Cynical Dave to relay updates to us on their journey, which as the crow flies was only 10 miles shorter than our one to Amsterdam. Trivia fact number 53.

Unbeaten in the league since Tim O'Shea came onboard, the Rooks went into Somerset with some confidence of a long awaited away win.

Weston-Super-Mare 0 Lewes 3 - Woodspring Stadium

Any of the twenty or so Lewes fans who were at the same game last season will have been worried in the opening few minutes that the game would pan out the same way. The home side dominated the first few exchanges, but the difference this year was that Weston did not have that man Dave Gilroy (last seen scoring a brace for Woking against the Rooks back in August), and that Tim O'Shea had added some bite and urgency into the team, which on occasions boiled over the surface.

O'Shea fielded the same side as had completed the previous game at Dartford, a blend of youth and experience with the accent on the former, featuring two teenagers in the starting line-up and four more on the bench. The attacking 4-4-2 with Murphy getting forward in support as much as he could was the order of the day. Chances in the first half hour were as sparse as the 212 crowd on the larg terrace behind the goal, with the only noise being generated by the travelling Rooks fans.

"Oh when the Rooks, go swooping in" sang the depleted Lewes Lunatic Fringe and to demonstrate the words Paul Olima wasted Lewes's best chance of the game after thirty minutes when it seemed easier to score rather than skying the ball out of the ground. Weston upped the pace in the last ten minutes of the half, building from the back, and creating a number of chances. The referee did nothing to endear himself to the few home fans when he failed to send off Chris Breach, after bringing down a flying Nat Pepperell on the edge of the box. The home team blew the resultant free-kick but looked destined to score three minutes later when a telling pass from Nayle Grubb split the Lewes defence leaving Marcus Duharty one-on-one with keeper Chris Winterton. The striker, unfathomably, decided a pass to an offside team-mate when a better option than a shot into a gaping goal, and the chance went begging.

Lewes once again took control in the second half, with the up-front pace of teenagers George Porter and Tom Murphy, playing further up the pitch, stretching the Weston defence. Murphy's pace led to the first goal, allied with a cool head and a fine shot, as he burst onto a perfect pass and slyly angled the ball past the keeper, in off the post. This was the first time this season that Lewes had taken the lead away from home and they didn't intend to throw it away. Lewes tried to close the game down, defending deep, and clearing long rather than attempting to pass out of defence. This gave Weston the chance to camp in the Rooks' half, and lay siege to Winterton's goal for a ten-minute period.

At this point a neutral might have surmised that the Seagulls (Weston-Super-Mare) deserved a draw, but Lewes, encouraged by a brilliant cameo from teenage Welsh midfielder Reece Jones on loan from AFC Wimbledon, took the initiative in the closing stages, and gave their win an emphatic scoreline. It was Jones' pass that set up Porter's goal, finished with some aplomb by the Orient loanee, who curled the ball past the keeper. The resulting celebration, as Porter ran behind the goal, involved both Lewes fans and players.

There was more to come, with Lewes now rampant, particularly down the right where Murphy had got the better of his man time and time again. The eighteen-year-old powered in his fourth of the season past a helpless keeper after a neat interchange of passes found him with space for a shot in the box.

In the last minute a flying Murphy was upended by the bemused Jamie Price, and Weston's frustration at their drubbing manifested itself when the resulting 'afters' led to a twenty man melee. In the brawl, Lewes' third in consecutive games, Porter seemed to be more sinned against than sinning, but nevertheless received a straight red card from the referee, along with Ingram who was dismissed for a second yellow.

So pleased with the victory was manager Tim O'Shea that on the way home he ordered the coach to stop at the services on the M4 and treated the players, and the travelling fans to a beer before catching up with Patrick Marber.

"It was another good, encouraging performance. It was a shame that the incident at the end tarnished the performance to an extent. George had done well up until then, and is still learning. George said afterwards that he was silly enough to get involved. But what it showed was the team were together with the way they reacted. Being away from home, this was an exceptional win. Even their fans said they couldn't believe where we are in the league. Rees Jones came on as a sub. He is only 17 years old and has just come back from the European Championships with Wales and looked excellent."

A small price to pay for the win? Possibly. A three nil away win is a great return in any circumstances but the ill-discipline has to be tempered. The team are full of youngsters who perhaps at times take the motivating team talks a step too far. Only time will tell if they have the right temperament for the game, but for now "We're on a march with ToSH's army"

Tuesday 9th November 2010
Bishop takes your Rook

Wander eastwards along Lewes High Street and just past the entrance to the Castle grounds you will come across a small alley, heading up the hill. Blocking the way on this fine sunny Wednesday afternoon was Lewes CFC Director Alex Leith, dressed all in black like a Milk Tray man, protecting the entrance to Viva Lewes, the high quality feature rich magazine about all things Lewes.

Alex is one of the founders of the publication, bringing his years of experience in writing and publishing to the Lewes community. He has a very interesting background in the game, laying claim to writing Ryan Giggs's autobiography, following David Beckham around Spain in his first season and ending up as Claudio Ranieri's translater at Chelsea for a number of seasons amongst his honours.

His involvement in the club came via fellow Lewes board member Ben Ward, although he had been a fan for quite some time. He had "ghost" written former Lewes manager Steve King's column in the match day programme during the championship year and had always been a fan, loving the whole "Lewes Experience". Looking back now whilst it is something to be very proud of that the club reached the pinnacle of Non League football, it was madness to go up, especially with the release of the whole first team squad and King himself in that close season.

Today he still sees himself as a fan first and a director second. You will never see Alex at the ground in a club tie, favouring his red and black stripy scarf. His proudest moments since taking over the club? Going in goal during the penalty shoot out at half time in the game against Dartford, or sneaking onto the snow covered pitch after the Boxing Day game was cancelled against Ebbsfleet United with a ball for a kick around. His greatest wish? A model pro's answer that he was taking each game as it came and that three points tonight would just be dandy.

Confidence was obviously high in the Rooks camp after their biggest, in fact, only away win of the season at Weston-super-Mare on Saturday. The team had discovered a hard belly, being prepared to fight to the death for their points. Exactly what the team had lacked in previous seasons, but a little over the top after mass brawls against Bromley, Dartford and Weston had resulted in two red cards and countless bookings.

Fixtures sometimes seem to conspire against teams, and after the longest away trip of the season to Weston on Saturday, Lewes headed north up the M11 for the 3rd longest road trip just 72 hours later. Despite it being a cold and wet Tuesday night, the number of Rooks who arrived at Woodside Park was surprisingly high. Of course the board were well represented with Mr Marber, Mr Williams, Mr Leith and Mr Dobres all wearing their colours and joining the dozen or so hard core regulars - well they could hardly all fit into Stortford's compact and bijous boardroom at the same time.

A surprisingly easy trip through the rush hour traffic saw me arrive at Woodside Park, in the shadow of Stansted Airport as the Lewes coach arrived. I headed into the bar and found the Lewes Lunatic Fringe propping up the bar along with Chairman Ibbo, complete with his mysterious Chairman's bag (similar to Danny Last's Non League Bag but with added cigars and fine wine I suspect) enjoying a fine pint of IPA. A perfect pre-match warm up.

Bishop's Stortford 1 Lewes 0 - Woodside Park

Last season when Lewes came to the furthest corner of Hertfordshire the home fans generated some atmosphere. Bash the Bishop, a member of the clergy who had a big drum and wasn't afraid to use it, generated some real noise for the "Blue Brazil" but it was sadly lacking tonight. A quick count of the crowd saw varying numbers close but ultimately under 200 (later "official" figures suggested it was 268 although I am sure you cannot count the players as part of the crowd) which was very disappointing. The draw of Lewes at home on a Tuesday night in November obviously didn't match an evening of Australian Masterchef - what is wrong with people today.

The Lewes players looked fit. Not in a FHM Swimwear special way but in an energetic way. They used the ball well, with Murphy in his fancy dan boots providing some tricks down the left. And it was the youngster who came closest to opening the scoring when his well struck free kick hit the foot of the post and rebounded too quickly for Hutchinson to take advantage of.

The response from the LLF was a Marber inspired rendition of "We are Community, I've got all my members with me" to the tune of We Are Family, although the take up rate was rather muted. Seconds left in the half and a rare slip in the Lewes defence saw a Stortford forward through on goal. Winterton tried to push him wide but clearly took him out. With the home crowd baying for a red it was with relief (and some laughter) that the referee produced a yellow for the keeper. And of course just to rub salt in the Stortford wounds, he proceeded to save the resulting penalty.

The second half was a battle of attrition with both teams flirting around the edge of the area. Lewes's new secret weapon, the "Rory Delap" throw in of Porter caused a few problems but not enough to really worry the Stortford keeper. Twenty minutes to go and a rare mix up in the Lewes defence saw Hutchinson dawdle, Winterton hesitate and Stortford's Duane Jackson pounce to score the only goal of the game.

Defeat is not a word in O'Shea's vocabulary at Lewes and so there would be no beer stops on the way home tonight, which meant that Deaks and Dave had no intention of travelling on the team coach, opting for Fuller's taxis back to Bromley. Instead he sat down in the Stortford manager's office and faced the questions of joint owner Patrick Marber.

"*The first twenty five minutes we looked comfortable, in control and Stortford's body language seemed to suggest they had run out of ideas. We were a good 25% short of where we were on Saturday. I thought we looked comfortable but we were let down with a few decisions in the last third of the pitch. We seemed to be scared to take a chance, taking one or two touches too many. We gifted them a lot of chances tonight - we didn't lose, we gave them the win. It is a thin dividing line and I think we deserved something out of the game. They haven't had to work hard for their goal. Tom (Hutchinson) tried to be too clever in heading it back and they scored.*"

As Alex Leith would say, let's just focus on the next ninety minutes.

Saturday 13th November 2010
Relegation form?

So three games gone under the new management team of O'Shea and Smith the Rooks had won one, drawn one and lost one. Four points from three games, which was ironically the same return Ibbitson had from the first three games of the season. Things went downhill from his fourth game in charge, and the run of one point from five home games since was alarming to say the least. However, a winnable game at home was just what the doctor ordered and three points from the game against fellow relegation candidates St Albans City was required.

As part of my commitment to a promise I made to Lolly at the start of the season, I would not be attending the Dripping Pan for this one. Instead I would be going to Upton Park to watch West Ham take on Blackpool. At the start of the season one of these was a shoe-in to be in the relegation zone after thirteen games - but few expected it to be the Hammers. After paying just £55 for the two tickets Lolly then came down with the flu and failed a late fitness test. Now I could have taken the simple option to not go, and head down to the Dripping Pan instead, but that would have made Sullivan and Gold the winners in my little personal spat about ticket prices so I decided to go. I am sure I was in for an afternoon of free flowing football played out by International superstars in a stadium full of passion and atmosphere right?

And what was I going to miss? An afternoon of Harveys ale, amusing conversation and 90 minutes of football played by two teams who wanted to put on a performance for the fans. Patrick Marber, himself no stranger to the Premier League with his comfy seat at The Emirates when time permits, castigated me for my decision, making me feel guilty that I had chosen Premier League over premier entertainment. Still a comfortable win over the Seasiders would surely make it all right, wouldn't it?

Lewes 3 St Albans City 1 - The Dripping Pan

So whilst I watched a Premier League bore draw, a brace from Paul Olima and a goal from debutant Ben Godfrey helped Lewes record their first home league win in nearly three months and move out of the relegation zone in the process. As with a few weeks ago when Dorchester Town were the visitors, the situation was remarkably similar to West Ham's. Both visitors came to the Pan almost within touching distance of Lewes at the bottom, and on both occasions West Ham were playing teams they should have beaten. However, on this occasion it was Lewes who rose to the occasion.

Lewes manager Tim O'Shea made two changes to the side which had lost 1-0 at Bishop's Stortford in their previous game, with Anthony Barness and Ben Godfrey replacing Nathan Green and Sam Butler in the starting line-up. Both sides started the game well, with a lot of possession being enjoyed by both sides in the opening exchanges.

The first chance of the game fell to Lewes. Jermaine Wright had a shot from the edge of the penalty area blocked after Tom Hutchinson had knocked down a long throw by George Porter and then Paul Olima received the ball twenty five yards from goal, turned past two players and sent a curling shot just wide. Meanwhile at Upton Park it was Blackpool who were making all the running, creating a number of chances against one of the most leaky defences in the Premier League. So far so good, I wasn't missing a thing.

It took a bit longer for St Albans to register their first attempt on goal, with Chris Benjamin sending a tame shot straight at Chris Winterton after a purposeful run. The Rooks continued to look the more dangerous side, though, and nearly took the lead when Tom Murphy out-paced St Albans right-back Ross Dedman, only to see his shot from a tight angle saved at the near post by Paul Bastock. The pace and trickery of Murphy was causing the visitors defence a number of problems, and the in-form winger was unfortunate to see a superb curling effort from the edge of the penalty area tipped over by Bastock. From the resulting corner taken by Lewis Ide, Ben Godfrey saw his powerful near-post header cleared off the line. How do I know all of these details? Twitter, of course. With West Ham simply failing to cope with Blackpool's midfield (Did I really just write that?), the chances of a home goal at Upton Park were as rare as Avram Grant cracking a joke.

Minutes later at The Dripping Pan, Lewes were unlucky not to take the lead, as George Porter saw a left-foot shot from twenty five yards deflected just wide. From the resulting in-swinging corner taken once again by Ide, Hutchinson saw his far-post header cleared off the line. Excitement aplenty at one of the two games - and it certainly wasn't in E13.

Finally, after forty one minutes, Lewes got the goal that their spell of pressure had deserved. The goal was scored by Olima, but owed much to the work of Godfrey, who after latching onto a long ball down the right wing by Andy Pearson, cut inside and played the ball across goal for Olima to tap home from inside the six-yard box. On the stroke of half-time, the Rooks increased their lead. Godfrey was the scorer, running onto another fine ball from Pearson, beating the offside trap and finishing calmly past Bastock.

Meanwhile in East London the referee's whistle for half time had woken up 34,000 fans who had been in a boredom-induced coma.

The second half began as the first half had finished, with Lewes on top. I punched the air when Godfrey scored, raising some strange looks from the West Ham fans around me.

West Ham had had three shots on target, none of which had troubled the Seasiders keeper. Lewes had had nine, two of which had hit the back of the net. And crowd noise? Well the seven hundred at Lewes would have been producing more noise than the thirty plus thousand at Upton Park - it wouldn't have been hard. After all, seven fans could have produced more noise than the collective Hammers fans at this stage.

Half time at West Ham used to be mildly amusing with the Hammerettes thrusting their way through a number of mistimed numbers. In their letter to West Ham fans at the end of last season, David Sullivan and David Gold assured us: "We want to bring the fun back. We want you to be excited on a match day, and not just about the style of football. We are looking at ways to improve our pre-match and half-time entertainment." So what did we have to lift the gloom today? An advert on the big screens for the highlights DVD from last season (i.e Scott Parker's goal v Wigan repeated from every conceivable angle) and an interview with "Mad Dog" Martin Allen. Hmm hardly groundbreaking or inspiring. But then what do you expect for £55?

Inside the first five minutes of the second half at the Dripping Pan Murphy had a goal-bound shot from a short corner headed clear by Harry Beautyman and Hutchinson sent a header from an Ide free-kick just wide. Moments after these two chances, the Rooks should really have made the game safe, as the impressive Godfrey was able to pick out Chris Breach unmarked at the back post. Unfortunately for Lewes, the centre-back sent a free header from inside the six-yard box over the bar.

The home supporters would not have to wait long for a third goal, though, as Lewes increased their lead after fifty four minutes. The goal was scored by Paul Olima, who received a pass from George Porter just inside the penalty area, beat three defenders, rounded Bastock and rolled the ball between two further St Albans players on the line to give the Rooks another goal which their performance deserved.

Unsurprisingly, the game began to peter out at this stage and despite the best efforts of both sides, goal-scoring chances were few and far between in the last half an hour or so. Meanwhile at Upton Park the closest we had come to a goal was a glaring miss from Luis Boa Morte when he pulled his shot wide when it was easier to score.

So all the goals were flying in at Lewes and a fourth of the afternoon came on the seventy sixth minute mark when St Albans scored a consolation effort with Adam Everitt sending a near-post header looping across goal and into the far corner. More drama at the Pan as within three minutes of pulling a goal back for his side, Everitt was sent off for a second bookable offence after cynically fouling Lewes substitute Tim Rivers.

Back at Upton Park and at last the game was coming to life, although not in favour of the Hammers. Ex-West Ham striker Marlon Harewood really should have won the game for the visitors when he miss hit his shot from six yards out, reminding Hammers fans of his miss in the last minutes of the FA Cup Final versus Liverpool in 2005 which would have won us the cup. But Harewood's miss was nothing compared to Gary Taylor-Fletcher's. Now double-barrelled named footballers always give off this air of superiority. You imagine that they went to a private school, breaking the rugby playing tradition to make a career as a footballer with the headmaster's words "You'll never make a career doing that boy" in their ears. But until June 2004 he was known simply as Gary Fletcher. Then he met Viv Taylor and as she was the last Taylor in her family they agreed a deal where he would take her name in return for a lifetime immunity from doing the washing up. Obviously pre-occupied with her next demands, GTF as I am referring to him for brevity skied the ball over the bar from an unmarked position on the six yard box with just fifteen minutes to go.

Both final whistles resulted in loud cheers from both grounds. At Upton Park it was the 2,500 Blackpool fans who were celebrating another excellent point from their travels, whilst the boos ringing out for another incredibly poor Avram Grant inspired performance were all to evident. Meanwhile back down in East Sussex the round of applause was for a Rooks performance that belied their lowly league position. It was too early in the season to talk about 'six-pointers', but the victory and performance to go with it for Lewes will certainly provide everybody associated with the club with some optimism after an encouraging start to Tim O'Shea's reign as manager.

After his birthday the day before, and the promise of a Harveys on the bar if the team won, manager Tim O'Shea was understandably a very happy man when he met up with Patrick Marber after the game.

"*It was an excellent game - just what the doctor ordered. Once we got through the opening fifteen minutes we looked strong. We looked dangerous from set pieces and corners. Murphy looked great - he is a real rough diamond and if we can work with him longer then he will be a great player. The team's performance deserved a clean sheet but it was a thrilling game. We are out of the drop zone for the first time this season. It is a great birthday present.*"

I was left to contemplate what I missed on my eight mile journey home that due to the ridiculous amounts of traffic in East London would take almost as long as the normal trip back from Lewes. I'd paid £45 more to watch less passion, less commitment and less entertainment. Who was the real loser here? M, of course. It would be different next time, honest.

Saturday 20th November 2010
Another avenue of pleasure closed down

The FA Trophy is a good opportunity for Non League clubs to go on a decent cup run and enjoy a day out at Wembley in May. Or is it? Like the FA Cup, the number of teams who have the resources to win the trophy are limited and on the very rare occasion the cup has gone to a team outside the Conference Premier can be counted on one hand in the past twenty years. If you look at the last few seasons, the final has always featured teams from the top division. AFC Barrow, Stevenage Borough, York City, Torquay United and Kidderminster Harriers have contested the last four finals at Wembley Stadium, and you have to go back to 2005 to find the last time a team from outside the top flight reached the final (Hucknall Town).

The simple fact is that league survival is more important and so if you can negotiate the opening rounds and then get that luck in a decent draw then you may just be able to put yourself within spitting distance of the final. When the draw was made for the Third qualifying round Lewes were paired with Salisbury City of the Zamaretto (Southern) League. Whilst they were one league below Lewes, they had been a Conference team until the end of last season when financial problems had seen them forcibly relegated two divisions.

So it was never going to be the easy game that people thought it was on paper although it did provide a brief distraction to the league campaign for Tim O'Shea and the Rooks.

Lewes 1 Salisbury City 3 - The Dripping Pan

It is fair to say that the five hundred and ninety eight fans who saw this game would be hard pushed to believe that Salisbury City were the lower ranked team. They came, they played, they conquered and went away from The Pan with a place in the next round without really breaking into a sweat.
The visitors Jake Reid's early chip in the third minute signalled Salisbury's intent and Tom Hutchinson had to make an accurate tackle to thwart the striker moments later as the visitors went for Lewes's throats from the first minute. Kayne McLaggon created something out of nothing after twenty minutes when his twenty five yard shot dipped late forcing Lewes keeper Chris Winterton to tip it over the bar. A minute later, Adam Kelly's excellent

looping shot from just inside the area edged City in front for a deserved lead which they took into the interval. Hardly a classic Lewes forty five minutes but with the players in the dressing room, Boss O'Shea had an opportunity to change things round.

Unfortunately, just four minutes into the second half Salisbury's lead was doubled when player-manager Darrell Clarke picked up a cross-field pass before striking the ball across the face of goal under Winterton. The collective sigh on the Jungle was enough to be heard around the ground. This wasn't going to plan. Jermaine Wright hit the bar as Lewes pushed forward and keeper Tommy Smith was at full stretch to keep out Tim Rivers' shot, and at last in the seventy second minute, the Rooks got some reward for their efforts when they pulled one back after substitute Lewis Hamilton.

Lewis Ide's free kick was tipped onto the upright by Smith and Rivers decided to take the ball on his own mazy run instead of passing and it looked like the home side could force a replay, but it was not to be when Salisbury boss Clarke scored his second with just three minutes left on the clock. .

After the game O'Shea could hardly disguise his annoyance with the performance when he chatted to Patrick Marber in the media centre at the Pan.

"*We are disappointed with the result. Chris had to make two saves, apart from the three times he picked the ball out of the net. They are a full time outfit and are riding high in the league below. Our guys will be going to work on Monday whilst they will be in training. Our fitness level was a positive, and when we brought it back to 2-1 I thought we deserved an equaliser. We have picked up two more injuries - Wormull has done his sciatic nerve and Murphs has done his ankle again.*"

A disappointing afternoon for the Rooks as the distraction of a cup run may have actually done the team good in the long run. Salisbury's reward was an away tie at Basingstoke Town whilst Lewes now had only one realistic chance of silverware - The Sussex Senior Cup.

Tuesday 23rd November 2010
The King of the County

County cup games are unknown these days to Premier and Football League fans. Many moons ago the clubs used to put teams into the regional competitions but that practice stopped at the creation of the gravy train known as the Premier League. Some league clubs still put a team into the competitions, although they rarely take it seriously, especially as it would fall somewhere below the Johnstone's Paint Trophy in the list of priorities. One such example is the Sussex Senior Cup. With only one league team in the county, you would have expected that Brighton & Hove Albion would have dominated this cup in recent years, and you would be right. The Seagulls have won three of the last four competitions, and in the fourth they had lost in the final to Eastbourne Borough after a replay.

Lewes have won the trophy three times in their history, the last being in 2006 when they beat Horsham in the final. So this season, with the FA Cup and FA Trophy consigned to the "been there, done that" folder, the only real hope of silverware was the Sussex Senior Cup. The first round was competed by the teams in the County league, with the Ryman, Blue Square and Brighton joining in round two in mid November.

Lewes had been drawn away to Shoreham. The Musselmen, as they are known, had finished in mid-table last season in the Sussex County League Division One and had high hopes of pulling off a shock, similar to that of Horsham who had beaten big spending Crawley Town the week before in this stage of the competition.

Shoreham 1 Lewes 3 - Middle Road

Cynical Dave again stuck his hand up and agreed to be one of the few Lewes fans to make the trip. Chelsea v Zilina was on the TV, the rain was lashing down but still Dave would rather suffer pneumonia than the Champions League anthem. He hates the commercialisation of the Champions League and I would suggest that if you ever offered him an all expenses paid trip to the final at Wembley in May he would take the ticket and use it as a roll up, putting his tobacco firmly over the logos of Ford, Sony and Amstel.

Just over a hundred fans watched the game unfold at Middle Road, the functional home of Shoreham FC since 1970. Lewes manager Tim O'Shea made six changes to the side which had lost 3-1 at home to Salisbury City on Saturday, with JJ Banasco-Zaragoza, Lewis Hamilton, Nathan Green, Reece Jones, Jordan Lang and Ben Godfrey effectively replacing Chris Winterton, Anthony Barness, Tom Hutchinson, Jermaine Wright, Lewis Ide and Tom Murphy in the starting line-up.

The game started slowly, but Lewes soon found their passing rhythm and went close when Sam Butler saw his thirty yard shot deflected just wide after cutting inside from the right wing. In a game with very little goal-mouth action, the Rooks continued to create the better openings and were unlucky to see Ben Godfrey send a header from a Lewis Hamilton cross just over the bar.

These openings paid off after thirty minutes, as Lewes went ahead. The goal was scored by Godfrey, who pounced on a rebound after Jack Adams in the Shoreham goal had only been able to parry a Butler free-kick, shooting in from a tight angle. Most people would have expected Lewes to take control of the game from this point, but a hard-working Shoreham side continued to impress and equalised five minutes before half-time after Graham Martin flicked a twenty five yard free kick up and sent a looping volley through the hands of JJ Banasco-Zaragoza to level the scores.

Lewes started the second half with purpose and were unlucky not to be ahead within a few minutes as Godfrey shot straight at Adams when clean through after latching onto a flick-on from Paul Olima. The Rooks nearly took the lead again soon after, but the impressive Nathan Green saw his long-range left-foot shot after a powerful run from inside his own half hit the far post, with Reece Jones scuffing the rebound wide.

After 66 minutes, the Lewes pressure told, as Tim Rivers sent a powerful shot from the edge of the penalty area into the roof of the net after Shoreham had been unable to clear a Butler corner. Just minutes later, Shoreham were unlucky not to find another equaliser, as Charlier Walker see his low shot well saved by Banasco-Zaragoza after the striker had taken the ball past Andy Pearson.

The game was made safe after seventy nine minutes, as Godfrey tapped home from inside the six-yard box after seeing his initial volley well saved by Adams following a good cross from Green. The game began to peter out at this stage and Tim O'Shea used the closing stages as an opportunity to give three under 18's in Max Howles, Harry Bowles and Layton Schaaf their first-team debuts.

The game was useful in giving the likes of Lewis Hamilton an opportunity to continue their return from injury in what was a very competitive game, as well as giving players such as Nathan Green and Reece Jones, who have not featured too much over the last few weeks, the opportunity to play. Manager Tim O'Shea spoke with Patrick Marber after the game.

"*In the end it was a fine win. It was always going to be a difficult game on a cold night with a bobbly pitch. A couple of cracking goals - Tim Rivers strike was excellent. It was good to see some of the youngsters get a game and it is a credit to the club and the youth system that we played so well, without putting a foot wrong.*

Roll on round three and a home game against Ryman League Bognor Regis Town and then just three games away from a final, almost surely against the Seagulls of Brighton & Hove Albion.

Not your average journalist

The Guardian's Paul Hayward is not your typical sports journalist. For one thing there are few amongst his peers that even have one Sports Journalist of the Year awards, let alone the two Paul has on his mantle piece. Secondly, there are few that actually support their local clubs, preferring to hobnob it in the plush confines of the Emirates or Old Trafford rather than the Rook Inn at Lewes. But that's not your Paul Hayward. Whenever the chance arises he will pay his tenner and take his place behind the goal at The Dripping Pan and support his local Non League team.

The honour of speaking to Paul fell to Lewes website and programme editor, James Boyes, in mid 2010 prior to the take over of the club.

Can I first ask you about your personal links with Lewes?
My family has been in Lewes for generations. My Grandfather was Mayor in the 1950s and my Dad played football and rugby in the town. My Uncle John was a fast-bowling stalwart of Lewes cricket club. I think of it as my home-town.

You're a keen follower of Brighton & Hove Albion, but how much do you follow Sussex sport in general?
I believe everything starts with grass-roots sport - with coaching, clubs and facilities, so I keep a close eye on events in Sussex. Withdean, the Dripping Pan, Hove (for the cricket) and Brighton racecourse are my main haunts. I just wish Lewes racecourse hadn't closed, because that's where I fell in love with racing, watching the horses on the gallops.

How aware were you of the plight of Lewes FC in recent years?
I've followed it closely. Some of my old school friends are able to go more often than me, and one - Nick Metcalfe - organised a fund to buy a share. I've a nasty feeling he bought a mountain bike with the money. Only joking! When clubs are in danger you see how much people care. The supporters saved the Albion for instance and look where they are now, and I hope they can do something similar with Lewes

I guess you're busy most Saturdays but do you ever get the chance to see much non-league football?
Only at Lewes, and occasionally Eastbourne Borough. I tell my colleagues

how good the football is at the Dripping Pan. Carpet football, as Bobby Robson liked to say. I couldn't enjoy it as much if it was kick and rush.

What do you think of the divide between the top echelons of the game and the lower levels like the Blue Square?
I've always felt the whole game needs to stay connected from top to bottom, so youngsters especially can see the path from non-league to Premier League. Football is embedded in our national culture and I hate it when people at the top think they can cut just the lower leagues adrift. Every player England took to the World Cup in South Africa started at a small club and worked his way up. Football's not a business, it's a passion.

Talking about the business side of things, we have seen a few Non League teams go out of business in the last season or so. How long do you think it'll be before we see a Premiership club go out of business?
Last season Portsmouth were in desperate trouble. Any organisation that pays out 80 per cent or more of its income in wages is dicing with death. I think we may have exhausted the wave of foreign 'investors' (I prefer to call them speculators, because most of them use other people's money). Would Abramovich have bought Chelsea now?

How did you get to the Guardian? Advice for any youngsters hoping to follow in your footsteps?
I started as a trainee journalist with the Racing Post and worked my way on to Fleet Street from there. My advice is to think beyond newspapers to multi-media careers. Get published wherever possible and always look for fresh ideas. The media is ideas-driven. You'll hit lots of walls but don't give up.

And finally, the $64,000,000 question: Do you know anyone with loads of money who wants to invest into Lewes?
I'll ask around! I interviewed Gareth Barry recently and asked him to ride to the rescue. It's painful but Lewes will emerge stronger and wiser.

Saturday 27th November 2010
A little frost and it all goes wrong

Today's football had been planned for week and was due to coincide with a nice family lunch as a starting point. CMF wanted to spend some of my money on Christmas presents and I had no intention of venturing into any of the Twenty first century cathedrals we have built in the South East of England. So I agreed to drop her off at Lakeside and pick her up afterwards, leaving me with a three and a half hour window. I hate to say that I was turning my back on Lewes, who were playing at Ship Lane against Lakeside but there is only so many cars you can count on the M25 there. Instead I had two options. Billericay Town and Concord Rangers. So I went to the God of all decisions. Twitter. I asked which one I should go to, and within minutes I had my answer:-

"Could unlimited tea/biscuits and an access all areas and guaranteed player/management interviews sway your decision? Direct from the horses, well press officers mouth at Concord. In truth he had us at unlimited tea.

But of course I didn't figure in the sudden and unexpected drop in temperatures. Games started to fall to the weather from 9am but Concord were holding out. A local referee came and visited the ground just before 11am and gave it the all clear. Both managers seemed happy and the message went out it was on. And then the proper referee turned up at 1.30pm, realised he didn't have his gloves with him and promptly called the game off.

Fortunately I was already north of the river when Concord let me know, and with the games at Billericay, Aveley, Ilford, Grays Athletic and Tilbury all gone the same way I had little choice but to head to Thurrock.

Now why my reluctance at going to see my beloved Lewes? Well, I have been to Thurrock a few times before, and it is not a ground that I really warm too. The small number of Thurrock fans are decent sorts but I think they could do much more to attract bigger crowds, but then so could so many other clubs. I didn't really fancy Lewes's chances either - despite climbing out of the bottom three recently, form on the road this season had been challenging.

So we met up with Deaks and Dave, who had managed to drag themselves out of Lakeside for the game, along with a guest visit from Dagenham Dan who like us had seen his plan A, B and C fall by the wayside.

I could go into great detail about the game but who really wants to hear about a game with a blow up doll, two penalties, another Lewes sending off, the long awaited return of David Wheeler, the longest queue for a cup of tea in the world, Patrick Marber wearing a hat with strange flaps on, Alex Leith being told he is not allowed to take pictures as it is "against the law" and a referee wearing gloves. You do? Oh OK then.

Thurrock 3 Lewes 1 - Ship Lane

After such a build up it was obvious that the performance on the pitch would be instantly forgettable as poor performance on a bitterly cold afternoon in Essex saw Lewes fall to a disappointing defeat at fellow strugglers Thurrock. I remember the same game last Christmas where Lewes were poor and it seems that as soon as they cross the Thames they go to pieces.

The game started slowly, with neither side really putting the other under a great deal of pressure. However, the first chance of the afternoon fell to the hosts, who saw David Knight send a stooping header at the near post from a Matt Bodkin cross against the cross-bar. The Thurrock fans, all twenty of them responded with a collective "oooh" which was barely audible against the noise of the M25 traffic. Lewes simply didn't look at the races and despite holding their own in midfield in the opening exchanges it was Thurrock took the lead after seventeen minutes. The goal was scored by Leon Lalite, who sent a volley from just inside the penalty area into the bottom corner after Anthony Barness had mis-placed a defensive header.

Patrick turned up at this point, resplendent in his Russian hat and army coat, looking like he had walked off the battlefields of Stalingrad. He wasn't happy to be greeted with the new of the goal but whether it was his presence or simply the threat of a ToSH rollocking at full time, Lewes did seem to wake up and begin to enjoy a bit more possession in midfield, without really causing the Thurrock defence any problems. However, Lewes nearly found an equaliser towards the end of the half, as Sam Butler sent a low shot from the left-hand side of the penalty area just wide of the far post after clever build-up play.

The Rooks suffered a major disappointment just before half-time, as Sam Butler left the pitch injured after pulling up while chasing a loose ball. Butler's replacement, our own David Wheeler, nearly got an equaliser on the stroke of the interval after seeing a close-range header fumbled by Joe Woolley at his near post and then seeing his rebound parried wide by the Thurrock goalkeeper.

Half time saw us take refuge in the club house and we did toy with the idea of whether we should go back out into the freezing cold. And the signs weren't good as the hosts nearly doubled their lead at the start of the second half, when Knight saw his low shot come back off the far post after being put clean through on goal. With the residents of the Bates Motel which sits high above the ground in an almost Scooby Doo like way, looking down on the game, Lewes came back into the game in the 54th minute when Paul Olima was brought down in the penalty area and he picked himself up and sent Woolley the wrong way from the penalty spot. A couple of minutes later, former Thurrock striker Olima shot straight at Woolley when he was put clean through after knocking Kenny Clark off the ball. It was the turning point of the game in some respects. A goal for Lewes would have certainly put them on the road to victory. The travelling Lewes fans thought they had a second goal when Tom Hutchinson's powerful header from a Wheeler corner was harshly judged to have swung out of play on its way over.

The game changed again after sixty nine minutes, as Thurrock were awarded a penalty themselves after Andy Pearson pulled the shirt of Knight at the far post. Dean Cracknell sent Winterton the wrong way from the spot to give the hosts an undeserved lead.

The game began to peter out at this stage, with Thurrock dealing comfortably with everything Lewes were trying to create.

Things got even worse for the Rooks in injury time, as Lewis Ide was harshly shown a straight red card for pushing a Thurrock player to try and retrieve the ball after he had won a free-kick. However, in the final minute of the three signalled by the fourth official, the hosts broke from a Lewes corner and scored an undeserved third goal through Knight, who sent a shot from the edge of the penalty area just over Winterton.

After the game, Tim O'Shea wrapped up warm and offered a few words of comfort to Patrick Marber in the shadow of the Bates Motel.

"*It was an ugly defeat. We didn't deserve anything from the game. Apart from that great spell in the second half we deserved to lose. The changing room was quiet before the game and we lost too many battles on the pitch. The incident leading up to the sending off played right into their hands. Some good news was the return of David Wheeler although I threw him on sooner than I would have liked to.*"

Although this was a disappointing performance for Lewes, they were no worse than Thurrock and were unlucky to come away with nothing. This was arguably the worst performance since Tim O'Shea took charge, but the hard work done in November against St Albans and Weston-Super-Mare has to be balanced with the disappointment of the away games north of the Thames at Bishops Stortford and Thurrock.

WELCOME TO
LEWES F.C.
PROUD MEMBERS OF
BLUE SQUARE BET
SOUTH

ABOVE Simon Wormull scores a trademark free-kick early in the season.

LEFT A rare Fuller Family moment on the terrace against Dorchester Town

RIGHT Standing room only on the terrace at the Pan in the sunshine.

LEFT As if you need another reason to visit Lewes

RIGHT Storm clouds gather over the Pan in October as another defeat beckons...

No pressure keeper - there's just a camera between your legs...

The fate of a season rests on one spot kick versus Maidenhead Town

Defeat on Easter Monday against Bishops Stortford condemns Lewes to relegation.

23rd March & league leaders Braintree Town are felled thanks to "our" David Wheeler's late goal...

...and celebrates with Cynical Dave and Big Deaksy

125 Not Out...enough cake to go round

"I see you stand like greyhounds in the slips. Straining upon the start. The games afoot: Follow your spirit and upon his charge cry God for Ibbo, Lewes & Saint George"

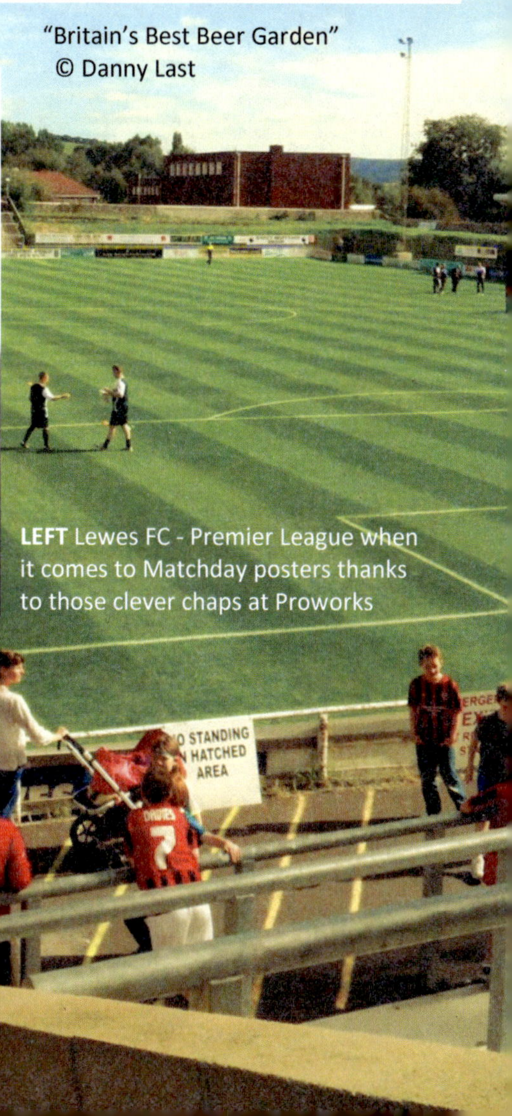

"Britain's Best Beer Garden"
© Danny Last

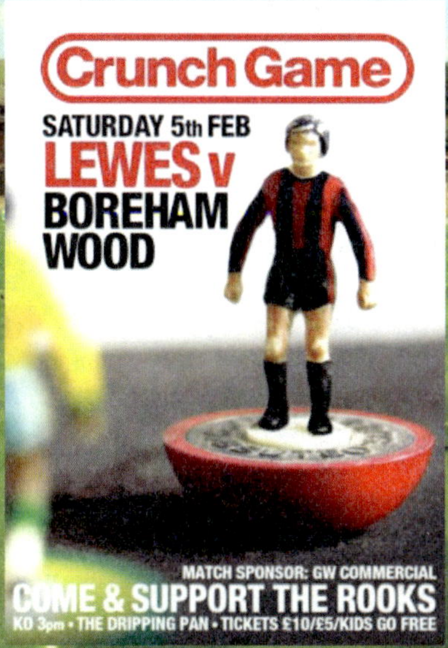

LEFT Lewes FC - Premier League when it comes to Matchday posters thanks to those clever chaps at Proworks

LEFT The return of the King. Ex-manager Steve King returns with Farnborough to the Dripping Pan...it wouldn't be the last time we would see him on the pitch at Lewes in 2011.

Wheeler wheels away at Basingstoke -scared of Cynical Dave's offer of a hug

LEFT Skipper Chris Breach's face says it all as the Rooks crash to another home defeat.

The legend moves upstairs...Charlie Dobres presents Ibbo with his life membership of the club.

Almost a spectacular end to the season. The nearest we get to a goal at Boreham Wood on the last day of the season.

It's never too early to enjoy a pint of Harvey's. Lolly on beer minding duty again.

The worst view in the house?

The view from the Gents at Ebbsfleet Utd on New Year's Day as Lewes start 2011 as they finished 2010.

Finally the season is over. The team applaud the support at Boreham Wood.

Hope? Gareth Hall is mobbed after his spectacular winner at Hampton & Richmond Borough

The Rooks 125 (L-R) Alex Leith, Ben Ward, Nick Williams, Patrick Marber, Charlie Dobres and Eddie Ramsden (hidden)

Saturday 11th December 2010
Friendly fire

Every year the UK greets the sight of snow with huge surprise. Our transport system grinds to a halt as we are vastly unprepared for this sudden deluge of snow and ice, which is normally forecast weeks in advance. Unfortunately this weather has a massive impact on sporting fixtures, none more so than in the Non Leagues. The freezing temperatures a few weeks ago had put pay to virtually all games, apart from Lewes's ill-fated trip to Thurrock. Then last week the huge dump of snow during the week had led to the pre-mature cancellation of the game versus Bromley at the Pan. The decision, as with most clubs (under pressure from the league to make an "early decision no doubt" had cancelled the game versus Bromley on the Friday, only to see a sudden rise in temperatures, and an amazing thaw overnight. We ended up finding a game at Ashford Town in Middlesex on a pitch that was complete free from snow.

With their exit from the FA Trophy at the hands of Salisbury Town, Lewes faced another empty weekend. With five games due in just 16 days over Christmas this was hardly ideal preparation, so the club arranged a friendly against Margate who were also game-less in a match which would see a number of players get a run out as well as the opportunity to try out some new formations.

The game co-incided with our annual Christmas party away day. Danny and I are lucky to have such understanding wives, who recognising how hard we work allowed us to have one last Jolly Boys Outing before Christmas. We thought long and hard about our destination, finally deciding on a trip up north to see fellow Community Club pioneers, FC United of Manchester. For once our rail network delivered value for money plus a reliable service and less than two hours after leaving London, Danny, Cynical Dave and myself were in the Waldorf pub in Manchester having a beer with our Manchester correspondents.

So it was going to be left to Mr Boyes to take pictures, tweet updates, write a report and then conduct all the interviews as a one man media machine.

Lewes 0 Margate 1 - The Dripping Pan

O'Shea fielded a side that was individually strong but still showed signs of needing to gel - another reason for arranging this fixture.

The game was well contested by both sides but Margate looked the better side throughout, belying their respective league performances. Worringly for boss O'Shea was the lack of attacking threat from his team, despite a number of more attack minded players in the team.

Margate scored the only goal of the game two minutes before the half time break. Margate's Curtis Robinson broke well on the left and was given the time and space to send a great cross to the far post from where Shaun Welford beat his marker to head the ball beyond Chris Winterton in the Lewes goal. With the exception of a ten minute spell after half time and the final quarter of an hour when the home side pressured for the equaliser it was a comfortable performance for the Ryman League team. .

The result wasn't the only disappointment for the Rooks support, as Lewis Hamilton was bizarrely dismissed immediately after being booked for dissent, and Lewis Ide sustained a serious knee injury which could see him miss a significant number of games.

The main highpoint for Lewes was the debut of assistant manager Neil Smith who had the final moments of the game having replaced Ide, with the Rooks having fielded all their substitutes by that point.

The Margate boss Iain O'Connell was pleased with the performance, and particularly at the back. *"The boys did really well, especially at the back. We were very, very comfortable,"* he said. That just summed it up better than anything I can say.

Thursday 16th December
A new chapter for Jason

Since the new management team took over the old pairing of Ibbo and Jason had continued to work tirelessly in the background to support them. It is rare in football that when a new manager is appointed, the old team still stay around to help, but then again Lewes is no ordinary football club. However, there does come a time when a change is needed, and in early December Lewes were approached for permission to talk to Jason Hopkinson about the vacant position down the road at Ryman Premier League Hastings United. What many people would not know outside of Lewes is that Jason, along with Ibbo had been working free of charge for the club for a few seasons. He had flatly refused to take a wage for the job he was doing. In an interview the day after the announcement was made, Steve Ibbitson summed up his feelings on losing his right hand man.

"It's with a very strange mixture of delight and dejection I have to report that Jason Hopkinson has accepted an offer to become the new First Team Manager at Hastings United. Delight because I know it would take something that Jason really wanted to do to tempt him away from Lewes, as he's turned down a number of offers over the years and particularly recently.

It's great for him to be going to a job with Hastings, a club with great traditions, to be doing a job he's really looking forward to.
Dejection because we're losing somebody who's done such a fantastic job for us. He's one of the best coaches in the County and did a phenomenal job with our under 18's and carried that on with the first team.

I know as much as anybody about the running of Lewes FC over the past 2 years. Believe me, without Jason, we wouldn't be here today. He's given up hours and hours of his own time and unbelievable commitment for the club. In all the time he's been with us, he's never asked for, or received, any pay. Quite the opposite, it's cost him money. At the beginning of this year, the new Board wanted to start paying Jason and I was asked to talk to him. He said exactly what I knew he would which was that the Club couldn't afford it yet and that, if he was paid, we'd have less money to build a squad. He never needed money to drive him to give his very best – he did that without hesitation.

I'm probably most dejected because I'm going to miss the camaraderie and fun we've enjoyed over the past six years. I think we'd both particularly remember taking the under 18's to Jersey for pre-season tours and the tremendous experience of looking after the first team for a couple of months in the Conference Premier. We've consoled each other when things haven't gone well but we've then sat down and tried to plan together how we can make them go better. We've also shared lots of great moments and, for two heterosexual (some would say Neanderthal) men, have spent too much time at various football grounds hugging each other.

My only disappointment with him was that he always disappeared when we were making substitutions, leaving me to hold up the electronic substitution board with all the wrong numbers on, as neither of us could ever to work out how to use it.

It's been a pleasure to work with Jason and the club has properly recognised the debt it owes him by making him a Life Member. On behalf of everyone at Lewes FC, I thank him, and his lovely wife Nikki, for giving most of the last six years of his life to the Club and wish him the very best of luck in his new role. I hope that we're only lending him to Hastings and that, following success there, some day he'll be back working for Lewes again."

There can be little higher praise than that. In some ways many fans will now be rooting for Hastings United, wanting Jason to do well so that a regular fixture can become their trip back to the Dripping Pan in seasons to come.

Tuesday 28th December 2010
History repeats itself, repeats itself

2010 was a dramatic year for Lewes FC, probably the most eventful in the club's history. The year started on a freezing cold day with an away game at Dover Athletic, where the team were well beaten and the game ending with fog rolling down the valley making visibility almost impossible for the dozen or so away fans who had braved the journey. And would you believe it, the fixture computer only picked out the very same game for the Rooks to end the year with.

Traditionally, the games over Christmas are local derbies. Unfortunately, Lewes no longer have any local teams to play. Once upon a time the Boxing Day fixture would have been Eastbourne Borough, or Crawley Town, the former almost guaranteeing a 2,000 plus home attendance. Sitting in the leagues below Lewes are Hastings United, Bognor Regis Town and of course Eastbourne Town but hopefully unless they move up then it will be a dream of a return to a game against Eastbourne Borough next Christmas.

The fixture list had given Lewes a home and away tie to Ebbsfleet United as thier "prime" Christmas games, plus a home game against Welling United and a trip to the Crabble Athletic Ground in Dover for the other. However, as you will have noticed from the two week plus lack of writing activity the weather had other ideas. In the run up to Christmas Lewes's games against Bromley and Hampton & Richmond Borough were cancelled due to the freezing conditions, and despite a massive effort by everyone at the club the Boxing Day game at home to Ebbsfleet United went the same way too.

Two days later and conditions in Kent had started to improve. This was good for two reasons. Firstly it would mean that the return fixture at Ebbsfleet's Stonebridge Road ground on New Year's Day would be on, but more importantly it would mean that the game away to Dover would go ahead, thus being Lewes' first league game for over a month.

Unfortunately both Danny and I would be missing, due to family holidays. We couldn't really pick more contrasting venues. He was in the winter sunshine of his wife's village, about an hour east of Madrid, helping himself to €1 beers from his Father-in-Law's bar downstairs from his apartment, whilst I would be freezing my butt off in sub zero temperatures of

Copenhagen nursing my €10 beer. Still, good old Big Deaks would ensure that we didn't miss a kick thanks to his lively and detailed Twitter commentary.

Dover Athletic 4 Lewes 0 - The Crabble Ground

At 3.01pm as I sat at London Stansted for Easyjet to make up a reason why our flight had been delayed I got my first update from Deaksy.

"Dover 1 Lewes 0 - 49 seconds gone - Start the car"

The Whites made a blistering start, and whilst most fans were still changing ends, Harry Baker played a neat one-two with Donovan Simmonds on the edge of the area, and Baker drilled his shot through the legs of Chris Winterton to the delight of the Dover fans. Bugger, that wasn't in the script. But a minute later the Rooks could have equalised. The ball came to David Wheeler down the right side of the area and his well-struck shot was superbly saved by Lee Hook, showing no rustiness after his lengthy spell on the sidelines.

Dover went close to adding to their lead, as Simmonds sent Baker through on goal but he was pulled back by Tom Hutchinson and John Scarborough made a vital block. Baker was having a great game though, and he showed vision to slide the ball through to Birchall in the area, but his shot from a tight angle was well saved by the feet of Winterton. It was fair to say by this point that Dover were dominating, and Birchall saw a shot deflected behind for a corner by Hutchinson. From the resulting set-piece, Baker almost got his name on the score sheet again, but his shot from the edge of the box was expertly palmed away by the keeper. It was no surprise that with five minutes to go before the interval, Dover doubled their lead. Cogan and Birchall combined down the left, with the latter dinking a cross to the far post. Baker had time to chest the ball down and fire into the net from twelve yards.

"Right on HT 2-0, a few chances for Lewes but a make shift midfield not helping, fast forward to Saturday. I saw that goal from the toilets, seems a long half, must have been about 42nd minute."

Baker had a chance to grab his hat-trick when Scarborough made another fine saving tackle, but with half-time looming, the Rooks almost found a way back into the game. Ben Godfrey then hit the post from close range after a quick throw-in from George Porter but it was the whites of Dover who went in at half time with their tails up.

O'Shea made changes at half time, but Dover came out stronger than they had finished the first half. Dover had a penalty appeal turned down when Birchall looked to be fouled in the box, but Mr. Venamore failed to award the spot kick. Lewes's first opening came when Hook had to save bravely at the feet of Wheeler but a minute later Dover raced down the other end and effectively sewed the game up.

"3-0 61st minute , say no more. Probably the lack of central midfield options has caused Tim a headache today, give him a couple of games to sort this out"

Simmonds was again involved, spreading the play from left to right, giving Baker the chance to run rings around substitute Nathan Green. Baker then slid the ball to Birchall, who dropped a shoulder and turned his marker before firing into the top corner of the net. Another fine strike from Whites' leading scorer. The Lewes fans by this stage were struggling to see events at the far end, with a spooky fog enveloping the ground similar to the end of the game last season.

An abandonment was the Rooks' best hope by this stage but there was still enough light for the referee to award a weak penalty. Long fed Birchall, who was adjudged to have been brought down by Andy Pearson. Despite the Lewes defender looking to have won the ball, the referee perhaps felt it made up for the two earlier penalty decisions that he hadn't given. Baker was given the chance to grab his hat-trick, but his penalty was saved by Winterton, but Birchall followed up to poke the rebound home.

"Penalty to Dover saved but scored on follow up, 4-0 game set and match"

To add insult to injury, the Rooks dropped into the relegation zone after this defeat by virtue of an inferior goal difference, with Thurrock leap-frogging to safety despite not having a game.

Christmas is always a pivotal time in a season and this is no different for

Lewes. With two tough games to go against high flying Ebbsfleet and in form Welling United, a zero point festive season is not the present that anyone at the club want. Manager Tim O'Shea faced the camera after the game and was as candid as he could be.

"*We wanted to start very solid in the middle of the park and that is why we started with Breach and Pearson in midfield. But when you concede a goal in 49 seconds you have to put your hand up and say we were still at the Christmas table eating turkey. I don't think the pair did anything wrong, they battled hard.*

As a manager you looked at the first half and saw that we created chances and that we didn't look like a fourth from bottom team. We gave them two soft gifted goals, and the individuals have been spoken to.

I want us to believe that we can compete with any side in the league. I asked them in the changing room after the game who thought Chris would save their penalty. Two hands went up, one of which was Winterton. Their player believed it could have been saved and that is why he followed up and scored. That is disappointing that we don't have the belief.

The performances against Weston and St Albans were not flukes, that is how we should be playing. I want to see a reaction from the team in the next two games over Christmas."

Saturday 1st January 2011
One foot in the Grave..send

Now if you are reading this it means that for once Easyjet actually managed to fly one of the those airplane things from Copenhagen to London Stansted on time.

Everything was on time so at 2.30pm I was walking through the turnstiles of Stonebridge Road, home of Ebbsfleet United ready to watch Lewes try and claw their way out of relegation trouble. This was always be a game that the Rooks would have marked up as a zero return one. Ebbsfleet had surprisingly been relegated on the last day of the season from the Conference Premier last season, and few would have backed against them making an immediate return. With their games in hand due to the poor weather, the club would have been within a point of Braintree Town at the top of the table, whilst Lewes would have been bottom if Boreham Wood and St Albans City would have played all of their games.

So virtual top versus virtual bottom was not the start that Lewes probably wanted to 2011. 2010 had been a bit of a nightmare to say the least, starting and ending the year with defeats away to Dover Athletic. In between there were also quite a few bits that the fans would want to forget, although there is still a sense of optimism about what the club is trying to achieve on and off the pitch.

Due to the weather, this was to be our first Lewes game in five weeks. In that time they had played just one league game (versus Dover on Tuesday) so you could understand some of the rustiness the team will have felt. It also has an impact on the fans too, with double handbag winner Deaksy (he won them both in the Lewes Christmas draw if you believe him although why he has to now take them to all away games "just to tell people" is baffling) and Cynical making their second trip to Kent in just a few days.

My first "hats off" award for the New Year goes to Ebbsfleet for charging just £5 for adults and £1 for children for this game. Coming off the back of the bumper attendance for the "keenly fought" local derby with Dartford where the crowd was well over 2,000, they could have been complacent and kept admission the same, but instead they slashed it. The club is still groaning along under the control of Myfootballclub. The internet fad that had started off with such a bang back in 2008 had lost its way in recent months and it was clear from standing in the bar pre-match with signs placed on the wall that every penny counts now, and the club is absolutely desperate to get back into the Blue Square Premier.

Ebbsfleet United 1 Lewes 0 - Stonebridge Road

After the goal in the first minute at Dover Athletic on Tuesday the travelling dozen or so fans breathed a sigh of relief when the big hand passed the sixty second mark. O'Shea had put out an attacking side with George Porter and Paul Olima up front, and David Wheeler back in his favourite advanced right midfield role. And despite the gap in points and league position, Lewes took the game to Ebbsfleet, pushing them onto the back foot as the ball pinged around a wet midfield. The highlight of the opening ten minutes had to be my very tasty jacket potato with chilli from the food cabin - a highly unusual combination to be found at a football ground, and served by a girl who was talking on her mobile throughout the transaction. Was it wrong of me to wish she would drop her Blackberry into the steaming hot pot of chilli?

Lolly was not impressed with such "exotic" football food as a purist and decided she wanted chips so went across to the other side of the ground to queue there. The first bit of excitement came when Deaksy found his hot sausage roll was actually frozen in the middle. He took it back and waited for another for a few minutes, before one of the girls actually asked him if he wanted a replacement, or was he just there as a public service announcement that frozen pork is not good for the stomach (Charlie says, for those old enough to remember).

But back to the football. Ebbsfleet came close to opening the scoring on twelve minutes when Anthony Barness had to clear off the line, and then huffed and puffed for the rest of the half. Apart from a shot from distance by Nathan Green in the dying seconds of the half it was relatively tame; for tame read dull. And for those amongst you questioning my parental responsibilities, I didn't just leave Lolly queuing up for thirty five minutes for her chips on her own in the rain, I did go to the bar and get her a Coke (and then went back into the bar myself).

The second half started much the same as the first really. Ebbsfleet tried to push forward but Lewes's defence, bolstered by new signing Jon

Stephenson seemed to be able to cope with their approach. Fleet managed Liam Daish made changes on the hour mark, bringing on Scott Ginty whilst ToSH had to take off the injured Porter, replacing him with live wire Tom Murphy.

Lewes seemed to have done enough to get a point as the game entered the final few minutes. However, they were to leave empty handed as for the seventh away league game this season (out of eleven) they were to lose by a single goal.

An uncharacteristic mistake from Hutchinson allowed a cross from the right to evade him and grateful sub Scott Ginty was able to capitalize and turn the ball past Winterton, much to the delight of the whole team with even keeper Edwards running half the pitch to join in the wild celebrations.

Ironically, Lewes made the most of the closing moments. Substitute Tom Murphy was just beaten to a long ball by Edwards, but in the next attack, a hopeful punt upfield found its way to Murphy again but his clever angled near-post header was pushed away by Edwards to preserve all three points for the hosts.

Lewes's rotten away form in the Garden of England continues. It is now almost three years since the Rooks won in Kent, and with three defeats out of three so far this season, with only Dartford still to face the hopes are not high to stop that run.

After the game Assistant Manager Neil Smith spoke to Patrick Marber. "*The boys were fully committed and we were very disappointed to concede such a late goal. Ebbsfleet is always going to be a tough place to come. We missed that little bit from Ben Godfrey today, injured just before the game. The lads are disappointed in there (*The dressing room) *as they battled hard. The spirit was fantastic and we will go straight into the Welling game and give it a real go.*"

So my mammoth six hundred and fifty mile trip to a football match was over, and it was the train back home for me. Easyjet had been on time. Stansted airport had treated me well. The M11/M25 had been as calm as a mill pond now could. A perfect day apart from the three points we all so badly needed.

Monday 3rd January 2011
Where's the midfield?

For all those who played Sunday League football, the above sentence will ring so true for you. Every goal that your team concedes will somehow be blamed by the lack of midfielders in defensive positions. Sod the fact that the keeper could have let the ball through his legs from a back pass from the half way line, it would still be blamed by the lack of midfielders. Now granted, at the age of forty and carrying a little more timber than I was some fifteen years ago, my "box to box" days are long gone, I prefer to take up the role where I do not move from the centre circle. The only issue with this is that my centre midfield partner also takes up the same position. A tricky one.

But the sentence wasn't shouted by the gobby keeper of Hole In The Wall (Chiswick) FC, but by the Lewes fans who saw another midfielder leave the club. On Friday, Jermaine Wright told boss Tim O'Shea he was retiring from football for family reasons.

The former Wolves, Ipswich Town, Leeds United, Southampton and Blackpool midfielder added tremendous experience to the squad after becoming one of O'Shea's first signings when he took over at the end of October. His departure came soon after losing fellow central midfielder Lewis Ide for the rest of the season with a knee injury.

With Simon Wormull, Sam Butler, Ross Sutton and Scott Manning all having left the club in recent weeks, the Rooks were desperately short on numbers in the centre of the park. O'Shea said: *"Jermaine has retired due to personal family reasons. It was a real bombshell when he told me and we missed him on Saturday at Ebbsfleet"*

So who would line up today in midfield against Welling United. Lewes always seem to be playing teams who are bang on form, and this Bank Holiday clash was no different. Despite some recent financial problems off the pitch, Welling had remained focused on it, beating Dartford on Saturday to move into the Play Off zone for the first time this season, a contrast to Lewes's situation where results elsewhere had pushed them into the relegation zone.

Once again, due to work commitments both Danny and I would be missing this one. In fact for one reason or another I had been absent from The Pan since October. However, I would be there in spirit, and with Big Deaks again providing the incisively cutting commentary via Twitter I would not miss a moment.

Lewes 1 Welling United 3 - The Dripping Pan

Good old Tim O'Shea. Just hours before the kick off he got his little black book out of contacts and two hours later a couple of fresh new faces alighted off the train at Lewes, boots in hand. James Rowe, of Reading and Ashley Robinson from down the road at Eastbourne Town had been persuaded to join the cause for the next month and went straight into the starting XI for the match against Welling.

With three straight defeats stretching back to November today was the ideal time to get back to winning ways. With Boreham Wood and Thurrock also going through mini wobble three points would keep the Rooks head above water. However, they were to finish the Christmas period pointless as Welling United continued their great run of form with an easy victory.

Welling United started the game brightly, with Lee Clarke sending an effort wide on the half-volley from just inside the penalty area after Luis Cumbers had flicked the ball back to him from a long free-kick in the first few minutes.

However, Lewes also impressed in the early stages and were unlucky when debutant Ashley Robinson sent a shot from the edge of the area wide. Robinson was again at the heart of Lewes' next move, as he linked up well with Ben Godfrey, only to see the striker drag his shot from the edge of the area comfortably wide after an intricate passing move.

Godfrey nearly gave the Rooks the lead minutes later, as he saw his looping header from a Nathan Green cross go straight at Gareth Stewart in the Welling goal but these misses proved costly as after thirty three minutes the visitors took the lead when Andy Pugh's shot from just inside the area curled beyond Chris Winterton and into the top corner.

"Bugger. One nil Welling. David Beckham with the goal" Always one to joke in the face of adversity is old Deaks.

Three minutes later, Welling doubled their lead when Lee Clarke converted a pull-back from Jack Obersteller to give the visitors an undeserved second goal on the balance of play.

"We're going to win 3-2..Remember Boxing Day last year?" Last season Lewes found themselves 2-0 down at home to Dover Athletic before somehow running out 6-2 winners. I didn't log onto my Bet365 app on my iPhone when I heard this news.

Tim O'Shea was obviously not happy and made the bold move of bringing on two substitutes with barely forty minutes on the clock. Tom Murphy and Paul Olima were added to the attacking options with Andy Pearson and Robinson the two players sacrificed.

The changes paid off within minutes as in the second of three minutes of first-half injury-time Godfrey latched onto a David Wheeler header back across goal from a Nathan Green cross, held off his marker and drilled a low shot through the legs of Stewart. Game on.

Unfortunately, Lewes could not translate the end of half momentum into something positive at the start of the second period. David Wheeler almost scored a bizarre own goal when he sent an attempted clearance against his own post. But a few words of encouragement from the sidelines soon saw the nervousness disappear.

Lewes continued to look quite dangerous going forward and another long ball from Nathan Green almost put in Ben Godfrey as he ran into the penalty area. However, it was a familiar story of not converting chances that saw Welling increase their lead on the hour. Pugh was the scorer once again, converting a cross from Cumbers.

The Rooks did not let their heads drop and went close to pulling a goal back twice in quick succession. On both occasions, Tom Hutchinson was the player denied, as he saw a stooping header cleared off the line by Joe Healy and then sent a header from the resulting corner just wide. Olima also went as close as you could when his header in the final minute hit the bar.

But 3-1 it ended and the Rooks miserable run continues. Welling had come into the game as one of the division's form sides, but had found it far too easy for themselves in the opening thirty five minutes. Tim O'Shea faced up to the questions some 45 minutes after the game:-

"I am very grim to be honest. I was disappointed today by the level of performance and commitment and it hurts a bit. Welling are a good side but I think we allowed them to perform too easily. What summed it up was that we hit the foot of our own post - a comedy of errors. Welling were worthy winners."

Saturday 8th January 2011
Mr Chairman

If you asked any Lewes fan who saved the club last season one name would come to the fore time and time again. A man who kept the team going on the pitch as well as a club off it. Steve Ibbitson may not have been a legend as a player, but as the figurehead for the survival of Lewes FC he was akin to the messiah himself. This season he decided to step down from team affairs, becoming the club's chairman back in October. So we did what all fans should do, we bought him a beer and talked to him about football.

How did you end up at Lewes?
I had no intention of ever going into coaching. I played in the Non Leagues until I was in my mid-thirties, but actually continued playing Sunday League until I was fifty two. I hated just running. I originally packed it in because I didn't want to come down in standards. I ended up at Bridgeview and sort of fell into coaching. Terry Parrish, who is still a Lewes legend persuaded me to come down to the club to meet Steve King, the manager at the time. Little did I know it was actually an interview and I ended up looking after the under 18s here, as well as latterly the reserves.

Who do you support?
Leeds United! It was great being there as a youngster. Juniors used to play across the road from Elland Road on a Saturday and after the game we used to go to chippy across the road then sit under the stand listening to atmosphere build. The nursery side used to include talent from all over the county and players would be put in the team for one or two games such as Jimmy Greenhof, Peter Lorimer, and Jimmy Lumsdon.

When you took over the team after Kevin Keehan's departure in March 2009 did you think that the club could survive the drop from the Conference?
If we'd been realistic - no. Happily football isn't always about being realistic and we wanted to try our best, so wouldn't let anybody concede we were down unless it was mathematically the case.

What are you most proud of at Lewes?
The under 18 teams Jason (Hopkinson) and I have produced. In particular the team that stepped up and kept us going for those last few months of the

Conference Premier season in 2008/9. Those kids performed in the best level of football outside the Football League and never for one moment let themselves or the Club down.

After how long can you determine if a player is good enough?
That is the problem today. You cannot determine when they will be good players. Players develop at different rates and physically and technically. We tend to take under 18's on at 16 years old and watch them mature. However, the ones that come through and succeed aren't necessarily the ones you thought would when you find found them.

Why do we fail to produce young talent as a nation?
We simply do not coach players well enough from seven or eight years old. They should be coached how to receive the ball, how to hold off opposition players and how to pass the ball in a simple way. I hate to say it but as a nation we are getting worse at coaching and developing the talent. We do not teach the basis like you see overseas. We do not have enough qualified coaches or facilities in this country. overseas. We need to be building good habits between the ages of five and ten years old.

Which player that has come through the ranks has the right attributes to go the furthest?
We've had some great under 18s but it's very difficult to make the permanent step up to adult football, especially at the level we play. All have had very positive things (or we wouldn't have signed them) and some negatives (or they'd be with League clubs). Perhaps the one most likely to go on and play league football is Grant Hall, who is still at the Brighton & Hove Albion. Grant is a great defender but is also quick and skilful for a big lad. I hope he gets his chance because he's a very capable player and a nice lad.

What does Lewes mean to you?
This is the most difficult question and I'm going to have to ramble to answer it. For me, it always starts with people. Initially Jason and the under18's - you want them to be the best they can be. Not just as players, but also in the way they conduct themselves. When you work so closely with people, especially kids, they almost become like your family. Then there's the people who come and support you and give you encouragement. When we became involved with the first team, it was the same process, not least with the supporters who've been brilliant with us, despite the hard times.

In addition, off the field, when you stand shoulder to shoulder with people to overcome the difficulties we've had to work through over the last few years, it creates a certain bond that will never be broken for me. Jason is an obvious example of this. Derrick Parris is another one. Derrick, more than anyone, loves the Club and wants it to survive and flourish. Between us we did all the accounts and finances for the Club last year. He's not getting any younger and I know that he had many sleepless nights worrying about things. It took its toll on him but he kept going and never gave up.

All the time this is going on, there's this history and tradition building up inside you and you realise that the Club is the people. Not just those running the Club and playing for it, but the supporters - without them there's nothing. Also not just those involved now but those who've fought similar battles for Lewes in the past. It's not just my Club or just your Club; it's our Club and that makes it more special. That means that it can be as good, or as bad, as we're all prepared to make it - which might help to understand what I'm saying in the next question.

What do you think the natural level is for the club?
I don't believe in natural levels. If we get enough good people involved with the Club, I believe we could get back in the Conference Premier. However, if we don't, the last few years have warned us that you could easily drop down several levels. The great thing is that the level we end up at is in our hands - but people have to get involved - it doesn't just fall in our lap.

I heard a saying yesterday talking about Non League clubs AND Crawley Town as if they are in a category of their own. What is your view on what is going on there?
I like to see all Sussex Clubs doing well and Crawley is a big enough place to support a league team. There are a number of clubs capable of gaining promotion from the Blue Square Bet Premier, including Crawley Town, and we'll have to wait and see who gets there. People have contrasted the community route we've gone down with what has happened at Crawley. I'm pleased with the way we've gone but I'm not an idealist - if somebody had come along last year and said they were going to throw a load of money at Lewes Football Club I would have snatched their hands off. So good luck to Crawley but I hope they have a Plan B because, at a slightly lower level than them, we know only too well how quickly things can change.

Did you always feel last season that the club would survive both on and off the pitch?
Definitely not. There are only a handful of people who understand how close we came to losing the club as we know it. To be quite honest, when we started the season, there was a massive doubt that we would get past the first three months. We decided that we'd give it the best shot we could and keep going unless somebody dragged us out of the Dripping Pan kicking and screaming. At virtually every Management Committee meeting somebody questioned whether we'd reached the end. I developed various different speeches all based on Winston Churchill's "we shall fight them on the beaches". I just wanted us to keep going as long as we could in the hope that something would turn up. The first glimmer of hope I had was a phone call out of the blue from Patrick Marber and he and the others have given the Club an opportunity to regroup and go forward. However, people should be under no illusions, there is still a lot of hard work to be done and help is needed.

What was the lowpoint of the season for you?
There were a few. Off the field, it was probably being led to believe that we'd be OK and given more time at a forthcoming winding up hearing provided we could raise £20,000 out of about £50,000 then still owed to Her Majesty's Revenue and Customs. I was delighted to phone our solicitor on the Friday night to tell him we had the £20,000, only to be told that we had to find another £30,000 to make it up to the full amount by Monday morning or else we were gone. Fortunately a number of great people came up with the goods and saved the club, but that was quite a weekend.

On the field, it was probably the evening draw with Worcester City in March 2010 at home when we were 3-0 up with twenty minutes to go. They brought on a big aggressive forward and we allowed him to bully us, with the result that we only drew 3-3. I'd thought before the game that a draw wouldn't be the end of the world but the way we drew made it seem like that and gave them a massive boost. For one night, me and Jason allowed ourselves to doubt whether we could stay up. However, we were speaking on the phone at 7.30 next morning, working out how we were going to get back on track.
However the very worst point was probably walking off at the last game at Bromley realising that despite two years of effort, coaching and sweat, neither me nor Jason had ever managed to work out how to use the

electronic substitution board.

What possessed you to agree to work for nothing last season?
That was never a difficult decision. Both Jason and I were never paid as under 18 management and knew the club was never in a position to pay us as first team managers. If we hadn't done it, all that we'd worked for over the previous four years would have just gone down the drain. The club is currently paying me back money I (along with others) loaned it last year to keep going. There were times we felt we wouldn't get that money back and so that's enough for me.

You have always worked so closely with Jason. How hard will it be not seeing him around the club anymore?
Very hard. We encouraged and inspired each other. Although I don't look it, I'm quite a bit older than Jason and I'm a bit long in the tooth to start forging new coaching partnerships and it probably signals the end of my involvement in that area.

Didn't you ever get cold standing on the touchline in your shorts, or are we all just southern softies?
When playing and training, I hated wearing track suit bottoms as they always made me feel as though my legs were cramping up. That just carried on in coaching. I don't think it was to do with Southern softies. Jason also rarely wore track suit bottoms but nobody noticed that because of the colour of his legs. I think it was the adrenalin that kept the cold at bay.

You seemed to find Tim O'Shea pretty quickly once you had decided to step aside, how did you identify him as a likely successor?
It wasn't really planned necessarily to happen as quickly as it did. I'd made it clear this was to be my last season as manager and wanted to make sure my successor was selected well before the season end to give him a chance to start planning for next season. Tim had built a reputation, especially at Croydon Athletic, and was identified, along with a couple of others, on an early possible short-list. The problem was that he was available at the time, due to Croydon's difficulties, but was unlikely to be jobless for long.

How emotional was your last game away to Bromley, and then the subsequent home game against Dartford?
Bromley was very emotional. Dartford was awful for me, and so has every

game been since then. Although I'm still sure I made the right decision, for me and the Club, I hate going to games and not being involved in the running of the team.

What did you say to Jason when you shared that "moment" in the dug-out at the end of the game in Bromley?
We talked about the game and how well we'd played using a 4-3-3 formation Jason had talked me into playing. We also thanked each other for the last couple of years we'd enjoyed so much, despite (or perhaps because of) some of the difficulties.

If you could have one wish granted for the club, what would it be?
New dressing rooms and a new bar facility which would help us to make income more on a par with our competitors.

What was the best team performance you oversaw in your time in charge of the team?
I couldn't pick just one, so hope you'll allow me to pick 3:-

1) Barrow away in the Premier where we lost narrowly but played magnificently with a squad made up of a few experienced players and loads of 16/17 year olds. Breachy was harshly sent off after fifteen minutes but, instead of trying to shut up shop, we decided to have a go and, especially for the last half hour, attacked them trying to get an equaliser. Our kids got a standing ovation from the Barrow supporters as we left their clubhouse.

2) Dover at home in December 2009 when we turned a 0-2 deficit into a 6-2 victory. There were a few groans when, despite being two down, we changed from two forwards to only one central striker. However, the plan was to get our two wide men, Dave Wheeler and Steve Brinkhurst, forward and running at their defence. Changes like that don't always come off but that one worked beautifully.

3) Worcester City away in April last year, where we only won 2-1 but played brilliantly on a terrible pitch, were by far the better side and undid the damage they'd inflicted on us by drawing at the Pan a couple of weeks earlier.

What does your typical day look like now?
I am mostly involved in administration now on a daily basis but it does vary

from day to day. The worst part is match days though. It is terrible not being involved in the team. I am not complaining though it was the right thing for me and the club to step down. I came into management too late to really make it an impact. I really enjoyed the training element though, having the opportunity to work with the youngsters and seeing them develop. However, it has given me the opportunity to see my family and re-introduce myself to them.

Do you still try and get in a few games?
Not really. In fact when I was in charge I/we (Jason and myself) would only go and see a game if there was a real reason such as we were looking at a player, or it was our under 18's side. That hasn't really changed actually. We have other teams watched for us and reports sent to particular players but as I said I am enjoying the opportunity to see my family. I work full time at the club so any games I go to are like overtime.

Finally, money being no object, which player would you loved to have seen playing for Lewes?
Realistically, Adam Birchall from Dover Athletic, a great little striker at our level, who tore us apart at The Crabble Ground this year. Including professionals, either my all time greatest player, Pele, or one of my Leeds United heroes, probably either Johnny Giles or John Charles.
With his beloved Leeds United putting up a great fight in the televised cup game Ibbo headed back upstairs to finish off his preparations for the game. No fuss, no bother, just getting on with things.

A week is a long time in football, but five days is even less. That is the time lapsed between the six hundred or so Lewes fans leaving the Dripping Pan on Monday after the defeat to Welling United, and the same group arriving back for the visit of Eastleigh. There are must win games, and there are real must win games. This was one of the latter.

It will have almost certainly escaped your notice (unless you are a die hard Lewes fan) that things on the pitch for the Rooks have not gone well since the end of November. The euphoria of the new management team of Tim O'Shea and Neil Smith has slowly ebbed away and a spate of injuries, suspensions, departures and in one case, retirements have caused headaches on the pitch. That is when the team has been able to actually get onto a pitch to play, with the Winter weather wiping out four weeks worth of fixtures. When they have been able to play defeats to Thurrock, Dover Athletic, Ebbsfleet United and Welling United have sent the Rooks back into the bottom three.

With games on the horizon against Staines Town, St Albans City and Boreham Wood there was hope. And unlike the "glamorous" Premier League there was no calling for the manager's head down in Blue Square Bet South. Instead there was a measure of calm coming into the game versus The Spitfires. In the past two seasons these teams have played four times in all competitions, with each game being keenly fought, and three of the four decided by a single goal. Would it be the same today? My money was on a sneaky 1-0 Lewes victory.

As a birthday treat CMF agreed to drive me down so that I could have a beer. In fact this was to be my first visit to the Pan since the end of October due to a number of reasons, so I intended to make the most of my trip with an early arrival and a late finsih.

Midweek had brought the usual spate of comings and goings at The Pan. Tim O'Shea had got his vast black book out and managed to negotiate the transfer of ex-England C international winger Ishmael Welsh from Grays Athletic. Welsh had played under O'Shea at Grays in the Conference Premier before moving onto Ebbsfleet United last season. Interesting enough he would potentially be competing with two of Lewes's most talented youngsters, David Wheeler and Tom Murphy for the wide berths in the side.

Lewes 1 Eastleigh 4 - The Dripping Pan

The omens weren't good for this from the moment we arrived at the ground. The Eastleigh team had arrived early, taking advantage of the prime spots in the Rook Inn for the televised Arsenal versus Leeds United clash. One solitary rook sat on the penalty spot, almost mocking us that today would be another world of pain. The good news was that Harveys Old Ale was back on draft. The bad news? Well, we will put that to one side for a few more minutes.

I was joined just before kick off by Deaks, Cynical and Kev. Danny had decided that the "Magic of the FA Cup" was too good to miss and was taking his place at the worst ground in England, the Withdean, for Brighton's game versus Portsmouth. The talk was of the forum, and the criticism being levelled at Tim O'Shea. People simply have no perspective on football, being completely subjective. Let's face it. Lewes have been in a relegation battle from day one, and the sooner they realise that, the better. This was going to be a tough game. Eastleigh had been punching above their weight on a style that was built on their physical presence. One look at the teams as they emerged onto the pitch confirmed this.

Lewes had started with a very attacking formation with Murphy, Wheeler and new signing Welsh pushing forward from the first minute. And it seemed to work. The team looked bright, full of energy and played with confidence that hasn't been seen for a few weeks. New signing Welsh put a couple of decent crosses in the box and it was a miracle that Godfrey didn't put away one of these chances when he found himself unmarked in the six yard box.

But then it became same-old, same-old. An Eastleigh player was hit hard on the halfway line and Lewes froze, expecting a free kick to be given, but the ref waved play on. Barness, was one of those caught out and he allowed the Eastleigh winger to control the ball, cross it and Danny Smith headed home with ease. With only twenty or so fans having braved the 657 line via Brighton (Portsmouth were playing at Brighton in the FA Cup) you could hear the collective groan from the terrace.

You could see the Rooks players heads go down. Only once this season have the team gone behind and then got something out of a game and it was as if the team knew it. Eight minutes later their wishful thinking came true as Brett Williams finished with ease after the ball was not cleared in the box.

Two almost became three just before half time but the one player who seems to realise the club need to fight Chris Winterton was switched on to the danger and saved superbly to keep the score relatively respectable.

It was tempting to stay in the warm Rook Inn at half time. After all I had a bit of maintenance to do on the scarves and I could have so easily got on with that. But in for a penny, in for a pound I was back out to support the club. O'Shea tried to narrow the game but this only served to isolate Wheeler and Welsh and they had to go looking for the ball instead of it coming to them out wide. The situation got even worse within fifteen minutes of the restart as firstly Tony Taggart and then another Williams strike (albeit one with a large Breach deflection) doubled the Eastleigh lead to four.

To say that we were stunned was an understatement. The fans hadn't seen an away team rip apart Lewes at the Pan for many a year and it could have been more. On 65 minutes Barness played a ball over the top, Murphy beat his man, rounded the keeper and slotted home. "*We're gonna win 5-4*" was the call from the terrace up until the final whistle but that sort of thing never happens to teams I support. Five consecutive defeats (six including Margate) now put the club in real trouble. The realisation that the league for Lewes was essentially now between five teams (Thurrock, St Albans, Boreham Wood and Dartford being the others) started to sink in for everyone. Results elsewhere would become irrelevant. It is as simple as that. Manager Tim O'Shea was equally unimpressed after the game.

"We had a bright start. We caused them problems and look the side that we are capable of being. Ishmael Welsh put some excellent balls into the box. But then we conceded not just one sloppy goal, but four. Teams simply do not have to work very hard against us at the moment to score goals. We're so frustrated on the sidelines because it's the basics we aren't doing.

Every game is important now and Bognor on Wednesday night will be no pushover. Whilst they are two leagues below us they are playing well and our confidence is low but we will be looking from a reaction to this result from the players in training on Monday and of course on Wednesday night."

Despite all of the pre-match optimism the Rooks had been shot down with ruthless efficiency by the Spitfires. Next up in the league? Only a trip to the league leaders Braintree Town. A walk in the park.

Wednesday 12th January 2011
Cross my palm with silver

The return of the Sussex Senior Cup for the Rooks could not have come at a worse time. On the back of a five game losing streak in the league, Lewes's last win had come in this competition back in December when they had won at Shoreham. Bognor Regis came to the Dripping Pan in fine form, having at last stopped their freefall that had seen them drop from the Conference South in 2009 to the Ryman League South in just over a year. Three seasons ago they looked forward to games against AFC Wimbledon and Newport County, whilst today it is games against Eastbourne Town and Whitehawk. However, the club have found their calm waters and are targeting a return to Step three of the non league pyramid next season.

The week before the game the draw was made for the next round. The Rooks had of course hoped for an easy-ish passage to the final where they could pit their wits against Brighton & Hove Albion, the strongest team in the cup. But it was not to be. "Number one – Arundel Town, Sidley United or Brighton & Hove Albion" will play "Number four - Lewes FC or Bognor Regis Town". Cancel the open top bus tour for now then. So even more incentive for "The Rocks" to upset "The Rooks".

The game co-incided with Big Deaks's birthday and thus both Danny and I made our excuses not to attend so that we wouldn't have to buy him a beer. It was touch and go in the run up to the game whether it would actually be played at all. Torrential rain had warranted a pitch inspection at 4pm, and part of me wanted to see a postponement to a date when I could make it, but with fixtures piling up from prior to Christmas it was probably for the best that the local referee said "game on" and battle could commence for the right to travel to play Brighton & Hove Albion, or Sidley United.

Lewes 1 Bognor Regis Town 0 - The Dripping Pan

Despite the club offering a VAT Busting 20% discount on admission, on a foul night only one hundred and eighty brave souls saw Lewes scrape through to the quarter finals thanks to a late own goal. In such circumstances everyone associated with the club will take that. It may not have been pretty, but at the end of the day it was all about getting through to the next round.

Both sides struggled with a sticky pitch and driving rain and neither forged any clear cut opportunities for most of the match. Dogged resistance from the Rocks eventually gave way three minutes from time when a David Wheeler cross was turned into his own net by substitute defender Stuart Axten. Tim Rivers almost doubled the lead moments later but his shot was well saved by keeper Craig Strong after fine work from sub Tom Murphy.

With the home supporters willing the final whistle, Bognor were inches from snatching a last-gasp equaliser but Dean Maynard's header sneaked over the bar to ensure a safe passage into the next round. Unsurprisingly, manager Tim O'Shea was smiling for the camera after the game.

"Horrible conditions for both sides, but it is nice to go through and it will be a good experience for the youngsters. The guys done well tonight, and in fairness to Bognor they did try and play some decent football.

Our recent run of defeats had lead to an unnecessary build up of pressure in the dressing room and tonight has helped relieve that. We are going in the right direction. Some may find it difficult to believe but I think we have had more than our fair share of bad luck recently."

Saturday 15th January 2011
Any old Iron

After a long run of consecutive league defeats, what better way to try and reverse the trend than a visit to the league leaders Braintree Town. Their form at home wasn't impressive at all - just the eleven wins at home so far this season – what Lewes wouldn't give for half of that. Last season they had come close to a play off spot, missing out on the last day of the season with a home defeat to Newport County. Heartbreaking as they had been in the top five for virtually the whole second half of the season. But that is football for you. So this season there was even more determination to go one better and secure a place in the Blue Square Bet Premier.

But who wants the boredom of chasing for promotion, winning week in, week out when you can have a relegation fight? The bottom of the table was starting to form into a small group, and despite the surge in crowds compared to last season, Lewes were well and truly in a relegation fight. Ironically enough, the comparable weekend last season saw Lewes in 21st spot with 17 points. As the team prepared to travel into the heart of white handbags and customised Vauxhall Nova's they had five points less. What the team needed was some of that latter season fight we saw in 2010.

Many fans would have simply written this game off as a certain defeat, focusing instead on the home games against Bromley and Staines Town in the next week. Fortunately Tim O'Shea and Neil Smith weren't. They were buillish in the lead up to the trip and added to the squad on the day before the game with the loan signing of highly rated Brighton & Hove Albion striker George Barker.
Once again it would be down to Big Deaksy to provide commentary on this one for us.

Braintree Town 1 Lewes 0 - Cressing Road Stadium

Now here is the first surprise of the afternoon. Jermaine Wright lining up in the centre of midfield. That is the same Jermaine Wright who just two weeks previously retired from football to spend more time with his family. I can only assume he dropped them off at Braintree Freeport Outlet Centre on the way to this one. "Just popping into Timberland store love. Won't be any longer than two hours". Still, a player of his quality was sure to give the team a boost, and with Wheeler and Welsh again on the flanks there was a glimmer of pre-match hope.

However it took just two minutes for the first groans to go up from the travelling Rooks fans as Braintree's Sean Marks headed home. Fortunately, the linesman had flagged for offside and there was a collective sigh of relief. Even Cynical Dave was seen to crack a smile at the irony of the home fans exuberant celebrations.

In the fifteenth minute Marks again had a goal disallowed, this time for fouling Winterton, although it did seem a tad harsh. However, perhaps it was time for a bit of luck to fall into the Lewes lap. Forty minutes in and the referee saw a handball that few else in the ground did and Braintree had a penalty. Of course it was Sean Marks who stepped up, and as if to sum up a torrid and frustrating first forty five minutes, Winterton guessed right and saved the spot kick. Nil-nil at half time against the league leaders? Who would have thought it. However, the smiles on the Lewes Lunatic Fringe were soon wiped off as news filtered through that Boreham Wood were beating Chelmsford City and Thurrock likewise winning against Welling United. Two coupon busting results if they stayed that way.

For once ToSH's half time team talk could build on the positives of a half of stout defending. But once again a single lapse in concentration just two minutes after the restart cost Lewes dear. Nicky Symons saw his effort well saved by Winterton, who could only palm the ball to the waiting Davis who then crossed for Marks to crash the ball home from close range. Of course it had to be Marks.

Braintree continued to pile on the pressure, with the Lewes goal leading a charmed life. On sixty four minutes new signing Craig Dobson crossed from the right for the unmarked Jai Reason at the far post, but his effort hit the post before skidding along the Lewes goal-line and away to safety. Winterton was having another blinder and kept the score to just the single effort with great saves from Reason and Marks in the latter stages.

The final whistle brought relief for Braintree and disappointment for Lewes. Interestingly enough the Rooks had fought hard and defended well, using the four players who had almost been the regular back four under previous manager Steve Ibbitson. Scoring is the problem for the team, it is as simple as that. For all the attacking flair of David Wheeler, Tom Murphy and new signing Ischmeal Welsh there is simply no one to put the ball in the net. Boreham Wood and Thurrock's wins over Chelmsford City and Welling United respectively not only saw Lewes hit rock bottom but also confirmed them as the lowest scorers in the league. However it wasn't all doom and gloom afterwards as Tim O'Shea explained.

"*There was alot more today to be enthused about. Commitment was better, motivation was better and I am now looking forward to Wednesday against Bromley. Two new debutants today who both did very well. We have tried desperately this week to get players in. Chris was outstanding, saving his third penalty of the season and pulling off two or three world class saves. There was enough in our performance to give us encouragement and stay positive*"

A one nil defeat to the league leaders is not a bad result. However, it is still a defeat and at this stage of the season points are the only thing that matters.

Wednesday 19th January 2011
It never rains but it pours

After the snow and ice of December, 2011 had brought rain, and plenty of it. Most teams had at some point become victim to waterlogged pitches, thus adding more pressure to already overloaded fixture schedules meaning that two games per week was going to be a regular occurrence between now and the end of the season. Great for people who could nip down the road for a game, rubbish when you have to work nights or are six hundred miles away as is the case for Danny and myself respectively.

There had been a noticeable reaction to the display away at Braintree from the fans who went to Essex, many saying the team appeared to have found that fighting spirit it had in the early ToSH days (all of two months ago). Was it co-incidence that the game marked the return from "retirement" of midfield general Jermaine Wright?

Cast your mind back to October when Lewes had visited Bromley in what was to be Ibbo's last game in charge. Going into that game Bromley were sitting at the top of the table without many cares in the world. Two months is a long time in football and since then Bromley's league form had been shocking to say the least, none more so than back to back away defeats to Weston-Super-Mare and Ebbsfleet United respectively, shipping in eleven goals in the process.

Rumours of financial issues at the club had not been quashed during the run up to Christmas, and when captain John Scarborough left the club alarm bells started to ring. Then just two days before this game, manager Mark Goldberg left the club, ending his second spell in charge of them.
Tim O'Shea had been busy in the days before the game, releasing Paul Olima and bringing in Michael Abnett. With injuries still jinxing the team he had to move quickly to fill the obvious gaps in the side, and that obviously requires a balanced squad. Rumours had been floating around with regard to Olima's influence on the side, and despite his four goals since joining in November, no one was too surprised that he had left the club.
Stockholm beckoned for me instead of The Dripping Pan, and try as I might I could not find one sports bar in the city showing the beam-back. Unfortunately the little matter of the Handball World Cup taking place in Sweden had hogged all the coverage. They have no idea of the important

things in life, so I was again thrown to the mercy of Big Deaks and his Twitter updates.

Lewes 0 Bromley 0 - The Dripping Pan

So at last the run of five straight league defeats had ended. That was the good news. The bad news was that the crowd had dropped to just under the three hundred and fifty mark. I know it was midweek, and I know it was a crappy night and few away fans made the journey, but even so the club must be a bit disappointed with the turn out.

O'Shea was able to welcome back George Porter and Ben Godfrey from injury as the attacking duo with David Wheeler dropping to the bench. Bromley started the game well, with their nice passing style which saw them keep possession of the ball for long periods and it was no surprise that they created the first chance when Henriques header just flashed wide of the post, with Winterton beaten.The Lewes keeper was then called into action shortly afterwards with two fine saves in quick succession. The first came from an effort by Wes Daly, who capitalised on a clearance from Nathan Green. The second came from a shot by centre-back Jerome Sobers, who saw his low shot stopped by Winterton diving down to his near post.

But it wasn't all Bromley. Just before the break George Barker saw his shot parried behind by Craig Holloway in the Bromley goal after Sobers had misplaced a pass inside his penalty area when under pressure from George Porter.

The terrace was lifted by the sight of David Wheeler lining up for the second half, replacing Porter who had been quiet and Wheeler was soon doing what Wheeler does best, taking on the full back and putting some quality balls into the box.

The move immediately paid dividends, as the Rooks began to enjoy more possession and cause the previously untroubled visiting defence one or two problems. Lewes continued to enjoy the majority of the possession, and were unlucky not to take the lead when Barker just failed to connect with one of those crosses to the far post.

However, Bromley were still in the game and they threatened twice in quick succession with twenty minutes to go when Harry Harding sent a glancing header just wide after a counter-attack, before the same player saw an effort from just inside the penalty area go wide.

Lewes had two chances of their own to seal the three points when Wheeler and then Tom Murphy saw shots well saved by Holloway after they had found space in the penalty area.

However, the final chance of the game fell to Bromley, who saw McBean fail to make a sufficient connection at the far post with a low cross from McKenzie when it seemed easier to score. But sometimes that is the luck you need and when the referee finally blew for full time the relieved home crowd cheered as if it was a long overdue win. There is still along way to go, and Deaksy's final 140 character tweet of the evening summed it up nicely. *"A great 0-0. Both teams attacking but failing to take chances. Bromley early on Lewes fought back with solid mid & Wheeler. Rot stopped"*

The after match interview with Tim O'Shea was unsurprisingly more upbeat than it had been in recent weeks.

"I told them to go out and be brave in the second half and they gave me 100%. Breachy was immense, and Nathan has a fantastic attitude, and you cannot fault his commitment. I think we saw the real David Wheeler tonight for the first time in months. We've missed someone in the middle who can organise things, which is what Jermaine has given us tonight. Another injury tonight means numbers again are thin on the ground. I get very frustrated when I see how we play on a match day after seeing them in training. We are a match for anyone if we put the same sort of commitment that we saw in the second half tonight."

The unbeaten run starts here. Next up Staines Town.

Saturday 22nd January 2011
The men that Fleet Street hate to love

There is no doubt that blogging is the future of journalism. Twitter especially has revolutionised the way that stories are broken and shared within seconds around the globe. It is no wonder that twenty four of the twenty five biggest newspapers in the world are experiencing a significant downturn in sales. People want the news when it happens, not twenty four hours later. And that is what Social Media has given us news hungry people. We no longer have to go and look for the news, the news finds us. Never has a truer word been spoken in terms of football journalism.

Over the past year the number of websites and blogs dedicated to the general, and even better, the very specific subjects of the beautiful game has risen dramatically. This surge in interest is simple. Content is king. Unless you are producing relevant and interesting content then you may as well give up and use your computer for something else. The A-list of football blogging are all members of something called Socrates. It is not some kind of secret society, or the equivalent of the Brat Pack, but rather a regular meeting of the bloggers to share ideas, talk about, believe it or not football, and have a few beers.

At a meeting back in the summer of 2010 we floated the idea of holding one of these gatherings outside London. The room went silent, heads turned in our direction and pints of beer fell to the ground at our suggestion. But then we followed it up with an invite to hold it at The Dripping Pan. We didn't have a clue if the club would allow it, but what the heck.

Fast forward six months and Saturday dawned as the first ever Socrates meeting outside of the metropolis. Over twenty of the men that Fleet Street hate to love were on their way down to East Sussex to take in the game between Lewes and Staines Town before retiring to the bar for a few Harveys. All very civilised I am sure. Lewes FC had rolled out the red carpet to everyone, and in light of the positivity that just one draw could bring to the club it was sure to be a win win situation for all. Socrates would get a day out at a level of football few had ever experienced, and the club would get twenty people waxing lyrically about the club...hopefully.

Everyone was up for making this a great day. So when James Boyes came to Danny and I and asked us for our "best ever interview" for the Lewes FC programme we looked at each other knowingly and decided that the ULTIMATE interview would be with each other - after all we really can talk absolute crap for hours. Unfortunately work commitments mean that we are normally six hundred miles apart during the week. No problems though – after all we have technology on our side. Or so we thought....

Danny – Earth calling Denners

Stuart – Got you!

D – I can't see you on MSN

S – I am not on messenger, I am on Google Chat

D – I don't use Google Chat – what on earth is that?

S – OK, I will go onto MSN....nope can't do that on my Mac

D – Shall we do this by phone?

S – Carrier Pigeon

D – Post

S – Yeah 'cos that will get there...I know a bloke at the Gatwick sorting office....ah there you are

D – Right, shall we kick off?

S – So, crop rotation in the 14th century – what was all that about?

D – The Young Ones – Grade A funny!

S - I am impressed you remembered it! OK - having been away from the "league" scene for a while, how has it been going back to Brighton and Hove Albion a couple of times recently?

D – Both bitter and sweet. Bitter in that it costs an arm and two legs, you can't get a beer in the ground, you get told what you can and can't do every five minutes and there is no lettuce in their burgers. Sweet in that they beat Portsmouth, handsomely, and that made it all worth the while.

S - So next season in a new stadium, with potential home games against West Ham and Aston Villa (based on current form), would you be tempted to start going again?

D - I shall pick and choose the games I go to. Hopefully, Lewes and Brighton will do the sensible thing and have home games on alternate Saturdays. Then I can pitch up at both, in between my jaunty trips abroad. I thought we were here to celebrate a classical Greek Athenian philosopher, right?

S - Just a warm up and then we can get onto that famous Garforth Town reject. Taking of trips abroad, on the FIFA star index, what would gain a five star trip these days? Obviously the bar has been raised in previous years.

D - I don't dish out the coveted FIFA five stars too easily these days. It would have to be something very special. How about a trip to Berlin for a derby between Hertha and FC Union in Division Two - watched by a sell out crowd of seventy five thousand followed by the Leipzig derby the very next day?

S - The Leipzig thing is amazing - great stadium as well. So this football blogging thing. How, why and when for you?

D - How is anyone's guess, I'm still try to work out how to use a computer properly. Why? Because at the time there wasn't anything quite like European Football Weekends. All of the (deep breath now) "ground hopping" blogs were more concerned with how they were going to keep their programme in mint condition and what time the last bus left from Chester-Le-Street. I just wanted to get likeminded folk, those who enjoy a beer, and a giggle and didn't take life or football too seriously together in one place. And I think that's worked. When? About three years ago, but only really seriously in the last twelve months. And I think that has worked!

S - What was your first trip you published? Do you look back at what you wrote and cringe? I am thinking of republishing all of mine from day one. A sort of a retro look back

D - The first one I published was from a trip to Romania to see them tackle Holland followed by a Division four game in Bucharest the next day. And yes, it was shocking, as were the rest of them around that time. I think the polite way of describing them would be "rough around the edges". Rubbish in other words. But good fun.

S - I learnt yesterday the origins of the term "pushing the envelope". How can we (as in The Ball Is Round/European Football Weekends) push the envelope even further based on our past year?

D - I only started taking a camera to games two years ago. Before then, I thought anyone who snapped away at games was radio rental. Like those who wave their mobile phones around at gigs. No need. Can we upgrade the envelope to a jiffy bag? That's the six million dollar question. And will we still be able to push that through the letter box? But to do that I have to put in more effort and invest more time to learn new skills. And I quite like my fix of Homes Under the Hammer in the morning. That'll have to give.

S - So what are your aims for 2011 for European Football Weekends?

D - As for 2011, all that I know is that I know nothing. Another nod to Socrates there, did you notice? More of the same, really. Other writers have climbed on board the good ship EFW, and they're really talented chaps. I'm chuffed to bits that someone else would want to write for EFW.

S - You have pulled in some big names in 2010. Who have you in your sites for 2011 and how do you managed to get so many big names to agree?

D - It was a concertina-effect, once The Guardian's Football Weekly star

Barry Glendenning agreed to answer a few questions and set the standard, it was easier to get others to say yes, culminating in getting James Richardson on, which was the highlight of 2010 on EFW. I belong to Jimbo. Oh and Dave Lamb (The voice of Come Dine With Me) was brilliant but only if he's reading this. As for 2011, I don't know - Gareth Gates? Patrick Marber?

S - You mention other writers - do you see a day when European Football Weekends will just be a portal for new writers?

D - That would be brilliant. If someone can get a bit of recognition by virtue of penning an article on EFW, then my work here would have been done. I missed my calling, but if I can help another person get a leg up, then I will.

S - It is certainly a long term ambition of mine to create a site for young writing talent

D - Aye, and not two old duffers like us. Talking of Duffers...Terry Duffelyn (one of the organisers of Socrates) has done a great job to bring the football blogging community together, no?

S - Yes indeed - how much power do you think the blogging community has nowadays?

D - Not too much power. But a fair amount of increasing respect I think. Initially, the perception was probably of a bunch of nerds hiding behind keyboards. And now, due to the likes of Michael Cox of Zonal Marketing and Kieran O'Conner from the Swiss Ramble, bloggers seem to be all the rage at the moment, the best of which will probably turn their hobby into a living.

D – I suppose I should ask you a few questions then? How do you get a golden pass from the Current Mrs. Fuller to attend all these matches?

S - I've always travelled for business, being away for days on end. I think I would drive her mad if I was at home every night. She doesn't want for much being a simple northern lass - a bottle of stout and a greasy chip butty. She reads all my stuff and is actually an inspiration behind some of my best work

D - Open the windows, why did you start The Ball is Round?

S - Well the forerunner was BudgetAirlineFootball.co.uk and that was set up to help fans go and get to games abroad. I have travelled for years going to football and used to take handwritten notes and keep them in a file, now taking pride of place in the Museum (my shed in the garden). Then I would see amusing stuff or get into situations where I thought "that would be funny to read about" so I started blogging in 2006

D – Hypothetical situation time. You've got a free pass next Saturday; would you prefer to go and see Lewes, West Ham United, a new non league ground, the Milan derby or a division three match in Bulgaria?

S - 1. A visit to a new non league, 2. Lewes FC, 3. The Milan derby 4. Bulgaria and finally 5. West Ham unless Avram had gone and then it may just move above Milan and Bulgaria

D - So West Ham have slipped down the pecking order. You gained infamy by penning an open letter to the board at Upton Park. Is modern football rubbish?

S - Modern football isn't rubbish per say - the club owners are businessmen and need to make money for their stakeholders, and like all businesses that means trying to gain more ARPU (Average revenue per user). So that means higher ticket prices, more crap merchandise, more paid for internet content etc. But unlike other businesses they seem to think that the quality of their product on offer does not matter - in fact they can reduce the quality and still expect people to pay more - bit like our trains really. After all clubs feel they have a monopoly on a fan's support but here is the secret. They don't - fans have a choice!

D - So what is this Socrates all about and why are all these football bloggers nodding in approval of the Harveys in the Rook Inn?

S - A meeting of some of the finest minds in the independent football writing community. And where better than at a community club drinking some of the best independent beer in England!

D - And at the best ground, no? What is so special about an afternoon at the Dripping Pan?

S - The surroundings, the fans, the banter - all friendly, nothing confrontational. Lewes fans are simply friends you have never met!

D - I think it's the best beer garden in England. So being Devil's Advocate here, Lewes isn't your local Non League club is it? Why not follow them?

S - I used to - Welling United is my local team and I did get involved with them, helping out on the programme, doing some match reports and even bringing in a couple of corporate sponsors. But they didn't appreciate it. No one ever said "thank you" for the free time I had given up so I thought "sod that"

D - So their loss was Lewes's gain then. And you're involved in the Lewes FC programme now as well?

S - Yes - and that is really enjoyable. I love writing about the unusual stuff around football and the fans seem to enjoy the stuff we are putting in there. And with the Community Share Scheme in place I will become a part owner of the club soon. And of course there is our ongoing work to turn The Rook Inn into a shrine to football. That project is far from finished and all donations from any club are still gratefully accepted

D - You spend part of your working week in Denmark. How does watching football in Denners compare with games back in dear old Blighty?

S - Football in Denners varies so much based on the levels you watch - even in the Superliga. FCK and Brondby are very corporate, akin to our Premier League clubs with your branded popcorn and fizzy drinks, whilst a visit to Lyngby in the same league is like a visit to a League One club. Go down a division or two in Denmark and it is the same level as Lewes. Funnily enough, the Danish equivalent of Myfootballclub has actually invested in Croydon Athletic of the Ryman League

D - Final question. Do you have a spare plastic wallet to keep my Bognor Regis programme in so it doesn't get creased?

S - Only if you tell me the return times from Braintree Freeport on Saturday evening!

Surprisingly, both Danny and I are married, hold down regular jobs and can use a mobile phone. Lord help us all. Moving on switftly then.

Lewes 0 Staines Town 1 - The Dripping Pan

Everyone had arrived without a problem and with the assembled masses of the full weight of Socrates we started to make a dent in the fantastic Harvey's Old Ale. The club had produced special limited edition posters for all attendees and it wasn't long before topical issues of the day were being put right. Organiser Terry Dufflyn of The Onion Bag and Football Fairground had brought a fine cast together including Supporters Direct's Dave Boyle who of course had an interest in seeing how Lewes's transformation to a Community Club was going, Jamie Cutteridge who had recently been writing for EFW, Ian King of the fantastic Two Hundred Percent and more. And then there was Lizzy. Dear, dear Lizzy. Football is not her game – cricket is. She commentates on the excellent Test Match Sofa, but we don't care – she is always a welcome addition to any gathering.

After a run of five consecutive defeats the Rooks had put in battling performances against two of the top teams in the league, narrowly losing to Braintree last week before gaining a valuable scoreless draw at home to Bromley on Wednesday. Manager Tim O'Shea had got his little black book out again in mid week and brought in more new recruits to bolster the injury ravaged squad. In came Gareth Hall, an ex-Lewes youngster Ibbo developed youngster from down the A27 at Brighton as well as ex-Millwall midfielder Ali Fuseini..

All looked promising then. That was until the twelth minute when Anthony Barness was forced to limp out of proceedings. Up until this point the Rooks had looked adventurous. The Socrates collective seemed impressed and despite news filtering through that some of Lewes's relegation rivals were winning, spirits in The Jungle were high. Then in the blink of an eye it all went wrong.

Staines had a free kick on the touchline about forty yards out. The ball was lofted into the area, Winterton came to collect and appeared to be impeded by Staines forward Griffiths and the ball sailed into the net. I would suggest 99% of similar incidents you will see would be deemed as a foul against the keeper. Harsh to say the least and the reaction of the Lewes players to the decision was understandable.

To give them their dues, the Rooks kept up the tempo and Chris Breach was desperately unlucky not to see one of his two goal bound efforts beat the man on the line.

Half time and a chance to refill our glasses with Harveys and discuss the goings on up and down the country. West Ham were unbelievably winning away from home at Everton, but scores elsewhere in the Blue Square Bet South were concerning. Still, fate is in the hands of the Rooks and all they can do is beat the teams put in front of them. Unfortunately, this was not one of those incidences as despite a further forty five minutes of positive forward momentum they rarely tested Louis Wells in the Staines goal apart from one deflected David Wheeler shot.

Manager O'Shea didn't know what to say when he met Patrick Marber after the game.
*"For the first time I feel a little bit down. I've seen the results around us and they are not good. The commitment and belief was there today but we conceded a soft goal and that hurt us. I am genuinely down for the players and supporters today. They did their utmost. I just hope we get our fair share of good luck and injuries to players like Barnie (*Anthony Barness) *and Chris Breach haven't helped.*

Even the Staines players were telling us after the game they didn't deserve to come away with all three points. David Wheeler had his best game under me for Lewes, and you go around the side and it is hard to pick out any individuals who had a poor game. There are still plenty of points to play for and we are all up for the fight."

So another three points dropped, and with St Albans City, Dartford and Thurrock all winning, the prognosis for the Rooks looks bleak. There was only one thing for it. Beer. We may be bottom of the league, but I am sure twenty of the most influential bloggers will agree, we are Champions League material when it comes to hospitality. If only leagues were decided on such criteria.

Saturday 29th January 2011
When the going gets tough....

The tough gets going. Apart from in football. In the crazy world we live in we all crave for a tough head on some tough shoulders when Mr Tough comes to the door and asks for his weekly protection money. Times couldn't be more tougher for The Rooks at the moment. This time last year the club came within hours of going out of business, and with Leyton and now Windsor and Eaton adding to the list of football clubs that are no more in the past ten days there has never been a more pertinent time to reflect on what could have been. Roll forward twelve months and the off the field problems have either been eliminated, or are under control. Unfortunately problems on the pitch have continued to mount.

Football fans are a pessimistic bunch. Win ten games on the spin and someone will be critical that the club haven't scored enough goals or that the formation at corners is all wrong. We all like to be armchair managers, and we all have selective memories. All of the talk on the Lewes Forum was about the tactics, formation and player recruitment of Tim O'Shea. On the eve of the vital away trip to St Albans City it had been announced that Rob Gradwell had been released. The news had not gone down very well.

Gradwell's vital goals in the away games at Worcester City and Hampton & Richmond Borough last season had been instrumental in keeping the club up, but his contribution so far this season had been disappointing. Pre-season had seen him fail to make his mark, missing a penalty away to Eastbourne Town to highlight his lack of form. He was sent out on loan when O'Shea arrived to Dulwich Hamlet in the Ryman League to try and get some much needed confidence in front of goal, and that is exactly what he did - he scored goals. However, despite the fact that Lewes had scored the lowest number of league goals in the Blue Square Bet South by some margin AND played more games than most, ToSH had decided to release him.

Cue all sorts of conspiracy theories about the management team and what their motives were. With a must-win game just around the corner, any players who read some of the comments would have hardly been motivated by the views of the fans. Of course everyone is entitled to an opinion, but there were some real rose-tinted ones going on. Some suggested that the board should sack ToSH and Neil Smith and replace them with Ibbo and

Jason again. So that would be the Club President and the manager of Hastings United then? Actually prior to this game ToSH's record in his first twelve games was better than Ibbo's but let's not get facts in the way of a good debate.

One thing is sure and that is that the club needed more fans to get behind the side away from home. More often than not it has been the same dozen or so away fans who have been following the club this season, including of course most of the Directors, who prefer to stand with the fans rather than sit on the directors box. Go to the games and then have an opinion sure, but do not whine and whinge if you cannot be bothered to go to the game to see the team first hand.

The trains heading north from the South Coast were sure to be packed though for the trip to St Albans City, but alas not filled with Lewes fans. Brighton & Hove Albion were continuing their FA Cup run away to Watford and were taking a good couple of thousand to Hertfordshire for this. As an added treat Southern trains had put on a special Rail replacement bus for part of the route as well of course.

With a trip to Los Angeles on the cards for me I unfortunately was putting in some quality family time and so sat back and awaited the usual Deaksy updates as he stood on the chilly open terrace at Clarence Park, one of my favourite non league grounds in the South of England.

St Albans City 0 Lewes 0 - Clarence Park

Tim O'Shea made four changes to the starting line-up from the 1-0 defeat against Staines Town, with Anthony Barness, Sonny Cobbs, Ali Fuseini and Ben Godfrey being replaced in the starting line-up by Callum Davies, who had signed on work experience terms from Gillingham, Nathan Green, Rory Hill, signed from Tonbridge Angels, and Tom Murphy.

During the opening exchanges, both sides showed why they were in the relegation zone with some poor defending but eventually it was the Rooks who created the first chance with Tom Murphy seeing a shot deflected wide by Adam Everitt after latching onto a long through-ball by the "born again" Jermaine Wright.

There was very little goal-mouth action in the rest of the half, with the defences dominating proceedings. In a sign of things to come later on Nathan Green made two crunching challenges to prevent St Albans players finding space in the penalty area..

The second half started with two substitutions by Lewes, with Jamie Crellin and Ben Godfrey replacing Welsh and George Barker as ToSH went for a more attacking slant although it was still the solid defences who were winning the day. At this stage I do not thing any bookie would have any further taken bets on a scoreless draw.

Almost all of the chances were from long range, with St Albans right-back James Fisher sending a thirty five yard shot straight at Winterton after a purposeful run from inside his own half.

The game began to peter out, mainly due to a referee who seemed incredibly reluctant to let the game flow at times, making it difficult for either side to create any real goal-scoring opportunities although the impressive Chris Breach sent a looping header over the cross-bar from a set-piece.

The game boiled over in the final few minutes of normal time, with Green receiving a straight red card for a high challenge on Adam Martin. Discipline has not been good under O'Shea as this was the fifth red card gained since November. From the resulting free-kick on the edge of the penalty area, Everitt saw a close-range header superbly saved by Winterton.

This was the last meaningful action of the game, meaning that a game which both sides probably felt they needed to win ended in a stale-mate. Despite this, the Lewes performance was a vast improvement on the display against Staines seven days previously.

And then the results start rolling in and the collective groans could be heard as far away as TBIR towers in South East London. Thurrock had beaten Eastleigh, Dorchester had managed a draw at home to high flying Welling United, Hampton & Richmond had drawn with Basingstoke Town and then the biggest disappointment. Boreham Wood had beaten Maidenhead United 4-2. Bugger.
Neil Smith spoke to Patrick Marber after the game.

"*We asked them to put a fight up and not get beaten and we did that. We got into situations where we worked it well but the final ball just wasn't there. Defensively we have had to be better and we have worked on that. It is just in the final third where the magic isn't happening at the moment.*"

The week ahead would prove defining for the Rooks. Boreham Wood were travelling to St Albans City in midweek in a real relegation six pointer before visiting The Dripping Pan on Saturday.

Saturday 5th February 2011
To live and die in LA

It had been a long week. One punctuated by jet lag, and long dull meetings, working from 8am to 8pm. But please don't feel sorry for me. After all, I was in Santa Monica, the laid back beach resort of Los Angeles - oh and did I mention I also partied at the Playboy Mansion? Well, let me tell you all about it. Oh hang on, there is that restraining order in place isn't there. Never mind. Let's just say it involved lots of free drink, women who started off in underwear and progressively lost it and sushi. Yes, sushi!

On Wednesday I headed off to the "Ye Olde English Pub" to see if I could find the St Albans City versus Boreham Wood game on any of the TV's. They told me that it was too expensive to buy in the feed so instead I had to make do with Blackpool v West Ham United.

A 1-0 win for Boreham Wood may not have seemed the best result for Lewes on the night (day) but events would take another turn later in the week.

I was lucky enough to be invited down to Carson City, home to LA Galaxy to watch them train. As I sat in the taxi on the way down to the training ground, James Boyes sent me a text that made my jaw drop. "St Albans docked 10 pts. Financial irregularities". Rewind on that? I knew St Albans had been skating on thin ice for awhile - in fact when we had visited there in August 2009 they appeared to be on the edge of extinction, according to their fans. Well it appears this incident related to events in season 2008/09 and the past had finally caught up with them and the ten point penalty had sent them to the bottom of the league.

So, the game on Saturday was going to take on even more significance. Second to bottom Lewes, against third from bottom, and in form, Boreham Wood. And would I be there? Well, if the pilot of VS008 from LAX to LHR put his foot down over the Atlantic I would be.

Lewes 2 Boreham Wood 2 - The Dripping Pan

Virgin Atlantic did their bit. They got me into Heathrow at 1pm, but Heathrow is not known as one of the busiest airports in the world for nothing. So after a twenty minute walk to the "UK Border", then a twenty minute queue to actually enter my country of birth and finally a forty minute wait for my luggage, there was no way I would make any of the first half. And as I had been away from the Fuller homestead for over a week, including a visit to the most decedent address on earth I really couldn't push my luck with a one hundred and twenty mile detour to the game.

What made this worse was that Danny and Big Deaksy, my usual sources of minute by minute information were in Germany, watching the Berlin derby no less, so I had to rely on updates from Mr Boyes in between snapping away on the touchline.

Tim O'Shea had been busy on transfer deadline day. A last minute attempt to derail the Torres deal to Chelsea had not come off, and instead he had managed to capture Lyle Taylor on loan from high flying League One side Bournemouth. Taylor had netted thirty four goals last season for Concord Rangers in the Ryman League so he certainly knew where the non league net was.

As we know in this league, you have to balance the books so with Taylor coming in then out went Nathan Green and Tom Hutchinson. Green, had not only impressed the Rooks in the past few weeks with his energy, if not for his tackling, had been watched by a Cypriot club who had seen enough to offer him sun, sand and soccer on the Island. Hutchinson, on the other hand decided that the Mediterranean weather was over rated and so headed off to Kingstonian instead.

In the build up to the game the club also waved goodbye to loanees George Porter (back to Leyton Orient) and James Rowe (Reading), whilst Joe Tabiri and Gary Noel came in from Dover Athletic and Carshalton Athletic.

So at 3pm when the teams came out onto the pitch there was an unfamiliar look to the starting eleven for Lewes. By 3.15pm, the news reaching me wasn't good. Two nil down, the trap door was very firmly open beneath the Rooks feet.

It was therefore against the run of play when Boreham Wood took the lead after just eight minutes. Ola Sogbanmu latched onto a wind-assisted long punt up field and poked the ball past Chris Winterton who had decided to venture out of his area.

Winterton was at fault for the second when Ali Chaaban sent a looping header past him after connecting with a cross from Elliott Godfrey.

It took Lewes until the half-hour mark to have their best attempt on goal, with new signing Taylor seeing his half-volley well saved by Elvijs Putnins in the Boreham Wood goal.

However, the Rooks pulled a goal back after thirty three minutes when Taylor cut inside two defenders and sent a twenty five yard shot past Putnins for an excellent debut goal. Minutes later, Lewes were nearly level when Noel turned Ryan Moran on the edge of the penalty area but his shot went just wide.

Having the strong wind on their side in the second half should have given Lewes an immediate advantage, but it was Boreham Wood who created the first opportunity of the half when Anthony Barness was forced to clear a Luke Wilkinson header..

But it didn't take too long for Lewes to get back on top when the new Taylor/Noel partnership combined well with David Wheeler to create a number of chances. Finally on sixty nine minutes, the Rooks equalised when Noel connected with one of those Wheeler crosses to slot home from close range, injuring himself in the process.

The Rooks went close in the final ten minutes of the game with Callum Davies, unable to make sufficient contact with a Wheeler flick-on from a Hill corner. Then Jermaine Wright then sent a thirty yard shot just wide, before Chris Breach had a shot cleared off the line from another Hill corner. The final whistle was greeted with a mixed reaction. The team had shown some real spirit in coming back into the game, but defensive lapses had given the visitors a two goal advantage.

Patrick Marber spoke to Tim O'Shea in the dressing room after the game. "*Frustration is the word of the day. We gave away two silly goals and apart from that they (*Boreham Wood) *didn't contribute alot to the game. There was an element of offside in their first goal although Breachie put his hand up at half time and said sorry. The second one was another defensive lapse. The youngsters did excellent for us today. All around the team there was passion and spirit. For the first time in my time here I feel that things are in* *place. We are due a win soon. we will get through this. There is a determination and a belief in this changing room to get out of this."*

A point gained or a two points dropped? Three draws in the last four was progress to a point but would it be enough come end of April?

Saturday 12th February 2011
Thames side

It was another week of surprises. Not only had England performed well in a pre-season friendly, beating an impressive Denmark team in Copenhagen, but one of the players who seemed to have a bright future at Lewes left by "mutual consent". That is a funny term as no decision in football is "mutually acceptable". One party always ends up better off than the other. In this case it referred to young winger Tom Murphy.

Lewes manager Tim O'Shea takes up the story: "*Tom called me over the weekend and said that he wanted a regular run in the side. I can understand why a player would want that but I told him that at the moment, it's something I can't guarantee.*"
"*I've bought in Lyle Taylor and Gary Noel upfront who both scored on Saturday and Tom felt that he couldn't see much chance of a guaranteed run of games.*"
"*I raised the option of a loan deal with him which he declined, but instead asked to be released from his contract which I have accepted.*"
O'Shea added: "*He's a young lad with a chance but still learning his trade. I would like to go on record in thanking him for his time here and wish him well for the future.*"

Murphy was a confidence player, a confidence that gave him a bit of a swagger. This sometimes came over as arrogance and I get the feeling that he had tried to call ToSH's bluff on this one and failed.

With midweek results sort of going Lewes's way the next two fixtures all of a sudden took on more meaning. Maidenhead United and then Hampton & Richmond Borough sat in the two places immediately above the relegation zone. Sure they had points and games in hand, but you can only beat what is put in front of you and so first up was a trip down the Thames to Maidenhead.

Last season the Lewes Lunatic Fringe had enjoyed their trip to York Road, the oldest football ground in the world still in continuous use (and they have a blue plaque to prove it!). With their own lap dancing bar, Maidenhead is a favourite for away fans. Easy to get to, being a few minutes walk from the station, town centre and dozens of decent pubs. This season it would be Cynical Dave and Big Deaks holding the flares in the away end. Would the flame fade and die like our survival hopes? Ninety minutes of nail-biting tension would tell us.

Maidenhead United 0 Lewes 2 - York Road

It had been ten games since Lewes last experienced a win, and longer since they took maximum points away from home at Weston-Super-Mare but the resolute performance that was on display at St Albans City and at home against Boreham Wood continued in Maidenhead.

Lewes looked solid at the back and this was as much to do with the fine central defensive partnership that is being forged between Chris Breach and Callum Davies as was the return of Lewis Hamilton after his suspension or the injured Grant Hall. A settled back four is almost as unheard of in these parts as an Avram Grant motivational half time speech.

Part of the reason for the upturn in recent form has been due to the return of Jermaine Wright but he was absent through sickness for this one. ToSh decided to field both wide men, Ishmael Welsh and David Wheeler, in the hope that they could create chances.

Wheeler took advantage of a defender's slip in the tenth minute but his cross was too quick for new singing Gary Noel who could not get his foot to the ball quick enough.

Both keepers were kept busy, with Chris Winterton parrying Mark Nisbet's shot off the line and former Rook Steve Williams saving bravely at the feet of Wheeler when the midfielder was clean through.

Things did not look rosy for the home side and that was summed up by the dressing down they got at half time from manager Johnson Hippolyte which was audible to the fans outside on the terrace.

This seemed to have the desired affect after five minutes when Cliff Akurang played in Kieron St.Aimie but Winterton stood up to the challenge and expertly pushed the shot away.

It was Lewes who looked more likely to score with the new forward partnership of Lyle Taylor and Gary Noel clicking straight away. Despite this, the Magpies nearly scored with sixteen minutes left when substitute Alex Wall forced a fine save from Winterton.

The breakthrough came at last in the seventy eighth minute after Maidenhead failed to clear a Lewes free kick and the ball fell to Joe Tabiri who found the target through the crowded area.

Any doubters about the passion and commitment the Lewes players have for the fight to stay in the division should have witnessed the whole team bar Winterton running over to Tabiri to celebrate his strike much to the annoyance of the referee.

Substitute Barker capped off a fantastic team performance when he struck a magnificent shop from twenty yards into the top corner of the net. Cue another team celebration, this time encompassing the other substitutes as well, but Lewes weren't finished and Taylor was unlucky in injury time when he broke free but failed to control the ball with the keeper advancing. Matter did it not as a two nil win was a fantastic result, and all of a sudden green shoots of hope could be seen in the frozen tundra of the relegation zone.

Unsurprisingly the management duo were very upbeat after the game when they stood in front of Patrick Marber's microphone.
"*We are now creating chances. The whole back four were very strong and great to see Lewis Hamilton back. It was an inspired substitution to bring on Barker (*Neil Smith laughs as it appears his was decision) *and he scored a magnificent goal. We have a nice squad now. It was a much needed win but we aren't getting carried away. This win was for the true believers out there, the supporters who are backing us in every away game.*"

Tuesday 15th February 2011
Beavering away

In any team there will always be one sensible person and one who is the creative brains. The one who lives in the clouds, looking at ideas from a different angle, always prepared to ask the "what if" questions. For Lewes FC this is Charlie Dobres.

Charlie is a man of leisure. I caught up with him, obviously, at The Dripping Pan. Shirt and tie? Nope, t-shirt and jeans. Meeting in the boardroom? You must be joking! The sunshine was shining, the pitch looked beautiful, so what did we do? Three and in of course on the hallowed turf.

His involvement in the club came at a time when the club had used up all of its goodwill with the local business community. He was introduced to Patrick Marber through a mutual friend at his son's school where he was a governor. They discussed a need to do something but he was reticent to get involved outright.

"*Running a football club is a money pit*" Charlie remembered "*So I didn't really see myself as a football club owner*"

However, he started to ponder the idea in his head and spent time understanding the workings of the club. He engaged with Supporters Direct and met with FC United's General Manager Andy Walsh. Over the course of a few months he presented the idea of a Community Club scheme to the management committee, and one by one they seemed to buy into the idea. The actual transition between a club owned by a few to one with a mandate to be owned by many has been documented earlier but by early July the deal was done. Charlie had become the part owner of a football club, although never in a way he imagined was possible, owning an equal share with the other pioneer shareholders.

The strategy from day one was very clear. To evolve the club after 125 years of existence into a self-sustaining organisation, rather like a foundation. The biggest challenge was obviously to make the transition of a loss making organisation into a position of stability. Considering the traumatic year the club had been through it was going to be no walk in the park.

Once the immediate danger had been starved off, and plans put in place for a sensible budget, the thoughts started to turn to what the club could do differently. As far as Charlie was (and still is) concerned, there is no limit to what can be tried. The Dripping Pan is essentially the biggest meeting place in the town, so it is only right that the facilities are in place to match. His plan has always been to "open the gates and leave them open". It is a community club so why shouldn't the club be open? However, there wasn't a motivating vision to get people through the door. So first came themed matches such as the 125th Anniversary, the Bonfire Day game, Boxing Day in February and the planned beat the leprechaun penalty shoot out for St Patricks Day.

In his eyes it is getting a different understanding of what football is actually all about. It is a release from the day to day grind. It should be fun, irrespective of the fayre on show on the pitch. Using a favourite saying of Danny and mine, "A great day out irrespective of the ninety minutes of football".

His vision is slightly different to the rest of the board. Whilst they see the club naturally performing at the current level, Charlie thinks they could go higher. His ambition is to see them compete in the Football League. Note the word there is compete, not just play. And ideal FA Cup opponents? Manchester United of course, here on our terms and at the heart of our community.

Valentines Day. The most overhyped commercialised day in our calendar. The pressure we all feel to try and go one better each year to prove our love. As the years roll on, and our relationships mature, why do you need one day to try and prove your love. I do it everyday with CMF by picking up my socks off the floor, or occasionally boiling the kettle so that she can make me a cup of tea. Little things like that show that I still love her.
It wasn't always so romantic. Once I flew her to Monaco just for lunch, swooping in and out of the principality by helicopter from Nice airport. She looked down downright bored all day, unsure of what to do with that third fork at the dinner table. I am sure she would have rather had a box of Milk Tray or some petrol station flowers.

But what a modern girl really wants is a trip to football on Valentines Day right? The magic of the game under lights, the smell of liniment, burgers and horse shit and the roar of the crowd as they call the opposing keeper a c*nt for daring to delay a goal kick by a second. And what a choice you had this year too!

The Sloane Square and Belgravia set no doubt headed down the Kings Road, or over Putney Bridge for the West London derby between Fulham and Chelsea, ultimately enjoying the view of the Thames at night more than the game on offer. But the real action for those wanting to be romantic was in the Blue Square North and South. Take your pick from a visit to Chelmsford, Eastleigh, Worcester or even Hinckley. If that is not enough to prove your love then I do not know what is.

At full time it appeared to be a mixed bag of success. Chelmsford City's crowd of nearly seven hundred for their game with Boreham Wood was slightly down on average but actually up by 12% on their game the previous Monday, whilst Eastleigh's Cupid themed event at home to St Albans City saw crowds down by 50% on a normal league game. In the Blue Square North Worcester City's crowd was down by 30% on normal, but around the same for their previous Monday night game last month, and Hinckley United, well I haven't got a clue as I cannot find the basics like a website to check from.

So what does that tell us? People from Hampshire are more romantic than those in Essex or Worcestershire and thus stayed at home or, dare I say it, went out for a meal rather than go to the game? Or is it simply that people cannot be arsed to go to midweek games?

We were due to put the theory to the test in some part as Lewes were due to travel to Hampton & Richmond Borough twenty four hours later, known as Realisation of Disappointment Day. After the Rooks fantastic win at Maidenhead United on Saturday, the momentum was back, especially as relegation rivals St Albans City and Boreham Wood had suffered St Valentines Day massacres at the hands of Eastleigh and Chelmsford City respectively. In fact the Rooks were now unbeaten in February, showing some nice touches as well as some steel in the team. Tim O'Shea, the Lewes manager had wheeled and dealed since taking over in October, trying to find the balance that would keep them in the division. With time running out it appeared he had turned a corner, but with Hampton & Richmond just one place above the Rooks it was sure to be a test.

We love going to The Beveree, home of Hampton & Richmond Borough. It is one of our favourite non league grounds, frequented by some of the best fans. They are also managed by West Ham legend Alan Devonshire who is always around for a quick word about the good old days post match. One of Lewes's finest performances in previous years had been at the Beveree in April 2010 when they pulled the rabbit out of the hat and stayed up on the last day of the season with a 2-1 win.

It's Tuesday, it's 5.35pm, it's time for FOOTBALL! I had driven into work, paying £10 for the privilege to drive through the congestion zone for thirty yards so I would be travelling in style to TW12. Tense, nervous? You could say that. But that is the romance of football. Who needs one day of the year to show your feelings to the one you love when non league football is happening all around. After all we all love football, right?

Hampton & Richmond Borough 1 Lewes 2 – The Beveree

They say the best things in life are free, but I would argue otherwise. Because tonight the best thing you could have done was spend £18.50 in TW12 last night. For that you would have got entry into the Beveree, a programme, hot dog and chips (with onions of course) and a beer. Oh and a goal that rivalled Wayne Rooney's for brilliance, but was far far more important than just a winner in a Manchester derby.

After a reminder of why I don't drive into London in the rush hour anymore (eleven miles in seventy minutes and too many close shaves with suicidal cyclists) I reached the leafy suburb of Hampton. Is there anywhere more English (apart from Worcester) than Hampton? You could almost imagine Colin Firth walking down Church Road practising his lines for the Kings Speech and bumping into Dame Vera Lynn buying twenty Capstones at the newsagents. However, on a cold and wet February night it didn't fill me with the spirit of St George.

But the Lewes faithful were here in force. Count them one, two, three, four, five and six. A full house of the directors of the club were in attendance. This was going to be some night if they had all hoped on the bus and travelled up from Sussex by the Sea. And even Chairman Ibbo had a smile on his face in the bar before the game.

It was time to take our place in front of the Alan Simpson Stand. To add authenticity to the occasion Alan himself wandered past just before kick off and wished us a good evening. A true gent, and for those who do not know who Alan Simpson is, well shame on you. A comedy genius who brought us Hancock's Half Hour and Steptoe and Son amongst other things.

No sooner had Alan taken his season in his own stand than Lewes were one up. Quite how is a mystery to most of us as we were having a bit of a chat about what you would want named after yourself (A betting shop for Dave, although Cynical Betting may not take off). Neither did ace photographer James Boyes who was eyeing up a WAG no doubt in the main stand. Apparently what happened was that a Hampton clearance was scuffed and it appeared to hit/was hit by Lyle Taylor, on loan from AFC Bournemouth and fly into the net.

You cannot comprehend the difference a few weeks has made to Lewes. When we last saw them at home to Staines in late January they appeared light in midfield, lacking someone to get the ball wide and no one really up front. Fast forward three weeks and the team have drawn two and one won before tonight, and importantly all against relegation rivals. Credit must go to ToSH and Neil Smith for bringing in the right players. Obviously, some like the impressive Lyle Taylor are only on loan, but they have given the team some confidence and it was obvious from the first half that a few players were upping their game.

David Wheeler for instance. Sorry, OUR David Wheeler was in the thick of things, putting himself about like we have rarely seen him do before and being on the receiving end of a few "choice" tackles which of course somehow he ended up getting a yellow card for.

Half time and a chance to grab our breath. It wasn't a great game, with the pitch certainly causing some issues for both teams but hey, we were 1-0 up! And that lead lasted all of three minutes into the second half. Just as I left the warm comfy womb (aka the bar to us grown men) I saw the ball hit the back of the Lewes net when Barrie Matthews strike beat Winterton from the edge of the box. In fact Winterton's task of picking the ball out of the net was one of the first things he had had to do all night.

We had a fight on our hands and the game bubbled under for the rest of the half, one tackle away from a mass brawl at times. However, it was Lewes who seemed to have the energy and after Hampton had again illegally stopped a Lewes assault on goal. After a yellow card was issued the ball was played deep into the Hampton box by Rory Hill. Gary Noel tried a bicycle kick that hit a defender and the ball flew out of the area until Grant Hall jumped and executed the perfect overhead kick. The ball flew into the corner and to say the place went wild was an understatement. Players, substitutes and the manager ran onto the pitch to jump on Hall. The referee simply didn't know what to do. But we did. We cheered, clapped, screamed and basically let out six months worth of emotion.

The last few minutes were of course spent camped in the Lewes penalty area but the team held on, and when the final whistle sounded it wasn't met with relief as it was ten months ago when we stood in the very same spot, but in triumph. This was another step in the direction of survival. Eight points from four games against relegation rivals, three of which had been played away from the Pan marked the best run for the club of the season.

Doom clouds hang over the Hampton fans in Hammonds Bar afterwards as their winless streak in the league stretched back to October. But it was the Rooks who were flying high. Where there is hope there is belief. Two men who have that belief are Patrick Marber and Tim O'Shea.

"It was a must win game and we had to take advantage of the situation. The spirit in the team has changed and that has come through improving performances and the belief in the changing room. The squad sacrificed a Valentine's night with their loved ones to train and this is the reward.
We have tried very hard to extend George Barker and Grant Hall's loan deals but Brighton want them back. It will be a shame as they have really added to the squad. But we knew this would happen.
Back to back wins mean that we will be going into the game against Havant & Waterlooville with confidence."

It is amazing what this performance meant to the players, management and fans in the bar, whilst the home fans could only see doom and gloom on the horizon. With ten weeks still to go perhaps it was all just a little premature.

Saturday 19th February 2011
To Have or Havant

Confidence breeds confidence and for a team at the bottom of the league that is all that you need at this time of the season. That and a little bit of blooming luck. After the consecutive victories on the road at Maidenhead and Hampton it was time to return home to face a Havant & Waterlooville team, who despite their pre-season hype, had flattered to deceive and sat in mid table.

Just three years ago Havant & Waterlooville had won the hearts of the nation when they had reached round four of the FA Cup where they played Liverpool at Anfield. You could draw parallels between their game and Crawley Town's trip last weekend to Old Trafford to face Manchester United. Except, Havant were playing at the time in the Conference South, they played more games, and generally most people liked Havant. They even had the temerity to take the lead at Anfield when Richard Pacquette scored in the eighth minute. Of course they never really stood a chance, nor did Crawley really last weekend, and went out as gallant losers.

Since then the club haven't really progressed. Players have come and gone, and at the start of each season the bookies seem to think this would be their season, but so far their money had been safe. This season it has been a case of winning exactly the same has they had lost, putting them firmly in mid table.

Tim O'Shea had been busy again during the week, securing the services of Ben Hunt from Dover Athletic who went straight into the match day squad. With almost everyone fit and available it was a high flying Rooks team that took to the pitch against Havant & Waterlooville, looking for a third consecutive win, for the first time in three seasons.

Lewes 2 Havant & Waterlooville 1 - The Dripping Pan

In a season where the club have suffered so many injuries and suspensions it was amazing to see Tim O'Shea able to announce an unchanged side from the victory away at Hampton earlier in the week.

The Rooks started the game positively, with David Wheeler looking particularly lively down the right wing and putting two low crosses into the penalty area just ahead of Gary Noel. The new pairing of Noel and Lyle Taylor continued to look lively up front, and for the first time in a couple of seasons the team had two strikers who were in form and creating problems for opposing defenders.

Whilst Lewes's approach relied on slick passing, Havant adopted a far more direct approach and came close to opening the scoring when Manny Williams saw his shot blocked. In fact it was the visitors who created more chances than the Rooks during the first half, with Wes Fogden coming within a lick of paint of breaking the deadlock when his miss hit cross hit the top of the crossbar.

The game ebbed and flowed in the opening period of the second half with Winterton the busier of the two keepers. But just when we thought this was going to end in disappointment for Lewes Chris Breach again delivered the goods from a set piece. With Jermaine Wright again delivering a pin point delivery from a free kick, Breach rose above his marker and glanced the ball into the net.

This galvanised Lewes and it took a fine covering challenge from Havant's Jake Newton to prevent Noel creating a goal-scoring opportunity. But it only took a few more minutes before the game was made safe. David Wheeler, sorry OUR David Wheeler capped another fine performance by slamming the ball home from ten yards after Noel's effort was blocked on the line.

A lot of sides would have sat back at this stage and settled for 2-0, but Lewes continued to push forward and Wheeler was able to use his pace to beat Havant full-back Jon McDonald on a number of occasions. But as luck would have it the final minutes became nail biting for the fans and management alike when former Lewes (and Arsenal) midfielder Ian Selley scored from close range for the visitors.

Full time and Lewes celebrated in front of a crowd of over seven hundred. Eleven points from a possible fifteen was an outstanding achievement for a team that looked down and out just four weeks ago. Could they make it four in a row when Ebbsfleet came to town in midweek? We shall see. After the game Tim O'Shea was in a upbeat mood.

"This is a win against a top six side. They have a decent squad and they are as good as the top teams on their day. It was a good marker today to see how far we have come.

We prepared well, we knew that they would use the long throw and to be honest when that towel appeared on the side of the pitch we were a bit worried. But Chris Winterton was immaculate in dealing with that.

I would like to think we have progressed on from when we last played Ebbsfleet in January and we are really looking forward to it. And thanks very much to the crowd today who really got behind the team."

Wednesday 24th February 2011
Christmas comes but twice a year

Why let the pesky weather get in the way of your Christmas? Well in the case of Lewes FC it didn't. We were all very excited in the extended Fuller household at Christmas to be making the trek down to the Boxing Day game against Ebbsfleet United with our Northern cousins (aka Northern Steve and young Liam) for their first ever visit to The Dripping Pan. But then the weather got in the way and we were forced to watch a complete box set of Glee instead and eat the strange light blue sweets in the big tin of Quality Street - hardly a fair trade.

The game against Ebbsfleet was duly re-arranged for mid February and 99% of non league clubs would just have republished the programme with a photocopied insert and be done with it. But this is Lewes we are talking about so we like to be different. And so the directors decided that Christmas would not be cancelled and simply shifted it by nearly two months. All were welcome, Santa hats certainly obligatory and Cynical Dave promised to bring the mistletoe. The club even went as far as making a promotional video to encourage people to attend. My only concern was whether the mince pies may have fermented since being kept from Boxing Day.

This was to be my seventh game in just ten days after my mammoth Northern Roadtrip. Was I bored with football yet? Not a chance and as I battled my way through the rush hour gridlock on the M25 I thought that this game could be a defining moment in the Rooks season. A win tonight and it was possible to leapfrog over a number of teams and into safety, defeat would keep the pressure on. But as we know, "if" and "and" make odd bedfellows (like Eddie Murphy and Scary Spice I always feel).

Lewes 0 Ebbsfleet United 3 - The Dripping Pan

Baaah Humbug. Ebbsfleet became the Grinch that stole Christmas, taking all three points in a game played with swirling mist all around the Christmas decorations at The Dripping Pan.
Lewes faced a bit of an onslaught in the first half and the long ball game employed by Ebbsfleet meant that the Rooks defence had little respite although David Wheeler was a constant thorn in the side of Ebbsfleet's keeper who didn't like it "up 'im" as Dad's Army used to say. However,

despite Lewes's strong backbone, and attacking flair with Noel and Taylor it was Ebbsfleet who took the lead in route one fashion. A long punt upfield by keeper and Ashley Carew squeezed between Chris Breach and Sonny Cobbs to slot an angled shot past Chris Winterton. Ouch.

Lewes continued to probe for the remainder of the half but the Ebbsfleet physical approach limited chances to shots from distance. Even a trip to the food van for a homemade cheese burger couldn't lift my festive spirits. It was strange that Lewes attacked the Jungle in the second half, as in all my times of watching them at The Pan this had never happened. The crowd on the terrace was swelled with at least one Santa Claus (because kids there is only one, right?) and in truth Lewes took the game to the visitors with Ebbsfleet riding their luck during a couple of goal mouth scrambles. ToSH wanted at least a point so took off Anthony Barness and introduced a more attacking formation. It had two effects. Lewes peppered the Ebbsfleet goal mouth but simply could not find a way through, whilst they looked more exposed to the counter attack.

And it was this shortage of numbers that led to two late goals by Ebbsfleet as first Calum Willock took advantage of another route one approach with a fantastic finish and then as the game entered injury time Carew scored again to send Ebbsfleet into second place in the table and to leave the Rooks clearing up the wrapping paper and putting Granny's jumper back in the draw. A set back to the fight that is all, no more, no less. Bring on Woking on Saturday is what I say!

Manager Tim O'Shea couldn't really take any positives from the game when he spoke to Patrick Marber after the game.
"There were some good individual performances, with the midfield competing well with a very good side who have few weaknesses and that is why they are right up there. The free kick in that fantastic position towards the end of the game was very disappointing. That summed our evening up quite well.

We need a positive reaction on Saturday and look to bounce back. We should have Lewis Hamilton back by then and he has been outstanding for us. But let's put some positive spin on this. We've gone five unbeaten and won our last three so there is no reason why we cannot get back in that sort of form."
So a few weeks of good form had been put to one side. It would be

interesting to see how much the defeat would affect confidence on Saturday for the visit of Woking.

Saturday 26th February 2011
A house of cards

In the cold light of day the defeat in midweek to Ebbsfleet didn't seem that bad. Sure, the team were still in the bottom three in the league but other results had gone the Rooks way. After all, Ebbsfleet were one of the favourites for promotion after their shock relegation on the last day of the season from the Blue Square Bet Premier. It could all be put right with a win over Woking, "The Cards". It seems so simple when you write it down "a win over Woking". If only it was.

Woking were one of those teams who you always expect to be playing at a higher level. They have all the makings of a league team in the waiting. A good cup record, beating West Bromwich Albion in 1991 thanks to a hatrick from Tim Buzaglo. A good nickname, "The Cards", which is much better than "City", "United" or "Rovers. A decent ground, including the finest stand in Non League football, the Leslie Gosden Stand and of course a fan base that swells when Chelsea/Fulham/Arsenal (delete as appropriate) are playing away from home. But for some reason they have not been able to climb out of the division since they found themselves in the Conference South some seasons ago.

Last season they came oh so close. They were the form team coming into the Play Offs, disposing of Dover Athletic in the semi-finals and thus setting up a final with Bath City. On a wet and wild afternoon in Wiltshire/Avon Bath City surprised not only Woking but watching observers by winning 1-0. This season has been a mixed bag again. Decent home form, including a 2-1 win in August against Lewes but away from home they had lost too many times, a good omen perhaps for this one.

For once the dressing room revolving door had been shut this week, with no additions to the Lewes squad, meaning that Tim O'Shea had almost a full squad to choose from. Could there be any better omens for this one? Well how about the long awaited return of Danny Last, absent on writing duties since last month for starters? No? Well what about a new delivery of Harvey's Blue Label beer behind the bar in the Rook Inn or perhaps the absence of Dave “I always score against Lewes” Gilroy? Excellent, I knew you could be bought!

Lewes 0 Woking 4 - The Dripping Pan

I could go on about defeat being on the Cards against Woking or the fact that the deck was stacked against Lewes but quite frankly there is little you can say about a 4-0 thumping at home apart from "bollocks". It had all started so brightly. The weather on the way down to the south coast had been awful, with torrential rain causing many a game in the non leagues to be cancelled around lunchtime. But conditions in Lewes were perfect. The ground was firm, the sun was shining and the couple of hundred of Woking fans were in good voice.

Within a minute of the game starting Lyle Taylor had come within a lick of paint of opening the scoring for the Rooks when his powerful shot on the run had struck the post. Five minutes later he was clean through again but put too much power behind his shot and it sailed into the packed Jungle. Those two chances were the sum highlights of the game from a Lewes point of view.

Woking came into the game with a 100% record in February and their goals conceded tally standing at zero, and it was easy to see why. A few "motivational" words from the sidelines after those two chances saw a tactical change in midfield, with one man pushing closer to play maker Jermaine Wright and it effectively changed the game.

In the twelfth minute Lewes contributed another clanger to the inevitable end of season bloopers DVD somewhere when Callum Davies slipped, forcing Chris Winterton to dash off his line and try to clear the ball, which he did with power, but only into the back of Davies and the ball flew back over their heads and into the path of Woking's Craig Dobson and he tapped the ball into an empty net. Ouch.

It couldn't get any worse could it? Well how about giving Dobson another gift of a goal ten minutes later? OK, why not. This time Winterton charged from his line to try and get to the through ball before Dobson, but he lost out in the challenge and the Woking forward was allowed to walk the ball into an empty net. At this point Dobson ran off the pitch, out of the ground and to the newsagents opposite the station to buy his lottery ticket such was his run of good luck.

With that second goal the sky's darkened and the rain started to fall. And fall. The collective inhabitants of the Jungle ran for cover into the main stand, all bar Eddie Ramsden. The financial wizard behind the club wasn't going let a little bit of rain spoil his afternoon - after all two gifted goals had already done that so the only way was up, assuming the mantra of Yazz and her plastic people.

Half time saw the Rook Inn brimming at near capacity. The Woking fans were in good voice but quite why they decided to start chanting about "You are only here to watch the Woking" or "Shitty ground" was a mystery to most. After all, the attendance was marginally over average and even normalising the away support was up on the corresponding fixture last season. Oh and for such a shitty ground they certainly seemed to be enjoying the beer and food by the looks of it.

Lewes did improve in the opening minutes of the second half. Ben Hunt continues his impressive run in the side, but still there were too many players who weren't up for the fight. It seemed that the belief that had been built in the past few weeks had been beaten out of them by a combination of Ebbsfleet United on Wednesday and Woking today. With Woking pouring forward at every opportunity it was a question of how many they would score. Lewes held out until the eightieth minute without conceding any further goals before Kieran Murtagh added a third with a well taken shot from just inside the area. And as if to add insult to injury Asward Thomas scored a fourth a few minutes later when he finished a nice flowing move.

Results from elsewhere are only seen as positives at this stage of the season when Lewes have taken points so two consecutive home defeats meant that draws and defeats for the teams around the Rooks were irrelevant, a fact that Tim O'Shea picked up on in his regular post match interview with Patrick Marber.

"*We had too many players who today felt as soon as we had gone one down felt that was it for the day. We started brightly in the first fifteen minutes but as soon as that goal went in we felt that we had lost the game. Things need to be adjusted before next Saturday because we need to make some changes.*
Woking are in fine form, but Ebbsfleet apart, so were we. I am struggling

to find any positives from today apart from Ben Hunt's attitude when he came on and of course Breachie's attitude. Also bear in mind that a 17 year old made the mistake for the first goal but he then raised his game and kept his head up.

I feel there is an eleven out there who can compete for the club."

Saturday 5th March 2011
George and the Dragon

The days after the Woking defeat saw the doom mongers return to the Forum, ready to stick the knife into the team and management who had essentially been the same ones they were lauding a week before. The fickle nature of football was in full effect.

Manager Tim O'Shea felt it was necessary to ring some changes in the squad again in the days leading up to the game away in Hampshire against Basingstoke. Firstly, Lyle Taylor had returned to Bournemouth as his loan had finished. It is fair to say that he had made quite an impact on the team, adding some strength and pace upfront, and it was no co-incidence that his loan spell had come at a time when the club enjoyed their best form for nearly three seasons.

It was also announced that Sonny Cobbs had left the club and joined Burgess Hill on loan until the end of the season. Cobbs had had a run in the first team but had fallen out of favour recently.

O'Shea said "*I had a chat with Sonny on Monday and although like any player he was disappointed not to be playing in the first team regularly, I felt he would be happy to stay at the Pan with the run of important games coming up, support the squad and work hard to win his place back.*"

"However, he wanted to play football and I've now agreed a loan deal with Gary Croydon at Burgess Hill who will take Sonny until the end of the season."

But there was a couple of new faces at the training ground. Well, not quite new as Nathan Green returned to the club after a strangely short period playing in Cyprus, which to me suggests that he simply went on an extended package holiday and played a bit of football on the beach. Also joining the squad was striker Kieran St Aimie who had been with the Rooks back in January 2009 on loan and more recently played against Lewes in the victory at Maidenhead last month. Both new players went straight into the squad for the away trip down the M3 at Basingstoke Town.

In one of those strange quirks of the fixture computer Lewes travelled to Basingstoke a year minus a day from the corresponding fixture last season.

On that occasion the team were again on a bit of a roll and Joe Keehan's early header was cancelled out by the home side and the points were shared. A draw today wouldn't be a bad result but with fixtures running out three points were really the only acceptable result. More and more teams were being dragged down into the relegation fight but unless Lewes could take advantage of their misfortune it would be irrelevant come the 30th April.

Big Deaksy was to be our eyes and ears for the game and with the only remit to use Twitter for the updates he did us proud in updating the fans back in East Sussex.

Basingstoke 1 Lewes 1 - The Camrose

"Wheeler starts for Basingstoke, DW on the bench for Lewes :-("
We still hadn't seen the best of our David Wheeler this season. Far too often he had been isolated on the left wing, waiting for the ball. There is no doubt he has immense talent but there are those who wonder if he is the player we need at the moment. Interestingly enough two seasons ago he went on trial at Southampton under Alan Pardew and the club seemed keen on him, but a change in ownership at the Saints had seen any potential move fall through. With Basingstoke lacking pace in the full back areas it could have been the perfect moment for him to rediscover his mojo.
"Nothing happening so far, too hot at present for silky skills"
Someone needed to do something. The first half was "dour" in the words of Cynical Dave, and coming from such a, how do you say, pessimistic Scotsman, that is saying something. The smattering of Lewes away fans took to amusing themselves by taunting the Basingstoke mascot, Stokie the Dragon (who it has to be said is a pretty decent looking mascot. Not in a sexual way, but in a well made and looked after way!).
"As the temperature drops it has been encouraging from the Rooks, almost dominant"

The Lewes midfield had been given strict orders by the looks of things, simply not to give the ball away. And they were doing that effectively, although it did mean as a spectacle it was poor value for money. But what is more important at this stage, points? or pretty football? Shut up Arsene at the back!

"Approaching half time and looking forward to David Wheeler's introduction already"

Wheeler started to warm up with ten minutes to go left in the first half. The game was crying out for someone to be brave enough to take on players. The ball was seeing very little of the pitch and the only winner seemed to be the boys who were standing outside the ground by the side of the main road collecting the ball as it frequently sailed over the fence. This would certainly take the Stoke City slot on Match of the Day (talking of which The Potters were currently 2-0 down to West Ham at Upton Park - get in there!).

"It is 0-0 HT, we can win this with Wheeler on the pitch"

"Not much goal mouth action, time for Wheeler , repeat to fade"

With little going on upfront for Lewes the time to make changes at last came just on the hour mark.

"Here comes Wheeler and St Amie, Welsh and Noel off"

And as if by magic, Lewes looked a more balanced team, and even created a few chances at last, the best of which inevitably fell to David Wheeler on 70 minutes.

"Massive chance for Wheeler, weak shot cleared off the line"

Then against the run of play Basingstoke took the lead with just ten minutes to go as David Pratt's shot from 20 yards flew past Chris Winterton.

"1-0 Basingstoke after a chance for Lewes. Good finish, well struck. Get the Ryman map out"

It is fair to say that defeat here would have a massive impact on the morale of the squad. Whilst Ebbsfleet and Woking were challenging near the top, Basingstoke were floundering in mid-table, and with games coming up against three of the top six they faced a potential disastrous run of defeats, and almost certain relegation. But then as if by magic with time almost up Big Deaksy's insistence on Wheeler in the side paid off.

"Wheeler scores 1-1. I am a tactical genius"

It may not have been the prettiest goal, in fact it would have been one straight out of that football purist Tony Pullis's book. After the ball was bobbling around the six yard box, Wheeler reacted quickest and bundled it home. According to the official timekeeper, Cynical Dave, there were 6 seconds left in the game.

"FT 1-1 fair result, no time for a winner"

So it was only a point, but taking the whole game into context the team had got the defeats in the past week out of the way and had shown some of the fight they had before Christmas. Results elsewhere weren't bad, and with a couple of the relegation threatened teams in midweek action next weekend's table could look very different. The view from Tim O'Shea after the game was one of mild disappointment.

"*It is a point gained and deservedly so although their keeper has worked harder than ours overall. We probably deserved to win it on reflection. It was a flat game and we were looking for a spark and that didn't come until they put the ball in the back of our net.*

We've got to get busy this week in strengthening the squad with a couple of our players loan deals coming to an end. We are thin in a few areas, especially up front."

A draw away from home is never a bad result but with time running out the result left the Rooks fans praying for a miracle at home.

Saturday 12th March 2011
Are you watching David Gold?

If you have just opened this book at WH Smiths at the airport and found this chapter then you may not know my true love is West Ham United. Well I am, and if you are too tight to buy this book then you will never know why I am planning on heading up the A12 to Chelmsford to watch Lewes rather than West Ham's 6th round FA Cup tie at The Britannia Stadium in Stoke-on-Trent.

The thought of having to watch my football in a half empty athletics stadium is as appealing as watching a DVD box set of Kerry Katona and Katie Price's TV highlights. From significant experience of watching games overseas in grounds where you are up to thirty metres from the action I cannot remember one match which I can say was watchable when played in such a stadium. I've been to some of the best in the world - Berlin's Olympiastadion, Barcelona's Montjuïc, Istanbul's Ataturk and Vienna's Ernst Happel, and I've been to some of the worst - Rotherham's Don Valley, Brighton's Withdean and Moscow's Dinamo Stadium. And the one thing that links them all is the fact that there is very little atmosphere, and this translates to the players. Are you listening Sullivan, Gold et al? Of course not. Our good friend Ian King wrote in When Saturday Comes this month about the real losers in the whole Olympic Stadium farce were of course the fans who simply weren't consulted. As a club member at West Ham I can certainly agree with that, never once having been asked my opinion about the move.

Perhaps they should have spent some time lower down the leagues to see what it is like in England playing in such arenas? In the Blue Square Bet South there are some nice traditional stadiums such as Braintree Town's, Hampton and Richmond Borough's Beveree and of course the Dripping Pan. There are some identikit newer grounds such as Eastleigh's, Bishop Stortford's and Staines Town. And then there is Chelmsford City's Melbourne Park.

Yes I know the history, and yes I am sure the club are very pleased to have a ground to call home after their time as nomads playing in places like Billericay, but it still doesn't get round the fact that it is an athletics stadium. They had tried to be a bit different in the fact that behind both goals they had put in temporary small terrace areas so that fans here are close to the action, but the covered seats sat some twenty metres back from the pitch meaning binoculars were as essential as a scarf on a chilly afternoon in deepest, darkest Essex.

CMF had declared today as a "Girls day out", which initially I assumed to mean that she would be looking after the little Fullers and thus I could get the train to Chelmsford with the rest of the Lewes Lunatic Fringe and have a few beers. Oh no, "Girls day out" meant CMF and her chums going out from 12pm on the piss, returning with a thong of a male stripper in her pocket and whipped cream around her mouth at 3am. So the little Fullers would be also making the envious trip to Chelmsford. Not an issue for Lolly but for Littlest Fuller it meant I had to be a bit creative in selling to her the positives of watching football in a desperate venue instead of shopping for make up or whatever eight year old girls spent their pocket money on these days.

I had amused her a few weeks ago on a trip to the El Grande Classico Paradiso, aka The Canvey Island derby at Concord Rangers when I told that I had been asked to count the official attendance, and if she did it then she would get one pence for everyone in the ground. She took a good half an hour to use her fingers and toes to tell me it was one hundred and seventy eight and then demanding £1.78 as her fee. I gave her £2 before Lolly was able to tell her that the official attendance announced over the PA was just over a thousand.

With away trips running out for the Rooks this was going to be one of the last of the season for the whole Lewes Lunatic Fringe. Chelmsford doesn't have that many pubs that could tick all of our requirement boxes - dart board, decent beer, child friendly, buxom barmaids with inappropriate dress sense. That is except the Woolpack, with its multitude of awards, games room and beers on draft such as Olde Skipper, Milk Street Amarillo and Wibblers. It was sure to be home to the legendary Viz cartoon characters The Real Ale Twats, and us of course for a couple of hours. However, they missed one simple ingredient. Food. What pub in this day and age doesn't do food. After we had asked, another chap came in and then went straight out when told there wasn't any fayre on the menu.

So we headed north for a couple of hundred yards and ended up at O'Connor's. Decent looking bar, they served food (four full Irish breakfasts please) and a nice beer garden. Two other chaps arrived, who had also ordered the breakfast. First came the news that they had run out of eggs. Then sausages, and finally the toaster was broken. All highly embarrassing when ours arrived a few minutes later with said items on, plus what appeared to be a quarter of a burger (supposedly "White Pudding"). Still it filled a hole.

Thirty minutes later we were pulling up in the Athletics stadium. Danny and Dave flashed their Student cards but with the littlest Fuller's in tow it didn't worry me as I queued in the Concession queue.

"£18.50 please".

"WHAT? I said one adult and two under 10's"

"Yes, that's right. Unless you want to go in the stands where you have to pay an extra £1 each."

"Hang on. £18.50 is 85% higher than you would pay at Lewes."

"It's average price in this league"

"Er no its not" A quick look in the back of their own matchday programme confirmed that their next away trips to Maidenhead and Bishops Stortford would be £14 and £10 respectively for the best seats in the house.

Begrudgingly I handed over my cash and we entered the ground. In the distance we could just see the pitch, separated by not only an eight lane athletics track but also the high jump and long jump tracks.

"Get used to it Stu" said Deaks as we looked onwards "This will be your view at West Ham in two years time, although it will cost twenty times more".

This game was the start of an unenviable treble of games against teams going head to head for promotion. With Farnborough Town (second) and Braintree Town (top) coming up next, this was the most "winnable" game on paper. And with the Rooks unbeaten away from home since mid January when they narrowly lost to Braintree Town hopes were high of at least a point from this one. Chelmsford City seem to be in the playoffs every season, and this year was no exception but they were fallible as recent results against Eastleigh and Hampton & Richmond Borough had proved. Yeah right....

Chelmsford City 4 Lewes 0 - Melbourne Park

This was painful. Not painful because of the poor view, the expensive admission or even the scoreline but because if one or two decisions or chances went the other way it would have been a different afternoon.

Lewes started the stronger of the two although once the ball went into the box there was no one there with any semblance of an attacking instinct. Our Dave Wheeler had started this game and was a constant thorn in the side of the Chelmsford left back who took to bullying tactics. All old school stuff. Sly little kick, pulling him up by his shirt when he had clattered into him and generally annoying him.

After the initial attacking flurry it was business as usual. Winterton was soon called into action, making a couple of excellent saves from the unfeasibly tall Rob Edmans and Jordan Sanderson. By this stage the little Fullers had headed off to the tuck shop to spend my money on Cola Cubes, Rhubarb and Custards and Sherbert Flying Saucers, so much healthier than hotdogs I am sure.

I am quite sure that my Golden Goal time of seventeen minutes was a good one, but amazingly the Rooks held out until the twenty ninth minute when a knock down wasn't cleared in the box and Gray turned and shot only for Winterton to get a hand to the ball but still saw it trickle over the line. One became two a few minutes later when Dave Rainford's mistimed header took Winterton by surprise and looped over him. Game over? Well, certainly in the first half.

It was tempting to stay in the cavernous and impressive Supporters Bar after half time. Whilst I have been disparaging about the ground and the pricing policy, there is nothing wrong with the Chelmsford fans who passionately follow their team and the ones I spoke to wished Lewes well, commentating on how much they enjoyed their visits down to the Dripping Pan.

Lewes actually started the second half the brighter, although Gary Noel, with his poncy blue boots on needed to learn to stay on his feet. Twice he theatrically fell to the floor, although it took him so long to reach the deck that the referee was already up the other end of the pitch. The Rooks earned a couple of free kicks in decent positions around the box but seemed reluctant to shoot.

Twenty minutes to go and Edmans again showed how good his close control was for Peter Crouch's body double as he wandered through the defence, rounded Winterton and was about to shoot when the keeper took his ankle away. There was no option for referee Quelch, who was up until this point quite frankly crap, but to send off the keeper. And with no substitute on the bench it was Andy Pearson who stepped forward and put the gloves on. And his first job? Trying to save a penalty of course. Which he didn't and Rainford made it 3-0.

Five minutes later and Lewes's tactic to try and get the game abandoned stepped up a gear as Ben Hunt got a second yellow for, well, who knows. Referee Quelch again showed that he had no intention of refereeing at a higher level by being so inconsistent, allowing some crunching challenges to go unpunished (especially on Dave Wheeler) yet issuing two yellows to Ben "Kate Moss" Hunt for his strong tackling. To add insult to injury Hunt had to be accompanied to the dressing rooms by not one but two stewards "just in case he went postal" so another steward told us. Jobsworth more like.

So ten minutes left and only two more red cards needed. Although the plan seemed to change when Lewes's Callum Davies decided to aim an inch perfect shot into the corner of the net, although perhaps he shouldn't have chosen his own one for his first goal of the season. Four nil, and enough was enough.

Whilst the Lewes fans rued on ninety minutes of football spoiling a good day out, Tim O'Shea was left to explain his thoughts to Patrick Marber.

"It was a remarkably bad day at the office. The result looks dreadful but we actually played OK in parts.

I wont harp on about the officials but when they had to escort him off the pitch with stewards says alot doesn't it. I have no issue with Winterton's red card but in the first half we saw a couple of other incidents which were comparable. There was simply no common sense shown by the referee all over the pitch. However, we did gift them three of the four goals.

*I am hopeful that we will be able to add one or two new additions to the squad this week, especially a goalkeeper with Chris (*Winterton) *being banned for a game now."*

It had been a painful lesson and an insight into the future that I didn't like. Athletics stadiums are for athletics, football are football and never the two should meet.

Saturday 19th March 2011
A royal flush

After three heavy defeats in the past few weeks to teams in the top eight, what else would you need to regain your confidence? What about two more games in five days again two of the top three. Of course.

The mood on the fans forum during the week ranged from despair to acceptance that the Ryman Premier League would be welcoming us next season. Whilst some fans felt this was all the fault of Tim O'Shea and his revolving door policy, others were more philosophical in that this was the culmination of the significantly higher budgets made available to some of the other teams in the league, the legacy of the financial constraints on the club and simply the fact that sitting down in East Sussex there was less of a talent pool to choose from. Any decent local players were tempted by the bright lights of the Withdean down the road in Brighton.

Whatever the reason Farnborough Town were rolling into town all guns blazing. Their return to the Blue Square Bet South had gone better than they could have ever expected, hitting the heights of second place in early March. And do we need to mention that manager Steve King was the man who took Lewes into the Conference Premier just three years ago along with a fair few of the current Farnborough squad. Obviously he would tell his team to take it easy on the Rooks wouldn't he?

Lewes 1 Farnborough Town 5 - The Dripping Pan

No comment. I should just leave it there shouldn't I?

A fine spring afternoon, great music from the Barulho samba band and a pre-match presentation to the victorious Lewes Ladies side with the newly-acquired County Cup all failed to inspire the Rooks who were two goals behind even before some people (and some of the players) had left the bar.

Former Rook Paul Booth was up to his old tricks again, scoring in the third and fifth minute as the home side made a disastrous start to the afternoon. Another former Rook Dale Binns was causing havoc down the wing and he posed a danger every time he got the ball.

A brief spell for Lewes midway through the half saw Gary Noel pull a goal back and suddenly the afternoon didn't seem so bad. But the feel-good factor didn't last long, as first Jack King and then Booth scored again before the break to send the away team in 4-1 up. To say that this was forty five minutes of hell would be an understatement.

Things improved second half for Lewes who tightened up at the back in a real case of after the horse has bolted, yet they made little impression on the Farnborough goal apart from rare forays from David Wheeler and sub Jamie Crellin.

Lewes looked to take some comfort from the game by keep a clean sheet in the second half of the game but even that wasn't to be when Ibe's late strike added more embarrassment to the score line. After the game Patrick Marber put some very tough questions to Tim O'Shea not only as a director but also as a fan of Lewes FC.

"Horrible. Very very horrible. X-rated to be honest. Defensively we were inept. If you saw that on Sunday in Mini-Soccer as a parent you would be annoyed, but this is senior football. At the end of the day it wasn't good enough and things need to be changed.

There is a need for a calming more experienced defender to slip into the back four. They are looking frightened back there. I have been looking for an experienced defender, as well as a midfielder and a forward - a spine for the team. We had identified a striker but he decided to go to Braintree Town at the eleventh hour for reasons I am not going to go into.

The dressing room was an interesting place at half time with a number of players quick to express their opinion and we did come out a stronger team in the second half.

If anyone has any doubts about the team and the spirit come down and watch them train. You will go away enthused by the effort and that is what we will take into the game against league leaders Braintree Town on Wednesday."

After a torrid few weeks for the team this was the last thing the club needed. Still only leaders Braintree Town up next in just four days time!

Wednesday 23rd March 2011
The Only way is Essex

This chapter has NOTHING to do with that trashy reality TV programme of the same name. I have no interest in the fake tans, fake boobs, fake accents and the lives of people from Britain's most derided county (OK, fake boobs are alright if you insist). Instead this is about football. More specifically one of the biggest banker away victories known to man. Runaway (ish) leaders against second from bottom in the Blue Square Bet South. A team in form and nailed on for promotion against one that has lost heavily in four of their last five games.

Hardly ideal current form, although it has to be added that the four games where Lewes have lost in have been against second, third, fourth and fifth in the league. So it makes sense to get Braintree Town, top of the pile, out of the way before the serious business of avoiding relegation can start again.

Not that Lewes were suggesting that this game was a foregone conclusion. Far from it. When the two sides met back in January, The Rooks can count themselves unlucky to come away from Essex with nothing at all after a narrow 1-0 defeat. And of course there was the lucky omen coming into play. Lewes had not lost a single game when the sun was shining, on a midweek game, this season, to a team beginning with B. One has to clutch any straw at this time of the season.

The Rooks forum was full of doom and gloom leading up to the game. Knives were definitely out for the management duo of Tim O'Shea and Neil Smith. Fans have very short memories and if they could remember back just twelve months then they should (and I repeat should) feel lucky there was still a team to go and watch.

After this match Lewes have got seven games left, all against teams in the bottom half of the table (well, six plus one against current tenth) and all winnable. So forgive me for closing the door on the proverbial fat lady for now.

It wouldn't be a normal week at Lewes unless there was a few new players arriving. Last week Crystal Palace youngster Charlie Holness arrived on loan in time for the heavy defeat to Farnborough (trivia fact: Bob Holness was the first person to play James Bond in a 1954 radio production of Casino Royale AND his daughter was one of the members of 80's one hit wonders Toto Coelo). Prior to this game Joe Dolan arrived on loan from Basingstoke Town, although he is actually registered to Kingstonian, to add the much needed muscle to the back four.

So the sun was shining, the ground looked marvelous and there was still a few beers left over from the Real Ale festival last week. What more could a man want? What about the love of a good woman? That would be good, and as CMF had been away all week for business (I ask you, who would just abandon their family for work?) I was in need of some love and affection. But that could wait until full time surely? OK then let's compromise on three lovely points. Surely miracles do happen?

Lewes 2 Braintree Town 1 - The Dripping Pan

At 9.37pm there was proof that the God of Football (will we one day know him as Blatter?) was alive and well and smiling down on a small town in East Sussex. This was a shock result, make no bones about it. Not because Lewes were down and out, nor because Braintree rode into town in their pink Cadillac as unbeatable giants but because the difference four days makes.

On Saturday the atmosphere was flat, the team lethargic and the clouds of depression hung overhead. There was real doom and gloom in and around the club after the thumping home defeat against Farnborough. But the core of fans still believe. They believe in what the club is trying to do. One of my mantras in live is "Get big, get niche or get out" and I firmly believe that the club is going for the niche option. But all of the great stuff that is happening off the pitch requires some delivery on it, and with results marginally going in the favour of the Rooks on Tuesday night we knew a win would close the gap on fourth from bottom (and thus safety) to one point. One point from potential safety, repeat to fade.

The evening had started well for me as I arrived earlier than planned into Lewes. What could be better than the sun shining on an empty ground? Well how about finding a ball and practicing my twenty five yard free kicks with Charlie Dobres. I was hoping that Jermaine Wright was secretly watching as his efforts from similar distances in recent weeks weren't impressive at all. I was quite pleased with my efforts, and capped off the session with a Ravanelli style shirt over the head celebration, to the bemusement of a few people who were in the ground already.

Getting that out of my system I headed off, found Deaks and Cynical and started on the usual game of trying to work out the answers to Dave's usual fiendishly difficult quiz questions (Q: How many times has the European/Champions League final been played in Britain, and name six Scottish Premier League players who have played for West Ham United, were this week's posers). With the Lewes Lunatic Fringe Premier League darts championship out of the way we were walking down St. Swithun's Terrace to the ground with all the talk of a draw being a good result.

Words cannot describe the emotions of the next two hours. As if Jermaine Wright had been secretly watching me prior to the game he fired in a free kick from twenty five yards (sorry, twenty two point eight six metres as I was corrected on Twitter), which may or may not have got a touch from new signing Joe Dolan on the way through. Boyesy said it did, after the game Jermaine Wright said it didn't. Who do we believe? Who cares, Lewes were one nil up.

Patrick reminded us that we had never lost after being one nil up this season. I reminded him that we have never lost at home in midweek to a team beginning with B all season. We both nodded in agreement, scared to say anymore just in case it all went wrong. So what could go wrong?

Town equalised in the sixty fifth minute after a controversial free kick was turned in by Cliff Akurang, playing against Lewes for the third different team this season (Thurrock and Maidenhead being the other two) but that only spurred the Rooks on and both David Wheeler and Ben Hunt had chances blocked as they continued to press. The atmosphere in the ground was building and there was a sense that this would be our moment, as Martine McCutcheon had once whispered into my ear (via headphones before anyone goes running to CMF with a tail of adultery).

Chris Breach was denied a penalty after his goal bound header appeared to strike a defender's arm and then Braintree almost went ahead when Glenn Poole's shot across the face of goal bounced against the far post and into Winterton's arms who knew little about it until the ball hit him in the stomach.

Then with ten minutes to go Charlie Holness won a corner. The ball was delivered into the ruck of players, it bobbled around a bit before David Wheeler, sorry, OUR David Wheeler stuck out a leg and diverted the ball into the side of the net. To say the roof came off the terrace would be an understatement. Beer was thrown in the air and Wheeler rushed to Deaks, Dave and Kev in a sight that would have terrified most mortal men. As if that wasn't enough, Nick Williams ran along the terrace to join in too. That would be Chief Executive Office of Lewes FC Nick Williams.

The final few minutes played out in midfield with little of the nerves we have seen in the past such as against Dartford or Bromley. A final blast on the whistle brought hugs, cheers and massive applause from the three hundred and thirty or so Lewes fans. The hardcore. The believers. And talking of believers, Tim O'Shea and Chris Breach faced up to the questions of Patrick Marber.

"*It was an enjoyable performance out there today. The gaffer chose to take the positives out of the game against Farnborough on Saturday and gave it to us in training on Monday.*" Chris Breach started before ToSH took over.

"I think Joe Dolan came in tonight and slotted in beautifully at the back with Breachie. Whilst I am ecstatic tonight I am also frustrated as this is how we can play and we should have played like this over the past month. Whilst we rode out luck at times, we created chances. Our back four were brilliant tonight."

Breach finished off the conversation with his thoughts on where the team would go from here. *"We need to keep believing. We know we are more than capable. Earlier in the season we played the league leaders and only lost by the odd goal. Tonight will serve us well going into the game against Dartford on Saturday.*

In the Rook Inn afterwards the beer flowed. Reduced to £1 everyone was in the party mood. If there was an old Joanna (piano) I am sure there would have been a right ol' knees up. Jellied eels an' all. So one swallow does not make a summer, but one win breathes life, hope and spirit back into the team. Braintree will go on I am sure to be there or there abouts at the end of the season. But for one night only the only way for them to go was back to Essex licking their wounds after being savaged by a hungry story-telling of Rooks...

An interview with Patrick Marber

You would think Patrick would be a relieved man. Just eight hours after dropping him home from a night of high emotion after the win versus Braintree Town we were sitting opposite each other over breakfast in Smithfields Market. He was still on edge, worrying whether St Albans would get all or just some of their points back from their FA appeal. He had gone through each fixture in his head, sure that if we could beat x, draw with y and scrape a victory versus z we would be safe.

It is hard to believe that an Oscar nominated screen writer who has an address book with more A-list celebrities in than Imogen Thomas would be involved in such a small club as Lewes. My obvious first question was "Why?". The answer could not have been more beautifully crafted if Richard Curtis himself would have penned it.

"*One day I was in town with my son and we needed to park near the station. Of course I was aware of the football club, and had a vague idea of where they played. Being an Arsenal season ticket holder meant I didn't really pay much attention to the lower leagues but I knew that they had been relegated* (from the Blue Square Premier) *the previous season and were struggling a bit. As we got out of the car the gates were open. It was a fantastic late autumn day, with the sun shining and the pitch looked beautiful. By chance my son had a ball with him so we thought what the heck and jumped onto the pitch and had a kick around.*

I liked what I saw and so came to a game a few weeks later. I loved the refreshing atmosphere, and despite them winning I heard from friends who were regulars that the club were in trouble both on and off the pitch."

Patrick did a bit more research and got the number for manager Steve Ibbitson and rang him out of the blue one day in December 2009. They agreed to meet and on a cold wet day in mid December sat in the home dressing room for a couple of hours, talking about the club, Ibbo's dream and all the positives there was around the club. Patrick was transfixed. He had no idea on the workings of a football club, what sort of operational budget they worked on or what he would be letting himself in for but in his words decided that this was his "fedora" moment. He was introduced to Charlie (Dobres) at Christmas time and the two started working on what could be done.

In late January the tax bill and the immediate threat of winding up from HMRC was a real wake up call for the club. He was introduced through a friend to Eddie (Ramsden) and between them they gave the club some money to get over the immediate obstacles. However, at this stage there was no plan to take over the club. That came when Charlie started investigating the idea of a Community Benefit Society.

But as the weeks progressed the romantic vision of being a part owner in a football club began to germinate in his head. Without action there simply would have not been a club in twelve months time. And in Patrick's words, *"Without Ibbo we would have not got involved".*

It is fair to say that Lewes took over Patrick's every waking hour in the months after the summer take over. He would worry continuously about things at the club. Was there enough toilet rolls, what would visiting officials make of our half time spread, why do so many people get in without paying? He still worries now if he thinks anyone (supporters included) are unhappy. Whilst he may be sorely tempted to jump onto the forum to respond to some of the criticism that comes about team selection, style of play or lack of chips in the food van, He simply cannot because he knows that once he starts he will not be able to stop.

He has recently moved back to London so that he can try and actually work on non football related projects, finish a screen play here, writing a book there. But the obvious question is "Is there a screen play in there somewhere about your experiences?" and of course the answer is "*Yes. Not if but when.*" But who will play Ibbo?

Saturday 26th March 2011
Back to earth with a Dart

Ah Dartford. Let me count the ways I love you. The best stadium in Non League football bar Lewes's Dripping Pan. A great set of fans. An easy journey from TBIR Towers and almost walking distance from The Current Mrs Fuller Senior's house (aka my Mum) meaning I could drop my washing off pre-game and pick it up all washed, dried and ironed afterwards. It was going to be perfect. Apart from the fact that I was going to be in Belgium.

Actually as events transpired, Danny, Big Deaks and myself could have been at Princes Park and still been in Royal Antwerp for kick off for their game versus Bossou later in the evening. As Wales were hosting England in another dull international the game had been brought forward to 1pm. All a bit too little too late for us as we were heading away on the Eurostar at lunchtime, along with a dozen Forest Green Rovers, a Swindon Town, and a Tooting & Mitcham fan for a weekend of jolly japes in Antwerp. If we had known that the game was being brought forward we could have hot footed it away from Princes Park to Ebbsfleet International in time for the 3.30pm train.

So without Big Deaksy it would be up to Cynical Dave to give us updates. Dave, relishing in his new found fame as a media star after James Boyes's iconic pictures of him celebrating with David Wheeler after scoring (David not Dave) the winner against Braintree Town, doesn't really use his mobile meaning that text updates, let alone Facebook or Twitter updates may be a bit delayed. In fact some three hours after the final whistle we received the first update from Princes Park after he forgot to press the "send" button.

Dartford 3 Lewes 0 - Princess Park

Lewes were brought back down to earth with a bump after the midweek Braintree victory, as a disappointing performance saw them lose 3-0 at Dartford. Boss Tim O'Shea made two enforced changes to the starting line-up, with suspended duo Chris Winterton and Joe Dolan being replaced in the side by Conor Gough, who was making his debut after joining on work experience from Charlton Athletic, and Andy Pearson.

Having produced such an impressive, hard-working performance on

Wednesday night to beat the league leaders Braintree Town , it was always going to be difficult for the Rooks to replicate that level of performance. This became evident in the opening exchanges, when Conor Gough was forced into two fine saves to deny Lee Burns and Lee Noble inside the opening couple of minutes.

It was therefore not a surprise when the hosts took the lead after just four minutes. The goal was scored by Danny Harris, who capitalised on a moment of indecision between Lewis Hamilton and Ishmael Welsh, unleashing a superb half-volley across Gough and into the top corner from all of twenty five yards.

Harris nearly doubled Dartford's lead just minutes later, as he sent a far post header just wide following good build-up play down the left wing. It was all Dartford at this stage and there didn't seem to be any sign of the Lewes fighting spirit until the fifteenth minute when Jermaine Wright had a chance to equalise but his volley was tame.

The hosts should have doubled their lead soon after, as Burns scuffed his shot comfortably wide when clean through on goal but it was only a matter of time you felt before the second came and sure enough on twenty five minutes the goal was scored by Charlie Sheringham, who appeared to deflect a powerful header from Paul Goodacre past Gough. Well, if such efforts are worthy of his father in a Champions League final then they are surely worthy at this level too.

Half time gave O'Shea an opportunity to change things around as it was obvious to the twenty or so Lewes fans that there was no way back into this game with the same approach. And it has to be said that Lewes started the second half brightly, with Ben Hunt and Andy Pearson both seeing efforts saved by Young from set-pieces.

The best chance the Rooks created came just after the hour mark, when a swift counter-attack following a Dartford corner ended with David Wheeler sending a half-volley just wide of the near post. So close but this was really Lewes's last chance to get back into the game.

The hosts added a third goal in the fourth minute of injury time, as substitute Jon Main clipped a cross to the far post, where Sheringham was able to chest the ball down and finish well into the bottom corner. The three nil scoreline brought an unwelcome return to the recent form prior to the Braintree game. Lewes were below-par for much of this game, with Dartford able to see out the second half with ease after putting themselves in an excellent position to win the game inside the first twenty five minutes. Patrick Marber tried to get to the bottom as to why seventy two hours had proved so different in the team's fortunes with Tim O'Shea

"Is it about pressure? Nobody expected us to get a result on Wednesday yet today people thought we could get a result here at Dartford. Again, we conceded an early goal. I am disappointed at the goals we concede so early. The team leave the dressing room fully prepared. Whilst it was a good strike he should not have had an opportunity to take the shot.

On Wednesday I will field a strong side for the Sussex Senior Cup quarter final but I will also include every local player in the squad. This is their competition and I want to give them a chance to play against their local heroes and the biggest side in the county. Then we move onto Maidenhead on Saturday. We are awaiting some calls from other managers in the Football League to see who we can bring in on loan.

I do not think Wednesday was a fluke performance. They are all capable of those performances every week, but they can also have performances like today. But we are still fighting and we will not give up."

Back to the drawing board for O'Shea and Smith following this game you felt. With all of the teams around Lewes having an opportunity to gain points in midweek, it was not the result that they wanted or expected.

Wednesday 30th March 2011
American Express? Not today thank you

Three weeks ago the Sussex FA announced that this season's County Cup Final would be played in the American Express Community Stadium, the brand spanking new home of Brighton & Hove Albion located just a few miles from the Dripping Pan. Not only would the game be played there, but it was also due to be the first competitive game in the new stadium. The remaining eight teams in the competition licked their lips in anticipation at the prospect of a great occasion, none more so than Brighton & Hove Albion themselves who would be highly embarrassed if they were not taking part in the final.

All very commendable but Lewes stood in the way. The draw for the quarter finals had paired the neighbours some weeks before with the game being due to be played at Brighton's training ground in Lancing. However, this game with so much at stake allowed the Lewes board to convince Brighton & Hove Albion to switch the game to the Dripping Pan.

The cup arrived at a time when morale was at its lowest ebb for Lewes, whilst things could not be better in the Brighton camp. Top of nPower League One by some distance after a win at Dagenham & Redbridge the previous night, the Albion came into the game relishing the chance to put one over on the Rooks. Whilst the squad for the County Cup would be made up mainly of reserve and youth team players, they were still playing for the shirt. And with first team boss Gus Poyet parking up outside the ground an hour before kick off they wanted to make an impression.

Lewes 0 Brighton & Hove Albion 1 - The Dripping Pan

Lewes were knocked out the Sussex Senior Cup quarter final thanks to a narrow defeat by Brighton & Hove Albion reserves. The Rooks held their own throughout the game and on balance were unlucky not to have forced extra time as they finshed in control of the game.

As with recent home games Lewes went behind very early in the game when Leon Redwood finished off a move started by Ryan Simmonds to put Brighton one nil up with barely three minutes on the clock.

The early goal failed to spark the game into life with neither side able to take the initiative and the game was generally devoid of any further clear cut chances for either side. In fact there was little to cheer, talk or even write about until the thirty fifth minute when Lewes debutant Pat O'Connor was shown a straight red card after he squared up to Agusten Battipeldi. From the terraces it appeared that there was no contact between the two players, with the Brighton man falling easily to the ground holding his face. In fact the referee took time to consult with his assistant before brandishing the card must to the disgust of the home fans.

Two minutes later there was more controversy as former Rook and the hero of Hampton & Richmond Grant Hall brought down Gary Noel. It appeared the challenge was in the penalty area and certainly denied Noel a goal scoring opportunity but the referee did not see it that way, only booking Hall and awarding a free kick outside of the penalty area.

The second half followed the pattern of the first half with Brighton being content to play the ball around without threatening the Lewes goal, whilst Lewes did not do enough to put the Albion defence under pressure. Brighton's Gary Hart and substitute Torbjorn Agdestein both had half chances but neither were too much trouble for Lewes keeper Chris Winterton.

With fifteen minutes to go a strong run down the left wing from Lewes sub Nathan Green almost saw Noel convert at the near post but Seagulls keeper Mitchell Walker beat him to the ball.

Brighton were reduced to ten men when bad boy Battipeldi's challenge on David Wheeler earned him a second yellow in the 80th minute and suddenly the crowd were lifted as they sensed an equaliser. Lewes upped their game and piled forward, with Walker stopping a late Breach header, but their late charge was not enough and the final of the Senior Cup at the Amex won't be graced by the Rooks this season. However, with six cup finals still to play in the league Lewes will be hoping that league survival is the ultimate prize.

Neil Smith summed up the thoughts of the team after the game with Patrick Marber.

"*Another early goal conceded but we battled well for eight eight minutes.*

We have six cup finals left and we were very pleased with the performance apart from that first two minutes. We went down to ten men for a decision we will dispute. But the team stuck to the game plan.

We have a big twenty four hours ahead as after that we cannot sign anyone else for the rest of the season. We wont give up until the final whistle at every game. ToSH and I were at Thurrock v Bromley last night and it was a nail biting end to that game. But every week is going to be like that and we cannot rely on anyone helping us, we have to win our games to get out of this."

Well, who wanted to play in a brand new stadium, in front of ten thousand people anyway.

Saturday 2nd April 2011
All's fair in love and football

You do feel for clubs that are penalised with points penalties through no fault of the current players or management team. You feel even sorrier for the fans. I know from bitter experience as a West Ham fan over the whole Tevez affair that your name can be dragged through the mud and the team suffer (yes, yes I know we should have been relegated but can we let that go now Blades fans) for years to come.

But what happens if the penalty happens to a promotion or relegation rival of your team? What happens if the harsh penalty actually works significantly to your benefit? Where do you stand then? Deep down you may feel sorry for the club, but outwardly are you not just walking around with a smile that the Mona Lisa would be proud of?

Just such an event happened yesterday, April Fools Day. And whilst the FA are seen as a joke by many in the way they run our national game, especially at grass roots level, the decision was made after midday thus condemning them to another year of being the fool if it wasn't true (as if they would need an excuse to continue their bizarre running of the game anyway).

St Albans City, fighting relegation from the Blue Square Bet South had their ten point penalty for financial irregularities upheld. The decision, relating back to events from over three years ago (!) has effectively relegated the team from the division. They are now twelve points from safety with just six games to go. If they do manage to get out of the situation then they deserve a spot in the Champions League. It is hard to see where the club will go from here, as they have been on the brink of financial crisis for a few seasons now. In fact on our last visit there in August 2009 saw them at odds with their programme printers and a simple A4 photocopied sheet was available (Another ridiculous FA rule - if a programme isn't produced a club faces a fine or points penalties).

Their misfortune worked in the favour of the other teams at the bottom, including Lewes and Maidenhead United who were also in the bottom three. And guess what the next game of the season is? Yep, Lewes were hosting Maidenhead United.

So IF Lewes could win, perhaps rediscovering the Braintree rather than the Dartford /Farnborough /Woking /Ebbsfleet /Chelmsford form then they could potentially climb out of the relegation zone for the first time in months and put five and eleven points respectively between the other two teams in the drop zone. Six pointer? This was going to be a twelve pointer!

This week also saw the non league loan deadline day. With few teams able to afford long term signings, the loan system is the only way some teams can compete. Lewes have used it extensively this season (around thirty players had come in on loan) and so it was no surprise to welcome a few new faces into the squad for the relegation run in:-

- Millwall defender Pat O'Conner (sent off on his debut against Brighton & Hove Albion in midweek)
- Striker Andy Hutchinson from Lincoln City
- Defender Mitchell Nelson from Bournemouth
- Striker Danny Buckle from Walton Casuals
- Goalkeeper Josh Wills from Sussex League side Sidley United

The Pan needed some lifting after the disappointing defeat in midweek to Brighton & Hove Albion in the quarter final of the Sussex Senior Cup. With the final being the first competitive game to be played in the new Amex Community Stadium, the prize was tantilisingly good but a strong Rooks team could not overcome the Seagulls. So it was going to be left to the Lewes faithful to lift spirits as Maidenhead rolled into town.

Lewes had been in the news this week for a number of reasons. Firstly because the press had picked up on the fact Nigella Lawson (and husband Charles Saatchi) had invested in the club. Not exactly a lie but not exactly true either. They had both become pioneer shareholders in the club, investing a fixed sum of £1,000 in return for one share in the community club. Just like over sixty other people had. The constitution of Lewes FC means that no one can actually own more than one share so I would hardly call this a "proposed takeover" as some people speculated.

And then yesterday. April Fools Day. One of the best football related gags was the news that Internationally-renowned sculptor Antony Gormley had agreed to create a modern sculpture that would be positioned in the currently vacant south-east corner of the ground.

Based on the Angel of the North in Gateshead, the 'Rook of the South' would be a seventy foot high sculpture of a rook - Lewes FC's nickname - with a hundred foot wingspan, constructed of weather resistant corten steel. Before any NIMBYs got too excited the last line of the article said plans would be available for anyone to see at the club until midday. I wonder how many people actually turned up?

The sun was out and I was being joined for the match than none other that Tom "The Pie Man" Dickinson, a man who knows a thing about football grounds and football cuisine. Tom recently published the story of his monumental trip around the Ninety Tow Premier and Football League grounds, enjoying (well eating at least) a pie in each one. He was going to be disappointed at the Pan as pies are not on the agenda. Still a few Harvey's down his neck would be ample compensation I am sure.

Lewes 1 Maidenhead United 0 - The Dripping Pan

The question that was being tossed about in the Rook Inn pre-match was which Lewes team would turn up today. The Braintree bravehearts or the woeful Woking wasters. O'Shea was able to recall Winterton in goal and Joe Dolan at the back after suspension and also added in debutants Paul O'Conner, Andy Hutchinson and Mitchell Nelson.

Ninety minutes later we had our answer. Sure it wasn't pretty but most of the near seven hundred in the ground will have seen the improvement in the defence. Dolan, a man who someone said to be was "more of a donkey than an actual donkey" was immense for the second home game in a row and won a deserved man of the match award. Breach continues to impress with every game and Nelson added pace that veteran Anthony Barness once had in his Bolton days.

There was really only one talking point. As a relatively nondescript first half entered injury time Hutchinson managed to get in front of the defender after a long punt up field. From our vantage point at the top of the Jungle we could see him go down under a challenge from the Maidenhead centre back. At first the referee said "get up" but then out of the corner of his eye, and ours was a waving yellow flag. The linesman had seen what we had. PENALTY.ow correct me if I am wrong here but Hutchinson had got in front of the LAST MAN. He had been FOULED in the PENALTY AREA as he prepared to take a GOALSCORING OPPORTUNITY. Add those four facts together and you get......nothing. The referee did not even book the defender. Still we had a penalty and Gary Noel stepped up and sent the keeper the wrong way. As a dancing Patrick Marber informed me mid-embrace "We've never lost after taking a first half lead".

There wasn't the same confidence we had seen in the Rook Inn against Braintree Town at half time. There was an air of nervousness, especially as scores elsewhere were not as good as could be expected. But at this stage of the season the fate of Lewes still lay in their own hands. Four wins from six would almost certainly lead Lewes to the promised land of safety.

So what can I tell you about the second half. Not a lot really. I couldn't even blame the Harveys this week. It was simply not a good forty five minute period. Wheeler kept tormenting the full back, Dolan and Breach kept things tight and substitute Danny Buckle (the rather large Danny Buckle) gave the two Maidenhead centre backs a torrid time.

Ninety minutes were up and do you know what? There wasn't any of the nervousness on the pitch that we had seen against other sides earlier in the season. In fact it was all relatively calm. With four minutes of injury time up the Maidenhead keeper decided to go on a run with the ball. One of those that you try on FIFA 10 where you try and take on everyone in the whole team. Well he beat Hutchinson and then Wheeler. As he crossed the half way line the referee blew for full time. Good job too as he lost control of the ball and Charlie Holness shot just as the whistle went. The ball, for all it was worth slowly trickled towards the goal, eventually hitting the post and just sat there, like a forgotten toy at Christmas, all alone, wanting to take part in the party, but no one invited it in (enough now!).

It was now all about results elsewhere. Five years ago we would all be crowded around a terrace tranny (a radio not a cross dresser!) waiting for the other results, but today there we all were on our iPhones checking Livescore and NLN24 with the full times from Thurrock (won, booo), Dover (defeat for Stortford - yes!) and Hampton (draw - ok). Unsurprisingly there were smiles all round again after the game as Neil Smith spoke to Patrick Marber.

"*A very important and deserved win. It is not nice watching that big clock in the corner ticking down in circumstances like that. It was a definite penalty. He earnt the penalty by chasing it down. I didn't watch it - my head was in my hands. Dolan had a great game, he looked like a winner alongside Breachie. Saturday is a long trip but we need to roll our sleeves up and fight for the points."*

In the space of twenty four hours Lewes had gone from relegation certainties to survival fighters thanks to the FA, an eagle eyed linesman and two good old fashioned centre backs. All is not fair in life, but on a day like today who cares - sorry St Albans City!

Saturday 9th April 2011
The Diceman cometh

Dicemen, the plan: Two creatures (Danny and Stuart) whose actions for one day only will be decided by the roll of a dice, the dice choosing from among options created by men - whom have had too much time on their hands. Danny takes up the story.

"Stuart and I often revel in the thought of implementing silly ideas into practice (such as hiring a coach to take forty fans across two countries to watch a Slovakian Division Two game). So, when I suggested to him that we should set aside a precious Saturday, and leave it in the hands of dice, he agreed. He always agrees.

Within ten minutes (he's good like that), he had drawn up a list of thirty six potential games to attend and sectioned them off into regional zones.

So with the dice in position before us, we knelt silently a prayed. Prayed for a fixture not too close to Bermondsey; Millwall were at home to Leeds United and things could potentially get messy around the London Bridge area. Littlest Fuller picked up the dice and began shaking it gaily in the bowl of her hands. Holding the dice above her head she intoned aloud 'Great bleak Blocks of God, descend, quiver, create, Into your hands I commit our soul. Oh, and whilst you're on please don't send the lads back to Walton Casuals.'

The dice fell: it was a five. It rolled again: a three - we were off to Walton Casuals. At this point sense took over.

Dicemen, the reality: I've been to Walton Casuals. I've been there on derby day and did pretty much every pub in town in the process. It was all as good as gold and that, but I didn't fancy going back. How can you beat the Walton derby? You can't, obviously. So, thinking quickly, we decided to go our separate ways. Stuart was to head to the garden of England for a double dose of Kentish football, and I was to join the Lewes Lunatic Fringe in Dorset for the Rooks crucial game with fellow strugglers Dorchester Town. Don't worry, we're still talking.

Two things immediately struck me as I exited Dorchester South train station;

firstly, a magnificent building, namely, The Dorchester Brewery. As my old pal Alfred Barnard noted back in 1889: "..it is certainly the finest specimen of architecture in the district with its imposing structure combing the useful and the beautiful to an eminent degree." He knew his brewing and architectural onions did Mr B. Second thing worthy of note was the pub just down the road called The Station. A pretty dire looking establishment granted, but they had a tribute act on called The Stereoironics. Of course The Stereoironics. We chuckled, gave it a wide birth and moved on.

Tom Browns, 47 High East St, Dorchester: Live music, dartboard, jukebox, extensive pub garden, Dorest Brewing Company Ales plus Tom Brown's house bitter variety of guests own beer. How many pre-match boxes do you want to tick Tom old chap? In we went and lowered a couple of pints of Old Piddle.

The other place in town that embraced local ales was The Colliton Club. £4 for lunch, a skittle alley, choice of six local ales (as advertised) and a cheese and wine evening in the offering for just five English pounds. The latter had of course sold out. Twelve wines and cheese for a fiver? How do they do it? It's like stepping back in time entering the Colly, but hey, it suited our grumpy old cynical needs. More Old Piddle please landlord.

Suitably refreshed we set off like lionhearts to the ground. It was such a nice day we walked (walked!) the fifteen minutes down there from town with Cynical Dave even being heard to whistle a tune. Spring was certainly in the air.

The Avenue Stadium has been knocking around for just over twenty years, and is a thing of NLB (Non-League Beauty). Take away the slightly cramped bar and you have a ground that every club at this level would rip of their shirts, beat their chest and be proud of. Even bonnie Prince Charles had been waxing lyrical about it and he is very hard to please. Weymouth like it so much they wanted to share it. Then they didn't. Nothing is straight forward with Weymouth Football Club - located six miles down the road - and supporting them must be a nightmare. Last I heard was that the Terras' offer of some solar panels (no really) wasn't the deal-clincher they'd hoped for and the whole ground-sharing idea has been filed under bin.

Lewes came into this game in decent form. Two wins and one defeat from their previous three league games. Dorchester had similar mixed form but their mascot "Dinky" was confident of the score pre-match. The bear felt that there would be five goals in the game, with a 4-1 scoreline in the Magpies favour, but his forecast was somewhat inaccurate at the end of a scrappy game.

Dorchester Town 0 Lewes 0 - The Avenue Stadium

Lewes were slightly more desperate than their hosts for a win to lift them out of the relegation places. Ninety fairly uninspiring minutes later and both teams were a point better off thanks to a goalless draw. Highly rated defender Gary Bowles had the home sides best moment striking a post for the Magpies whilst on-loan striker Andy Hutchinson had the best chances of the first half for the Rooks, slicing one shot wide when clear through and agonisingly heading the same way with a point blank header after Gary Noel had distracted the keeper on the stroke of half time. How we grimaced.

The Rooks rode their luck at times, Dorchester being denied by the post and keeper Chris Winterton's reactions but even he could only watch as a Ryan Moss shot went the wrong side of the far post.

Chris Breach and David Wheeler had a chance each that their overall play deserved in the second period but the game was to end in a draw after a confident and at times nervy display for Lewes.

News elsewhere was favourable in terms of Lewes clinging on to their Conference South survival. Both Thurrock and The Bish lost, and so on reflection, this could well have been a good point well made. Two wins and a draw from the last four games may well be enough to ensure renewed acquaintances, rivalry and crowds in the thousands against Eastbourne Borough next season.

After the game in the Wessex sunshine Tim O'Shea chatted to Patrick Marber on the pitch about the game, and the fight in general to stay up.

"*It would have been a kick in the proverbials if we had have come away today with nothing. We had the better of the chances such as Andy Hutchinson's header in the first half. The draw was nothing less than we deserved. Chris* (Winterton) *was brilliant again, making a couple of excellent saves. We played our part in an entertaining game. We couldn't fault the team on commitment today.*

Let's hope that Weston-Super-Mare have already packed their cases for Magaluf next Saturday and we can take advantage of it."

Saturday 16th April 2011
Buckle up

Here is my tip of the year. If you are planning on having children, look to conceive them in October and November. That way you will not have to sacrifice a day of football to spend it in retail hell such as Build-a-Bear Workshop. Whilst I dearly love my youngest daughter, the idea of spending her eighth birthday with me at The Dripping Pan was never at the races. So whilst the rest of the Lewes Lunatic Fringe would be sipping Harvey's on the Jungle I would be standing like a plum in Claire's Accessories. However, with all that time on my hands I was able to work out the odds of missing a home game in her first eight years, as well as when I could expect to miss the next one. Fortunately it isn't until 2015 by which time I doubt she will want to be seen out in public with me!

At the start of the season the expectations were that Weston-Super-Mare would be fighting relegation. Last season they finished in the bottom three but were reprieved due to gaps in the leagues left by teams going to the wall. With crowds often failing to break the two hundred and fifty mark you have to wonder how they have managed to do so well this season. Home form has been impressive and this is what has kept them in the division. Their away form is actually the second worst in the division so it was with this in mind that Lewes had hyped the game up as the biggest of the season. "A real six pointer" Chief Executive Nick Williams Tweeted on the morning of the game.

So with my eyes firmly glued on NonLeague News's vidiprinter I headed into Hello Kitty hell...

Lewes 1 Weston Super Mare 1 - The Dripping Pan

As the referee blew the final whistle the optimists in the crowd saw this as a point gained in the fight for relegation. However, the majority saw an opportunity missed to close the gap and coupled with wins for Maidenhead United and Boreham Wood the number of teams involved in the dog fight had been reduced. The glimmer of hope was that Bishop Stortford's recent form continued to be poor and with the Bishops due to visit the Dripping Pan in just over a week it could all rest on the last ninety minutes of football at the Pan this season.

The Rooks were the hungrier side from the kick off and were unlucky not to have been awarded a first half penalty when Andy Hutchinson was brought down inside the area. Nerves could be felt all across the ground, affecting the manager, the players and of course the crowd. Even the presence of actor Rupert Graves, a (sorry should that read only) Weston-Super-Mare fan could provide any excitement. The first half came and went in a blink of an eye.

Lewes went ahead in the fifty sixth minute when a sustained attack down the right saw Gary Noel's header cleared as far as Rory Hill who's shot just squeezed in at the far post. It was no less than the hosts deserved with Weston giving the impression that they weren't all that bothered what happened during the game, an attitude which was compounded by time wasting from early in the first half. With their position in the division secure they literally had nothing to play for.

So could we rely on them to roll over? Er no. Someone didn't tell Kane Ingram this in the sixty fourth minute when he equalised, capitalising on some uncertainty in the Lewes penalty. It was almost even worse when they appeared to have a perfectly good goal disallowed for offside a few minutes later.

But the final controversy in the game came in the ninetieth minute when Lewes substitute Danny Buckle saw his spectacular overhead kick ruled out apparently for a foul committed by Joe Dolan in the run up to the goal. No one, apart from the referee saw the offence and after Weston's Nat Pepperrell had wasted the final chance of the game and the full time whistle blew, Lewes surrounded the officials to try and understand what he saw. Of course he refused to answer any questions. Respect works both ways. Instead Chris Breach won the honour of speaking to Patrick Marber after the game.

"*We are led to believe that Joe, who flicked the ball on, nudged the defender. There is contact all over the pitch and if you give that, you should have given us a penalty in the first half. Their players didn't exactly appeal against the decision did they?*

We all still believe that we will get out of this. The guys are frustrated in the dressing room. We haven't lost, but look at today and last week's and we only got two points and we should have got more. We are more than capable of going to Havant and winning next week though."

The mood after the game was somber as you can imagine. This was a must win game, and a draw just wasn't enough. For the first time even the most realistic fans started preparing for life in the Ryman League.

Saturday 23rd April 2011
The battle of Waterloo..ville

What is it with teams at the bottom of the league who start winning at the end of the season? Maidenhead United, Bishop Stortford, Boreham Wood and Dorchester Town all started picking up points during april. Maidenhead's resurgence in form after their defeat to Lewes was put down to the lifting of a gypsy curse on their York Road ground by their managing peeing in all four corners of the pitch. Desperate times call for desperate measures. Then all of a sudden, games in hand were converted to points, meaning that Lewes had to go along the A27 into Hampshire to get at least a point from the trip to Havant & Waterlooville.

Every season the Hawks seem to be mentioned as one of the favourites for promotion. Perhaps that is just a hang over from their miraculous run in the FA Cup a few seasons ago which we mentioned earlier in the book and the fact that there is an assumption that if they can play Liverpool at Anfield in the FA Cup then they should surely be able to negotiate their way out of the Conference South.

Football doesn't work like that and at the end of the season they will look back on another disappointing campaign of mid-table mediocrity. But ask any Lewes fan if they would rather be in the Hawks or the Rooks shoes coming into this game and you will get the answer that win one, draw one, lose one is a fine strategy.

Havant & Waterlooville 1 Lewes 2 - West Leigh Park

Late goals always add drama to a game, but actually when you think about it they are far less painless than an early goal and then defending for your life for the remainder of the game. So when Ben Hunt scored in the ninetieth minute to give Lewes the lead nervousness of conceding a losing goal evaporated and the fans could breathe a sigh of relief that Lewes lived to fight another day. The 2-1 away win ensured that the Rooks did the double over Havant and Waterlooville and set up an "all or nothing" encounter on Easter Monday against Bishop Stortford.

Lewes certainly rode their luck at times, but that is just the way football deals its cards. Some weeks lady luck is playing like Lionel Messi up front, other times like Gomes in goal. The opening exchanges were relatively equal although the Rooks were relieved to see Manny Williams' half volley direct from a corner cannon off the bar to safety.

But Lewes were never outclassed in the first half. With the midfield looking strong and the ball frequently finding its way out to David Wheeler on the right it was no surprise that they took the lead just before half time. Wheeler beat the full back and opted to get the ball in early, delivering it low and hard into the six yard box. Havant keeper Howe was caught in two minds whether to stay on his line or come out for it and in the end his hesitancy caused him to spill the ball into the path of Andy Hutchinson who headed the ball into the open net for his first goal for the club.

After the break Havant showed that they weren't going to lay down at let Lewes walk all over them. Keeper Winterton was the busier of the two goalies, saving the Rooks on a number of occasions, including a vital save from a misdirected back pass. The Lewes Lunatic Fringe knew what was coming next, and sure enough on sixty seven minutes Havant substitute Guiseppe Sole sent a cross in from the left which found Mustafa Tiryaki in front of goal and his side foot volley gave WInterton little chance.

With three of the four other teams in the relegation battle winning, Lewes knew that they had to go for all three points. Tim O'Shea sent on Danny "The Unit" Buckle and Ben Hunt and these two combined to create the winning goal in the last minute. Buckle's clever ball played Hunt in and his speculative shot trickled slowly from his foot, taking what seemed an age to squeeze between the post and Howe to secure a great win for Lewes and a fourth unbeaten game on the trot.

After the match Tim O'Shea was able to face Patrick Marber with a small smile on his face.

"Ninety four minutes of that at least proves my heart is in good working order. Yes we got a bit lucky today, but how many similar goals have we conceded this season like that?

It is ironic that we have done a double over a team who were tipped for better things at the start of the season. Let's look forward to doing it again on Monday."

So the relegation battle was going to go down to the wire. You couldn't write a better script for a film. Lewes faced Bishop Stortford in just forty eight hours at The Dripping Pan. Defeat would spell relegation, and almost certainly save the visitors, whilst a Lewes win would lift them out of the relegation zone and almost condemn both The Bish and Thurrock. And to make matters worse I would have to follow events from a hundred miles north via Twitter.

Monday 25th April 2011
Check mate

I think it is fair to say that few of the people involved in the evolution of Lewes Community Football Club slept very well in the two days between the win against Havant & Waterlooville and the visit of Bishop Stortford in the final home game of the season. Every permutation had been played out in the head, every scenario double checked. Every way you cut it it came down to the same fact. Lewes had to win to survive.

There was a subdued atmosphere around the town on the morning of the game. The Rooks forum was relatively silent. Fans didn't want to speculate on what would happen if the game was lost. And of course I needed a happy ending for this book. Relegation with a game to go wasn't a good story line and wouldn't get those Hollywood screenwriters interested in turning my story into a film would it?

It is fair to say that the atmosphere at kick off was nervous. Danny and I were some one hundred miles north on the Suffolk/Essex border and we could feel the tension by just looking at the Twitter feeds. As Big Deaksy wrote as the game kicked off:-

"Don't get out the Ryman Handbook just yet"

Lewes 1 Bishop Stortford 2 - The Dripping Pan

This was not in the script but then again when in life is there a truly happy ending? The disappointment as the referee called time on the game wasn't the fact that Lewes had lost, it was the fact that they had gone down without much of a fight. Whilst the squad could be called transient based on the number of players that came and went during the season, surely they had been motivated enough to know what a win or a defeat meant in this game not just for the club or the fans but also the people of Lewes.

Tim O'Shea made one change to the side which had won at Havant & Waterlooville two days previously, with Ishmael Welsh replacing Rory Hill in the starting line-up, hoping that the combination of his pace on the left and our David Wheeler on the right would upset the attacking intent of the Bishop Stortford full backs.

Both sides struggled to get the ball down and pass it on a very dry pitch which hadn't seen any rain for a number of weeks. The visitors created the first opening when Michael Bakare evaded the challenges of Chris Breach and Lewis Hamilton but could only then scuff his shot when he only had Chris Winterton to beat.

Just before the half hour mark we got very excited. A rogue tweet appeared on our timeline. Chris Breach, get in 1-0, Come on You Rooks! We jumped around like loons, high fiving the news from The Pan. And then I lost a wireless connection. For ten blissful minutes we believed that Lewes were on their way to safety. I rebooted my phone, clicked update and saw:-

"Breach goal disallowed. Dolan foul. Bollocks"

"Stortford score - unmarked header at far post"

"2-0 Stortford. Rance easy chance in box. Is there any point in having a second half?"

And then the tweet we did not want to see "Get the Ryman Handbook out"

We had gone from ecstasy to agony in the space of ten minutes. We had lived in a world where everything was right for six hundred seconds. We had planned trips to Truro City, promoted a few days previously from the Zamaretto Premier League, and started speculating on the attendance for the Boxing Day game against Eastbourne Borough who would be joining Lewes in the Blue Square Bet South next season after their relegation. And all that was now just a dream. Goodbye Sutton United away, hello East Thurrock United.

The visitors could not believe their luck. They had strolled to a two nil lead and almost had a third when Sanchez Ming sent a thirty yard effort just wide of Winterton's goal.

To say the mood in the Rook Inn was somber was an understatement. However, miracles happen every day so for forty five more minutes the fans expected the team to throw everything at The Bishops.

O'Shea replaced the ineffective Gary Noel with Danny "The Unit" Buckle at half-time to try and add a physical threat to the Lewes attack. However, Bishop's Stortford still looked the more dangerous side going forward and it took a fine challenge from Lewis Hamilton to prevent the dangerous Bakare scoring again after he took the ball past Breach with ease.

Ben Hunt was brought on just on the hour and at last they got the message that they needed to actually get the ball into the opposition penalty area to stand a chance of scoring a goal. He almost had an immediate impact when his goal-bound effort seemed to be blocked on the line by the arm of Max Lette-Jallow, only for the referee to see something different from the eight hundred or so spectators in the ground.

With time ticking away it was clear that the pressure was getting to the team. Bakare missed another chance for the visitors and as the ball went out of play, captain Chris Breach made his feelings clear to Winterton, resulting in the two needing to be separated. The referee decided that the pair were guilty of ungentlemanly conduct and booked them both.

Breach was substituted soon after, feeling the wrath of Tim O'Shea's glance as he passed him on the touchline. His replacement was Rory Hill and with just five minutes left on the clock he fired in a free kick from the edge of the penalty area to raise the noise level inside the Dripping Pan tenfold. Five minutes plus injury time to save their season.

As the clock ticked over the ninety minute mark, Danny Buckle saw his header from a Hunt flick-on fly straight at Nicky Eyre in the visitors' goal. But that was it. The final whistle saw the players sink to their knees, whilst the visitors breathed a huge sigh of relief. They were safe, to fight for another season whilst Lewes would be playing in the Ryman Premier League.

It would have been too easy for the manager to have kept the dressing room door shut after the game to wallow in self pity, but Tim O'Shea came out and faced the camera of Patrick Marber.

"The bit that has disappointed me the most is the team performance. Quite frankly that opening half was a huge step backwards. We haven't played that bad for a long time. Yes, some of that was the nerves of the occasion. People looked afraid of making a mistake, and then we go and give away

two in two minutes. Since Joe Dolan has arrived we have had a solid base at the back so it was inexplicable. To go and perform like we did on Saturday at Havant and then to put in that forty five minutes is the major disappointment."

Over the course of the season the Rooks had picked up a few impressive results especially on the road, but the form at home had been their undoing, especially the period after Christmas which saw heavy defeats to Eastleigh, Ebbsfleet United and Woking in quick succession.

There was still pride to play for in the final game at Boreham Wood, and perhaps the final game for a number of the squad and management. Only time would tell.

Saturday 30th April 2011
"Ladies and Gentlemen, please welcome the Fat Lady"

When the fixtures were published back in the summer, a few Lewes fans looked at the last game of the season away to Boreham Wood and felt that could be crucial to the survival of the team in the league. However, they (like I) believed it would be Boreham Wood who would be fighting for their survival. Having been promoted via the play offs last season, they had one of the lowest budgets in the league, and their average attendance was comparable to the likes of Thurrock and Weston-Super-Mare. When the two teams met in February Boreham Wood were below the Rooks in the bottom three, and a swift return to the Ryman looked odds on.

However, two months is a long time in football, and Boreham Wood's ex-Arsenal midfielder Ian Allinson was able to strengthen the squad, sending the team on an impressive run that saw them rise up the table, and guarantee Blue Square Bet South football for next season with an impressive 4-1 at Dartford in mid April. So this game meant little for both sides with Lewes's relegation already confirmed. Or was it.

The saying it is always darkest before the dawn holds so many truths. Us football fans cling to any possible hope. I personally refuse to believe relegation or promotion is confirmed until it is a mathematically certainly. So you may need to score forty goals in your last game, hoping that the team above you loses by a similar amount. Well if a group on monkeys can in theory produce the complete works of Shakespeare then I will believe that the record score in an English football match could be achieved twice on one afternoon. But what you need to factor in to the equation on Lewes's relegation is the impact of other teams financial predicament.

A quick glance at the record books highlights one outstanding fact. Never in the six year history of the Conference South has a team finishing in third from last place actually been relegated. In fact on only two occasions has the team finishing second from bottom experienced demotion. Take last season as a case in point. Weymouth, who finished in twenty second place fell into the Southern League, but Weston-Super-Mare who were in twenty first place did not go down as Worcester City (twentieth) moved from

Conference South to North to balance up the numbers. Confused? You should be.

So a win against Boreham Wood, and the inevitable Farnborough win at home to Thurrock would see The Rooks leap above the Lakesiders and sit in the quasi-relegation spot. And with an impressive run of form away from home, Lewes could just get out of this situation.

Exactly a year ago I had been in the bumper crowd at Meadow Park to see Boreham Wood beat Kingstonian to secure their place in the second tier of Non League football for the first game. The match had been marred by a Boreham Wood fan running onto the field of play and attempting to strike the Kingstonian captain when the scores were level. Two further pitch invasions may have had little effect on the final two nil score line but Kingstonian felt they had a case to at least have the game replayed.

But with the usual speed we see from the football authorities in England no decision was made until AFTER the new fixtures had been published. Boreham Wood would be taking their place in the Blue Square Bet South with a slap on their wrists.

A year later as we arrived it was hard to believe it was the same place, or that there was even a game on. I had read that the home side had launched a free season ticket scheme for youngsters in the local area, which should be applauded, but to charge all other under 16's £6 was unbelievable and perhaps explained why the only two youngsters in the ground apart from the ball boys were two Lewes fans. It seemed that the free season ticket holders had something better to do on a hot Saturday afternoon.

Boreham Wood 3 Lewes 0 - Meadow Park

Despite the poor attendance it was good to see a bigger than normal Lewes travelling contingent. My one main criticism this season has been the fans have been too quick to get on the back of the team and management based on a view from home games alone. It has been the same dozen or so faces at most away games but for the last game a few more faces had come out into the sunshine. And with the game just a minute or so old they nearly had something to cheer about as a David Wheeler free kick was flicked goalwards forcing the keeper to make a fantastic one handed save.

Lewes actually played quite well for long periods of the hot first half. Talisman Wheeler, undoubtably playing his last game for the club as he heads back off to college in West London for next season, kept sending the balls in for "The Unit" aka Danny Buckle, but the Boreham Wood back four looked quite solid and surely but slowly the home team got into the game, striking the woodwork in the twenty fifth minute from a shot from distance. With time running out in the half and the bar seeming the best option for us, Boreham Wood took the lead. A corner was floated into the Lewes box and the defence were obviously concentrating on their half term oranges as Risbridger headed home.

Half time scores were looking good for a third from bottom finish as long as they could turn around this game. But they couldn't. Wilkinson doubled the lead with another header from a set piece in the sixty eighth minute and three minutes later Garrard added a third. It was harsh on Lewes but on many an occasion since Christmas they had been put to the sword by teams in the second half of games.

So the referee brought an end to the game, and Lewes's season. Where we will end up is now completely out of our hands. Rumours are rife about clubs up and down the pyramid who are looking for a way out of their current financial situation by taking a voluntary relegation. But that is for another day. The team sat on the pitch in a circle as manager Tim O'Shea debriefed them. How many would be in a similar situation in just three months time? We can but speculate.

We said our goodbyes to David Wheeler, our David Wheeler who has shown commitment to the club in the past three years and he looked genuinely sad that he was (probably) leaving the club in such a circumstances. But he has to move on.

With Patrick Marber absent for the first time today it was left to Charlie Dobres to ask the questions to the manager Tim O'Shea.

"*It has been a disappointing last few days. We did all the hard work, so we thought, at Havant but then Monday happened.*

*The first goal was a kick in the preverbials. We came out and huffed and puffed, but with one eye on events down the road (*Thurrock*) we didn't* *defend set pieces and all of a sudden it was 3-0.*

The players have worked, trained well and no lack of fitness. For the last six or so weeks we have been in good form and that is why Monday was such a downer. They were all told on Thursday about the history of third from bottom finishers in this league so they were aware of what was to play for.

*I hope and pray that there is a reprieve. The genuine fans, the players and you guys (*the Directors) *I hope something does happen as you deserve it. I've told the players to bottle the feeling and learn about disappointments like this so that they know how to avoid it. It is the first time in my career I have experienced this. I know there are some fors and against us as a team and managers and everyone is entitled to their opinion.*

If I look back it is the manner of the games where we have lost that has been the most disappointing. There hasn't been many games where we have been unlucky and we've lost. On too many occasions we have conceded a goal and soon after another one has come along like a London red bus.

My parting message for the season is to thank the genuine fans, everyone at the club and the players."

So the season ended on a low. Lewes had been outclassed by a team who at the start of the season they had expected to finish above. Boreham Wood were organised, played with passion and took their chances. Lewes weren't. Ahead would be a long summer of rebuilding and studying the Ryman Handbook. Where is Concord Rangers again?

Postscript

In early May it was announced that Tim O'Shea and Neil Smith had left the club by mutual agreement. This was hardly surprising. They had lost the faith of the fans with the number of players that came and went during the season, and the constant tinkering with the team. There were mitigating circumstances that we have already covered in what they had to work with but fans rarely see that.

Relegation was never in the plan but the changes to the structure and organisation of the club meant that it had been prepared for.
The fans would be back, hopefully in similar numbers, and for all of the fun we have made of the "Ryman Handbook" there are some good away trips to look forward to. Lowestoft Town, Margate, Canvey Island, Leatherhead who be new places for many of us to travel to. It had been eight years since Lewes had played in the Isthmian league and teams had come and gone. Make no mistake it is not an easy league to get out of, and there would be strong challenges from the likes of Bury Town, Billericay Town and Harrow Borough. But come early August every team starts joint top and the hope of the club would be to be looking forward and not backwards for at least one season.

Off the pitch the club planned to launch the next phase of its ownership scheme. In mid May the directors announced an annual membership scheme, allowing any fan to own a share in the club from just £30 per annum. Taking forward similar community benefit schemes run by FC United of Manchester and AFC Wimbledon the aim was to have five hundred share holders by the time the first ball was kicked of the new season.

And then the news that every Lewes fan wanted to hear broke in early June. Steve King was returning as manager. The ex-Farnborough manager, and man who took The Rooks to the promised land of the Blue Square Premier back in 2008 was coming back to the club.

In one of his first interviews with the club he spoke with me as part of an interview for Viva Lewes magazine.

They say "never go back"....so guess what my first question is? Why did you agree to come back to Lewes?

The club has always been in my heart. My first period here was full of happy memories and I think I proved myself during that time in taking the club to the highest level it has ever been. When I left, I felt there was a different agenda as to what I had followed and it took time to get over that. However, once I was aware that Lewes were looking for a new manager and once I met the current owners I could see that they were the right guys to take the club forward both on and off the pitch. They had the interests of the future of the club and community in their hearts.

Sum up your management philosophy in a few sentences
In one word – Win! I always work hard and have built my knowledge up over many years of players in the non leagues so I have a good idea of who the winners are and what they can do for me. It is a trade where you are constantly learning though.

What do you know of the Ryman League? Who do you think the teams to watch out for are?
I spend every waking hour it seems watching football – about 150 games last season so I am very familiar with teams and players at this level. It is going to be a very tough league and hopefully we will be in the mix at the end of the season. I can see Lowestoft Town continuing their excellent form from last season and Carshalton Athletic seem to have some financial muscle behind them so I would not rule them two out from being up there.

What would it take for Lewes to climb into the Blue Square Bet Premier again?
A decent team with the right winning mentality. A bit of luck with injuries, some decisions going our way. We will put out a team that will be very competitive next season and we will know what we have to do.

What can the fans expect from your team next season?
I believe in playing football with style, allowing players to express themselves and above all instilling that winning mentality into all of them. We will score goals and I am determined to put the smile back on the faces of all of the fans. They haven't had the best couple of seasons so I am determined to give them something this season to make them proud to be a Lewes fan.

Lewes Community Football Club is in a period of evolution not revolution.

The aim still remains that it will be at the heart of a unique community as much as the community will be the heart of a unique football club. And few would disagree that there is a better place to watch a game of football in England.

WE WONT BE DRUV!

Acknowledgements

When I first had the idea to document Lewes FC's first season as a Community club I really didn't know what to expect. I certainly didn't expect a season long fight against relegation, nor the dramatic change of management. However, I was fortunate to be taken into the heart of the club by the new owners and was consulted on a number of matters. That made me feel very privileged and I would like to thank Alex Leith, Nick Williams, Charlie Dobres , Ed Ramsden and Ben Ward for their forthright opinions and views. I would especially like to thank Patrick Marber for nudging me along in the right direction – anyone would think he had written a thing or two in the past!

Thanks also to Steve "Ibbo" Ibbitson for this candid view on events at the club when a better man would have just given a "no comment". Huge thanks to James Boyes for his tireless work for the club and helping me out with the match reports during the season when I missed the odd game or three.

The Lewes Lunatic Fringe proved excellent value on the road, especially Big Deaks and Cynical Dave and they will be terrorising the Ryman Premier League this year with energy.

A huge debt of thanks goes to Danny Last for writing a few of the chapters here, diverting me away at frequent points during the season and essentially being responsible for my three digit phone bills every month. His attitude towards grass roots football is second to none and it is a privilege to have him as a friend.

Every good writer needs a great publisher and Matt Smith at Blackline Press has been just that. The enthusiasm for this project to see the light of day was overwhelming from day one and I hope the end product has done him proud.

I have to say that once again my girls have given me the opportunity, energy and reason to write. Without the fantastic Current Mrs Fuller, aka Bridget I would be a mere armchair fan. She has supported me through another venture with tireless enthusiasm as I disappeared off for a day trips to Chelmsford and Thurrock without a single complaint. Never has a man had such a wonderful companion in life to make his flask of tea and iron his programme when he returns home.

The Littlest Fullers have been inspirational in their own way. Lauren for her support of everything red and black and her critical view of chips served in the Blue Square Bet South, whilst Isabella has kept us all amused at some point with her very mature seven year olds views on the futility of the game we all love.

Finally, to you, the reader. I hope that you are sitting on a plane, train or even a beach reading this rather than in WH Smiths. It is the feedback I get from readers of my website that continues to drive me on, so thank you for making the journey so far most enjoyable.

About the author

Stuart Fuller used to love West Ham and Marmite. In the past few years both have been removed from his life, one through a general apathy at the commercialisation of the game at the top level and specifically his beloved Hammers, the other because he works in Denmark and they have banned the stuff.

He started getting his kicks lower down the leagues in 2007 and has never looked back. In 2008 he met Lewes FC and over a few pints of Harveys he has never looked back. He can be found on the terraces of the Dripping Pan every other Saturday with the rest of the Lewes Lunatic Fringe.

A prolific blogger through his website, The Ball is Round, he has written a number of books on football in the past decade. He also went to the Playboy Mansion in 2010 in case you are one of the 0.1% of the population he hasn't told.